Software Configuration Management Implementation Roadmap

Software Configuration Management Implementation Roadmap

Mario E. Moreira

John Wiley & Sons, Ltd

Published by   John Wiley & Sons Ltd, The Atrium, Southern Gate, Chichester,
West Sussex PO19 8SQ, England

Telephone (+44) 1243 779777

Email (for orders and customer service enquiries): cs-books@wiley.co.uk
Visit our Home Page on www.wileyeurope.com or www.wiley.com

Other Wiley Editorial Offices

John Wiley & Sons Inc., 111 River Street, Hoboken, NJ 07030, USA

Jossey-Bass, 989 Market Street, San Francisco, CA 94103-1741, USA

Wiley-VCH Verlag GmbH, Boschstr. 12, D-69469 Weinheim, Germany

John Wiley & Sons Australia Ltd, 33 Park Road, Milton, Queensland 4064, Australia

John Wiley & Sons (Asia) Pte Ltd, 2 Clementi Loop #02-01, Jin Xing Distripark, Singapore 129809

John Wiley & Sons Canada Ltd, 22 Worcester Road, Etobicoke, Ontario, Canada M9W 1L1

Wiley also publishes its books in a variety of electronic formats. Some content that appears
in print may not be available in electronic books.

British Library Cataloguing in Publication Data

A catalogue record for this book is available from the British Library

ISBN 0-470-86264-5 (HB)

Typeset in 10/12pt Times by Laserwords Private Limited, Chennai, India
Printed and bound in Great Britain by TJ International, Padstow, Cornwall
This book is printed on acid-free paper responsibly manufactured from sustainable forestry
in which at least two trees are planted for each one used for paper production.

I dedicate this book to those who have passed much too early, but have inspired beyond their years.

Carlos 'Caito' Moreira

Moinuddin Baqai

Contents

Preface

Years ago, when I entered the field of SCM, I was hard pressed to find SCM materials that focused on 'how-to' implement and perform SCM. Many books focused on defining what SCM is and many focused on SCM as it is applied to government or military sectors with few focusing on the commercial sectors.

Even after years in the field, many books continue to focus on what SCM is with a few including sections on 'how to do' SCM. This does not underestimate the quality of the SCM books on the market as well as an increase in SCM discussions amongst peers, via e-groups, websites, and conferences. But instead, it highlights that there is a gap to be filled.

Many SCM practitioners, particularly the junior to mid-level personnel, and those in small companies who must 'do-it-all' (you know who you are), get thrust into the SCM role (either willingly or unwillingly). You are the people who need down-to-earth assistance where tasks meet the everyday work life and ultimately those who may be looking for instruction and examples of how to establish an SCM infrastructure, create SCM processes, identify SCM tasks, and develop SCM implementation plans. In the early 1990s, seeing the need, I set out to begin this book.

Upon my journeys, many people to whom I have spoken either openly conveyed an interest in seeing a step-by-step practical guide for SCM or appeared interested in the idea when discussing this topic. Then in 1999, I was asked to be the tutorial speaker at SCM-9 (Ninth Annual International Symposium on System Configuration Management) to provide a tutorial on 'the implementation of SCM'. The session went very well and although I had three hours to give the tutorial, we ran out of time before completing it because of the interest, discussion, and questions the session generated.

It is with this in mind (and a continued interest by John Wiley & Sons Ltd.) that I finalized this book: an SCM book that provides customizable step-by-step guidance in implementing SCM. The unique aspect of this book is that it separates SCM tasks into three levels within the workplace (i.e., organization, application, and project levels). For example in one scenario, the objective is to get a 'project' release package into production while another scenario is to implement a new SCM system for an 'application'. A third scenario may be to establish an SCM policy for the 'organization'. All are SCM related, but using these levels to target the task may reduce some of the issues I have seen in implementing SCM which may lead to better chances of success.

I hope the materials in this book will make your role easier as you implement SCM and ultimately lead to a more successful level of SCM across your workplace. You may also find that the amount of time saved by using these step-by-step materials will easily make up for the cost of the book and quite possibly many times over. It is for you, the SCM professional and those who work in this and related fields, that I wrote this book. I hope you find it helpful.

Acknowledgements

I thank my loving family, Seeme, Aliya, and Iman for the sustenance and patience that made it possible for me to complete this book.

I thank Damon Poole, co-founder of AccuRev and a leader in the SCM industry for his encouragement, input, and friendship along the way.

I thank Stephen Berczuk, published author in the SCM and engineering field, for his thoughts during the making of this book.

I thank Birgit Gruber, Laura Kempster, Daniel Gill, and Sophie Evans from John Wiley & Son Ltd for their patience, direction, and support in helping me complete this book.

And I thank numerous others who over the years, have engaged me, encouraged me, challenged me, and stimulated my passion for SCM.

1

Overview

1. Introduction

"I know what Software Configuration Management is, but what I really need to know is how do I do it?" A person may be put into a position to implement SCM within their workplace. They may have some SCM understanding and skills, but need to know what to actually do to establish SCM in part or in whole. This is the main benefit of this book: to help the reader implement SCM and reduce the time it takes to do so.

1.1. Goals of this Book

This book provides the reader with the building blocks and concrete steps for implementing SCM. It does this by focusing on two goals:

- Align SCM Tasks to the Target Levels – this goal helps the reader align SCM tasks to the appropriate target level within the workplace. The three target levels are the organization, the application, and the project. Aligning SCM tasks to the appropriate level increases the chances of a more effective SCM implementation.
- Provide a Customizable Set of SCM Tasks – this goal provides the reader with a customizable set of SCM tasks and templates for establishing a unique roadmap for implementing SCM. Each task provides step-by-step guidance to implement the SCM need. It is also important to implement SCM in a practical sequence of events so that past SCM tasks can lead to more effective completion of future SCM tasks.

1.2. Customize, Customize, Customize

Overall, this book provides assistance in preparing a *customizable* planned approach for implementing SCM and the detailed steps needed in carrying out the plan at the appropriate target level within a workplace. It is important to understand that the reader is expected to customize the materials in this book in a manner that will be more effective for their customer and environment. What are some ways in which the materials may be

Software Configuration Management: Implementation Roadmap   M. E. Moreira
© 2004 Mario E. Moreira   ISBN: 0-470-86264-5 (HB)

customized? After reviewing the tasks, you can:

- Merge two (or more) tasks into one task or separate one task into two (or more) tasks
- Rename tasks (to better align with terminology within the workplace)
- Reorder tasks within a level (or from one level to another)
- Rewrite tasks to better align with terminology and approaches used within the workplace

As an SCM effort is approached, consider using complementary resources such as other SCM books, websites, and personnel for additional input, material, and advice to help with the implementation. Again, this book provides a strong foundation for an SCM implementation, but must be adapted to each effort in order for the implementation to be successful and for adoption to occur.

1.3. Going Global: Offshore and Distributed Development

This book also provides a focus on distributed development since development is more distributed than ever before. This can be viewed as global development, offshore development, multiple site development, or distributed development. Distributed development, whether it spans a country or continents requires special thought for the processes and infrastructure that can make it successful. SCM has a major role to play in this space. This book provides direction in this global space for selecting distributed access technologies, defining distributed development strategies, and implementing a distributed development infrastructure that is aligned with SCM objectives.

2. Who should use this Book

This book is intended for the individual or group that plans on implementing or performing SCM for an organization, application, or project.

- The **primary audience** who may benefit from this book includes junior to mid-level SCM personnel such as: SCM managers, SCM engineers, SCM coordinators, and release engineers (or people in similar roles). It will help them understand their roles, the variety of tasks in SCM, and provide a stepping stone to an easier and more effective implementation of the SCM tasks. This book will also benefit the individual within a small organization who has a number of roles and performing SCM tasks fits into one of the roles. It will become a valuable resource that eliminates or reduces the 'how do I make it happen' phase of implementing and performing quality SCM.
- The **secondary audience** who may benefit from using this book includes application owners (e.g., product or program managers), project managers, QA/test managers and personnel, senior management and project stakeholders, and senior SCM personnel. For application owners (product and program managers), project managers, and QA/test managers and personnel, it will help them understand what it means to implement and perform quality SCM and how it may support their needs. For senior management such as Director/VP/Senior VP level, it will help them understand the many facets of performing SCM and the benefits of quality SCM to their organization. Ultimately management in general should realize that SCM is a management resource that can

help them identify and control their product. For SCM personnel at the senior level, it may act as a refresher and reminder of how to implement and perform quality SCM and fill gaps in SCM areas they may not yet have experienced.

3. Benefits of this Book

The key benefit of this book is that it may help to significantly reduce the time it takes to plan and prepare for an SCM implementation or an SCM task. And time is money. How often do people get assigned new tasks, and end up spending a lot of time figuring out what must be done? Half of the challenge of getting started is knowing where to begin. And if something is not done correctly the first time, the task must be revisited. This book hopes to eliminate or significantly reduce this challenge. This book may also help those who are undertaking a CMM compliance effort where SCM is a component. This book may reduce the effort it takes by providing repeatable SCM processes and an understanding of which SCM tasks may be important.

If this book saves the reader a few hours because of the guidance it provides, then the material in this book pays for itself. And it may pay for itself many, many times over. For planning an effort, the reader simply selects the task(s) needed, customizes as appropriate, and begins.

4. Examining the Target Levels

For the purpose of improving comprehension, it is important to define the target levels (e.g., organization, application, and project) within a workplace and the differences between them. Also, the term 'release' will be discussed in the context of the target levels. If the reader (or the workplace in which they work) has different definitions for these terms, ensure the terms in this book are aligned with those within the workplace of the reader.

It is important to define these terms because many people within a workplace use some of these words interchangeably, when, in fact, they are different. Below are brief definitions as they relate to this discussion. Ultimately, it is important for the reader to define these terms for their workplace.

An *organization* can be:
- An entire workplace if it is small and has only one division head or area of focus.
- A division of a workplace if it is large enough and/or has multiple division heads with different market or product sector focuses or which operate relatively independently from other parts of the workplace.
- A sub-division that performs different functions from another sub-division within a division.

In all cases, an organization, as discussed in this book may have several applications being developed or supported.

An *application* can be:
- An accumulation of deliverables that make up a functioning system that is in a full state of operational readiness otherwise known as "in production" (which can be running on a server, on a client, or packaged on media).

- A *release* of an application is a changed set of deliverables. Each set of deliverables is typically the output of a project which defines the release number of the application (e.g., Release 2).
- An application lifecycle is the existence of the application from the first release in production, through to the last release, and until users are no longer using the application.
- An application may also be called a product if the product only includes that application. However, some products are collections of applications.

A *project* can be:
- A set of tasks/activities whose aim is to deliver a changed (new/modified/deleted) set of functionality, otherwise known as a *release*.
- A *release* of a project is a set of changes to the application functionality, in the form of deliverables, that is created from a set of tasks/activities (a project) that in turn is derived from requirements changes and/or bug fixes.
- A project lifecycle starts in the planning and requirements stage and ends when all project tasks are completed and the deliverables are released into production.

The following diagram may help illustrate these terms more clearly.

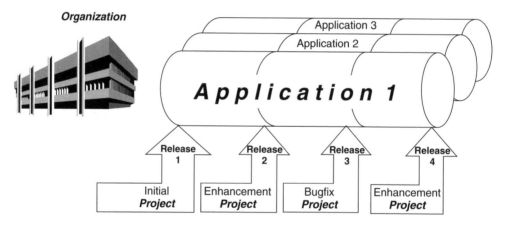

Figure 1.1   Relationship of a Project to an Application within an Organization

The beginning of an application lifecycle also coincides with the initial project that focuses on the Release 1 deliverable of the application. It is before and during this time (hopefully prior to coding) that the SCM infrastructure should be established. Although, in some cases, the application is already running in production when the need for SCM infrastructure becomes apparent.

4.1. Aligning SCM Tasks to the Target Levels

The primary method of identifying the proper target level of an SCM task is to identify the primary beneficiary of that task within a workplace. Consideration should also be given to who will work with SCM personnel to complete a task, the life expectancy of the output of the task (a.k.a., deliverable), and how repetitive a task may be to increase the change of success. The levels in which SCM can be focused to ensure an increased possibility of success include:

- *Organization* level – tasks targeted toward **upper management** that benefit the **organization** by ensuring that SCM is at a level that can change the culture. These tasks are usually *done once* (e.g., create a CM Policy, etc.), the deliverable(s) will live for the duration of the organization, but may need occasional updating.
- *Application* level – tasks targeted toward the **application owner or product manager** that benefit the **application** (typically SCM infrastructure tasks) by adding control mechanisms (technology and processes) that improve the stability of an application. These tasks are usually *done once* (e.g., build infrastructure, establish process, etc.), with occasional improvement, and the deliverable(s) will live for the duration of the application lifecycle.
- *Project* level – tasks targeted toward *project managers* (and their staff) that benefit the **project** that focus on the delivery of the project release. These tasks may be *performed numerous times*, are performed only in relation to a specific project release, and should be *repeatable* using processes defined at the application level.

Let us consider several brief use cases in examining the above:

- When you want to establish an SCM policy for a small company (e.g., a workplace), the primary beneficiary is the organization. Therefore, you should meet with the appropriate level of management to get buy-in and approval for that policy. In this case, the task may be targeted toward the president, CEO, CTO, or similar level personnel. However, if you believe that getting buy-in for an SCM policy at the organization level may be too difficult, then consider targeting the application level. Then the SCM policy task gets moved into the application level set of tasks.
- If you want to implement an SCM system (technology and process) for an application, then the beneficiary is the application, the application owner, and the application team. Therefore, you would want a specific SCM effort to implement the SCM system for the application. In this case, the task is targeted towards the application owner and application team.
- If you have a task where you want to create a set of deliverables from a build or baseline for testing purposes, then the immediate beneficiaries are members of the project team and the project manager. Also, this task may occur multiple times prior to releasing the deliverables into production. Therefore, it is a project level task.
- Many times, an SCM infrastructure task gets included in a project level plan (i.e., during the lifecycle of a project). What happens is the SCM infrastructure task impacts or takes a lower priority than the immediate project task of preparing release deliverables. This is because the SCM infrastructure task is not a 'project' level task focused on the project deliverables, but is an 'application' level task focused on the application environment.

Overall, this may help SCM professionals target their SCM tasks or effort more effectively, leading to better SCM planning and ultimately to a more successful implementation and adoption of SCM.

5. Examining the Customizable Set of SCM Tasks

This book hopes to provide the reader with a customizable set of SCM tasks and templates for establishing a unique roadmap for implementing SCM. Each task provides step-by-step guidance to implementing the SCM need. Below is an examination of the SCM tasks at each target level.

5.1. SCM Tasks at the Organization Level

This book provides a chapter that includes a step-by-step guide for establishing SCM at the organization level. It is the recommendation of the author that the reader consider implementing the following SCM tasks prior to or, at least, in parallel with the application level SCM tasks. By implementing SCM tasks at the organization level, it will improve the chances of implementing SCM at the lower levels (e.g., at the application and project level). If there is little focus on SCM at the organization level, these tasks may be completed at the application level. The tasks at this level are placed in phases based on how they contribute to establishing the groundwork for organizational SCM. The phases at the organization level include:

- SCM Commitment – This phase includes tasks that focus on establishing SCM commitment within the organization. Specific tasks include raising SCM awareness, assessing SCM risk, evaluating support and sponsorship for SCM, and defining an SCM budget. *Benefit*: establishes a common understanding of SCM and assesses if management is truly serious about SCM to determine if it is worth pursuing SCM at the organization level.
- SCM Direction – This phase includes tasks that focus on setting the organizational direction for SCM. Specific tasks include establishing an SCM policy and creating an SCM plan. *Benefit*: expresses management commitment to SCM by providing clarity on SCM objectives and guidance for all levels within the organization on how SCM will be enacted.
- SCM Foundation – This phase includes tasks that focus on establishing an organizational SCM infrastructure. Specific tasks include establishing an SCM personnel structure, defining SCM terminology, and establishing organization level SCM metrics. *Benefit*: provides consistency for SCM roles and SCM terminology, and a focus on how SCM objectives will be measured so it is clear on which aspects of SCM the organization should focus.

5.2. SCM Tasks at the Application Level

This book provides a chapter that includes a step-by-step guide for implementing and establishing an SCM system for an application. Every application must have a solid and effective SCM technology and process infrastructure. An application may remain viable for a number of years and through many releases. The more effective the SCM infrastructure, the better the chances for a more efficient, repeatable, and traceable project release process. The tasks at this level are placed in phases based on when they may occur in an SCM effort. The phases at the application level include:

- SCM Analysis – This phase focuses on reviewing the current environment (platform, tools, processes, etc.), determining the level of risk and readiness, and providing improvement opportunities that will allow for appropriate SCM planning. *Benefit*: provides important insight into the current state of SCM.

- SCM Implementation Planning – This phase focuses on establishing a roadmap of tasks and activities needed to implement an SCM system (technology and process) effectively. *Benefit*: provides a structured approach for managing the tasks.
- SCM Technology Selection – This phase focuses on an evaluation process to make an objective decision in determining the best SCM technology for the requirements of the application. This includes: determining SCM technology functionality, customer service, and cost requirements; evaluating tools; and determining benefits/risks of tools. SCM technology includes version control, as well as (but not limited to) problem management, change control, release engineering, and multiple site technologies. *Benefit*: provides a more rigorous and objective approach for selecting an SCM technology for the application.
- SCM Design – This phase provides a design approach to defining SCM roles and responsibilities, environment details, SCM system details, and training direction. *Benefit*: provides a methodical approach to the logistics and conventions of designing an SCM system.
- SCM Process – This phase focuses on establishing SCM processes for application development. *Benefit*: provides processes for repeatability and improves communication within the team.
- SCM Technology Implementation – This phase focuses on establishing an SCM technology environment. This includes installing the SCM technology, creating repositories, importing code, and refining the build process for application development. *Benefit*: provides an SCM infrastructure for managing application items.
- SCM Training – This phase focuses on ensuring the appropriate personnel get trained to perform their SCM roles. This includes SCM technology admin training, SCM technology user training, and change control board (CCB) training. *Benefit*: provides an organized way of getting personnel trained in SCM technology and processes that leads to a solid and consistent usage of SCM technologies and processes.
- SCM System Testing – This phase focuses on providing verification of the SCM technology and processes. *Benefit*: allows for confirming the integrity of the SCM environment prior to transitioning the application team to a live SCM system.
- SCM System Transition – This phase focuses on providing support during the transition of staff to new SCM technology. *Benefit*: provides support to those who are making the transition to the SCM infrastructure (technology and processes).

5.3. SCM Tasks at the Project Level

This book provides a chapter that includes a step-by-step guide for identifying and executing appropriate SCM tasks on a project to more effectively and efficiently create and deploy a quality release package. The objective at the project level is to define a consistent and customizable set of SCM tasks to be included in the project plan and to be performed during a project to produce the release. It also focuses on having a repeatable release process. The tasks at this level are meant to align with the phases in a project lifecycle and to be adapted for the lifecycle method used. The phases and their SCM tasks include:

- Project Planning and Requirements – This phase focuses on getting SCM tasks into the project plan, providing an overview of SCM, updating the CCB member list, and authorizing the requirements baseline for the project. *Benefit*: provides awareness of SCM and direction for the project.

- Design – This phase focuses on establishing the development baseline project branch, performing capacity planning, training personnel in using the SCM technology, and creating user workspaces. *Benefit*: ensures the SCM infrastructure is ready and capable of supporting the project needs.
- Development – This phase focuses on performing builds and merging activities (if applicable), creating release packages, creating draft release notes, and performing an SCM audit and review. *Benefit*: uses SCM processes to create release deliverables and assess if SCM is being performed appropriately to create quality deliverables.
- Test – This phase focuses on migrating the release package to the test region(s), finalizing the release package and release notes. *Benefit*: provides support to the test activities and finalizes the package for production.
- Release – This phase focuses on authorizing the release, installing and verifying the release, creating a bugfix branch, and performing cleanup of unneeded workspaces. *Benefit*: provides a final check prior to going live, gives consistent steps for installation, and focuses on supporting the release once in production.

6. How to Use this Book

6.1. Systematic Approach

Approaching an SCM effort is always a challenge. However, the key to a successful SCM implementation is to define and follow the roadmap (or plan) from the beginning of the effort to completion. In a nutshell, think of the SCM effort as a project and prepare an SCM work breakdown structure (WBS), task list, or plan. With this in mind, consider following these steps to build an SCM WBS that leads to an SCM project implementation plan:

- Review all the chapters in the book. This will allow you to be aware of all tasks available before determining which level(s) and tasks are appropriate for your SCM effort.
  It should be noted that each task is captured in a task table format. A task table provides the key components necessary to successfully complete a task. This includes the steps to perform the task (Key Steps), who has a role in implementing the task (Roles), additional insight into the task (Considerations), and the expected deliverable(s) of a task (Output). Immediately following a task table, there may be sections that provide more information to help complete the task. Each task table will look like the following example:

Key Steps – high level steps to get the task complete

Roles – who is best suited to perform the task

Considerations – other items to consider while performing the task

Output – what is the expected result of performing the task

- According to the SCM objective(s), determine the level(s) you are targeting. Since this book is divided into these levels (i.e., organization; application; and/or project), you can more thoroughly review the section where you will be working. For more on the topic of target levels, consider reviewing Section 4 in this chapter.

- Determine which tasks will be undertaken for the particular effort. Try not to take on more than an organization, application, or project can handle. Please note that some SCM tasks will require predecessor tasks in order for them to be completed successfully. Since this book takes a customized approach to your SCM effort, you can add, delete, or modify the tasks listed in this book.
- Create an SCM work breakdown structure (WBS) by including the tasks that have been selected. This can also be referred to as your plan, or task list. Consider using the task name from each task section that was selected to more easily map back to this book. However, you may customize the task name with a name more suitable or better understood within the organization. If you are working on project level tasks, it is recommended that you incorporate these SCM tasks into the project plan of the development project since these tasks should align with the project effort in which SCM tasks are being applied (see Chapter 5, Section 2.1).
- Customize the materials in the task sections to more appropriately suit the organization, application, or project needs. This is particularly the case where this book offers templates, processes, standards, policies, and plans. These items are meant to serve as a starting point and may be customized for the particular effort.
- Review the SCM WBS and supporting tasks with the personnel who will be working through the tasks and the group or organization in which it is being implemented. In effect, once an SCM WBS is in place, use good project management processes to manage the plan to completion.

6.2. Reference or Ad Hoc Approach

This book may be used as a reference guide or tasks in the book may be undertaken in an ad hoc manner. It may be used as a reference to supplement existing SCM materials. It may be used ad hoc when there is a specific need for an SCM artifact or practice: the reader may go to that specific task. For example, if the reader is interested in creating an SCM Change Control Process or an SCM Job Description, they may go to the chapter that contains the task focused on the specific area.

2

Introduction to SCM

This chapter provides a summary of SCM and presents the more common SCM definitions. The author recognizes that there are many other definitions of SCM and the reader must decide what is best for their needs. There may be specific SCM compliance standards (e.g., government, military, etc.) that must be followed within a workplace for application development. With this in mind, be aware that there are many good SCM resources that can provide the reader with more detail or differing views on this topic. Section 4 provides a selection of valuable SCM books, websites, and discussion groups that may be used to enhance SCM knowledge.

1. General Definition of SCM

SCM is a recognized engineering discipline that provides the processes and technologies to identify and control items. The basis for an SCM process includes a set of functions that improve the integrity and quality of code, tools, documents, designs, and virtually any item that an organization desires to manage. SCM focuses on four areas: identification, control, audit, and report (or status accounting). These are the four fundamental components of SCM and they are discussed in further detail in Section 2. Typically, the four components are realized by functions including version control, change control, problem management, release engineering, SCM audits, and reporting on SCM activities and baselines.

Simply put, the key to SCM is that it enables a person or group to identify the pieces that make up an application or organization. By identifying the pieces, an application or organization is better able to control changes to the pieces, therefore the environment. Changes can be planned and made after determining the impact of the change and the correct course of action, instead of having to figure out what was changed after the fact.

1.1. What is a Configuration Item?

In the SCM space, "configuration item" is a key term that is often used, but with varying definitions from workplace to workplace. Configuration items (CIs) may refer to the deliverables (e.g., the end product); the deliverables and the pieces that created the deliverables; or the deliverables, the pieces that created the deliverables, and the environment in which

Software Configuration Management: Implementation Roadmap   M. E. Moreira
© 2004 Mario E. Moreira   ISBN: 0-470-86264-5 (HB)

the deliverables are created. The key to defining a CI may be to recognize any item that is delivered to a customer (whether internal or external) and items that can impact the quality of the deliverables. As an example, CIs may include items such as deliverables (in the form of software) and user documents that are delivered to the external customer and any items such as project charters, project plans, requirements, technical specifications, architectural designs, code, training materials, tools used, test cases, and scripts that are delivered to internal customers in some manner. Or the definition of a CI may lie somewhere between that definition and simply the deliverables. The most important factor is to define the terminology with a definition that best supports the needs of the workplace.

2. Four Fundamentals of SCM

Traditional SCM is comprised of four fundamental components: Identification, Control, Audit, and Report (Status Accounting). It is important to communicate the definitions and interpretation of these components to those in the workplace.

Figure 2.1   Four Fundamentals of Software Configuration Management

Below are overviews of the four SCM components that may help in communicating the definitions in more general terms. This can help facilitate a quicker understanding of SCM throughout the organization.

2.1. Identification

Figure 2.2   Identification Component

The first component of Software Configuration Management is to *identify* all configuration items (CIs) related to the application. By identifying CIs, you establish a baseline of software-related items where you can then control, audit, and report the changes occurring to this baseline. Configuration items may include the product deliverables and the corresponding plans, requirements, specifications, designs, source code, executables, tools, system information (i.e., software and hardware platforms), and test cases, etc. Further consideration is given to the exact version of the tools you are using. Are you using release 4.1 of a tool or release 5.0? A different release of a tool can output different results.

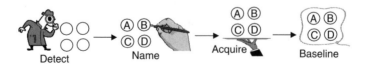

Figure 2.3   SCM Identification Sub-Process

The component of Identification may be divided into four areas: detect, name, acquire, and baseline. *Detect* refers to defining and identifying the CIs that make up your product. This is more than just source code. This may be webpages, documents, or even requirements. *Name* refers to developing a nomenclature that is unique, unambiguous, and traceable to easily identify and locate the CIs. *Acquire* is the process of collecting the CIs under SCM control. *Baseline* is the process of establishing a cohesive and meaningful set of CIs.

2.2. Control

Figure 2.4   Control Component

The second component of Software Configuration Management is to *control* changes to all configuration items (CIs) in your product. The processes of Control are version control, change control, build management, and release engineering.

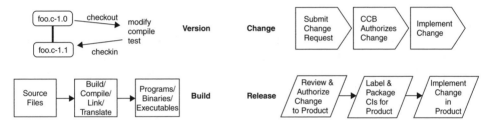

Figure 2.5   SCM Control Sub-Process

Version refers to the version control of configuration items. Changes are typically controlled by a 'version control' process and all changes are versioned incrementally. *Change* refers to an effective means of proactively controlling changes to your environment. An effective way of facilitating control over changes to your product is to implement a Change Control Board (CCB). This board represents the interests of the project manager and all groups who may be affected by the change to the software baseline. The CCB authorizes the establishment of a software baseline, reviews and authorizes changes to a baseline, and approves the creation of products (releases) from a software baseline. *Build* refers to a standard repeatable and measurable build and release packaging process. *Release* refers to a controlled way of acquiring approval for release deliverables and establishing the production baseline (e.g., making the product generally available to the customer).

2.3. Audit

Figure 2.6   Audit Component

The third component of Software Configuration Management is *audit*. The process of audit includes two steps. The first step is to analyze the baselines and processes. The second step is to assign action items for issues and non-compliance so that improvements can be made. In effect, this provides SCM with a continuous process improvement loop.

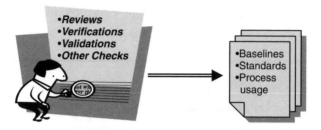

Figure 2.7   SCM Audit Sub-Process

SCM auditing may be implemented by selecting members from the project who work with SCM personnel to periodically audit different SCM areas. By carrying out the SCM auditing function, a more systematic improvement of the quality of the software assets may begin.

It is important to note the term 'audit' can bring about considerable resistance in an organization. You may consider changing the word 'audit' to 'analysis' or 'assessment' to make this task appear less threatening and start by performing limited analysis or assessments when the organization is very young or less mature and using the results for improvement and not punishment.

2.4. Report

Figure 2.8   Report Component

The fourth component of Software Configuration Management is to provide *reporting* on the events surrounding projects. More traditionally, reporting is referred to as **Status Accounting**. The primary benefit of reporting is that it affords an opportunity to systematically collect the data needed, record the data in a measurable, meaningful, and repeatable way, and then report on the data to the appropriate personnel for improvement opportunity goals.

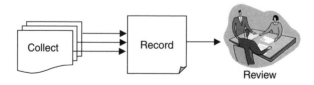

Figure 2.9   SCM Report Sub-Process

The process includes documenting and reporting changes, providing quality and productivity metrics, providing results of software baseline audits, version history of configuration items, and meeting minutes. If the generated SCM reports are important for tracking the efforts of a project, then these reports should be kept in a repository. This provides a traceable way of reviewing past reports and comparing them with current information.

3. Benefits of SCM

The perceived value and benefit of SCM depends on the audience that is being addressed. Some of the main roles that benefit from the SCM function may include management, development staff, and SCM and QA/test personnel (note: there are also other roles that derive benefits from SCM). What may be perceived as a benefit to the SCM personnel may be considered a hindrance to the development staff. With this in mind, when SCM benefits are stated in a presentation, ensure the audience is considered.

3.1. Benefits of SCM to Management

When discussing the benefits of SCM to management, it is important to note that SCM has an initial cost involved from both a technology and a personnel aspect. This cannot be ignored since management will evaluate the importance of an item based on the cost/benefit perspective. With this in mind, consider the cost avoidance that SCM provides. Some benefits of SCM to management include:

- SCM provides a means to control cost. This may offer management a way to identify the cost of a change prior to making the change.
- SCM offers a place to store and manage product assets. This may provide management with an understanding that the company's assets (i.e., products) are in a safe place. This avoids the cost of looking for lost assets.
- SCM reduces maintenance costs. Once a release package is delivered, management may be sure that the application is under control, can be recreated, and avoids the cost of functional regression.

Also it is important to note that when you are discussing SCM with management you should focus on the problems that can be solved. Gather the current issues and risks that SCM may solve or reduce.

3.2. Benefits of SCM to Development Staff

When discussing the benefits of SCM to development, it is important to provide them with the most streamlined process while still maintaining the integrity of SCM. It is often better to start with a straightforward process, rather than a complex one. Consider gathering input from development as to what issues SCM may solve and what improvements they would like to see with the SCM process. Some benefits of SCM to development include:

- SCM provides product integrity, reproducibility, and reliability. This lets development know that their changes are stored so that they do not have to reproduce the item and the items can be retrieved on demand. Effectively, it reduces the chances of losing code assets and the changes to code.

- SCM provides a technology that allows for easy access and control of items. This ensures that there is a streamlined process and integrity of the code and therefore, the released product.
- SCM provides a window into changes and visibility into the release process. This lets development know what has changed, where, and when.

3.3. Benefits of SCM to SCM and QA/Test Personnel

In most cases, little effort has to be made to express the benefits of SCM for SCM and QA personnel. However, it is important to identify a benefit for any SCM function or process to ensure that it has merit. Some benefits of SCM for SCM and QA personnel include:

- SCM provides traceability. This ensures that changes can be tracked from inception (requirement change or defect) to the completion of the change therefore reducing effort to track the item.
- SCM provides auditing capabilities. This ensures that SCM processes are followed, and that baselines and the changes to the baselines are identified.
- SCM provides reporting capabilities. This allows the SCM status to be reported for visibility and gives opportunity for improving the SCM system (technology and process).

4. SCM Resource Guide

There are numerous valuable materials available on SCM to help with definitions and further knowledge and information. This section will list a small subset of the resources available.

4.1. SCM Books

There are numerous SCM books available on the market. This book does not intend to provide in-depth SCM concepts or definitions. However, please consider reviewing one or more of the following books to get more details and information in this area.

- *Anti-Patterns and Patterns in Software Configuration Management*, by William J. Brown, Hays W. "Skip" McCormick, Scott W. Thomas, 1999, John Wiley & Sons Ltd.
- *Software Release Methodology*, by Michael E. Bays, 1999, Prentice Hall PTR.
- *Software Configuration Management Patterns: Effective Teamwork, Practical Integration*, by Stephen P. Berczuk with Brad Appleton, 2002, Addison Wesley Professional.
- *A Guide to Software Configuration Management*, by Alexis Leon, 2000, Artech House. (This book also includes a history of CM.)
- *Configuration Management: The Missing Link in Web Engineering*, by Susan Dart, 2000, Artech House.

Because there are other SCM and Configuration Management (CM) books on the market, consider visiting an online bookstore and performing a search on this topic.

4.2. SCM Websites

There are numerous SCM related websites available. The list included is only a very small subset. However there are numerous other SCM links within these websites.

- Configuration Management Today (CM Today): http://www.cmtoday.com/
  - CM Today Yellow Pages: http://www.cmtoday.com/yp/configuration_management.html
- CM Crossroads-Online Community and Resource Center for Configuration Management: http://www.cmcrossroads.com/
  - CMWiki: http://www.cmwiki.com/
  - Configuration Management Body of Knowledge: http://www.cmbok.com/
- Assembling Configuration Management Environments (ACME): http://www.cmcrossroads.com/bradapp/acme/
- Institute of Configuration Management: http://www.icmhq.com/
- The Association for Configuration and Data Management: http://www.acdm.org/

4.3. SCM Discussion Groups

There are several SCM online discussion groups of which a subset is included.

- CM Crossroads Discussion Forums: register for membership access at http://www.cmcrossroads.com
- CM Talk Newsgroup: go to http://www.cmtoday.com/mail_list.html

3

Establish SCM in an Organization

1. Focusing on the Organization Level

This chapter of the book focuses on SCM tasks that provide awareness, goals, structure, and direction for establishing a common organization-level SCM framework.

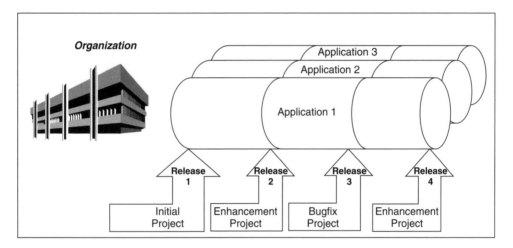

Figure 3.1   The Organization Level

1.1. Organization Level Phases

This chapter is divided into phases that focus on establishing a foundation for SCM at the organization level where there is commitment and direction for SCM. The phases include:

- SCM Commitment – tasks that focus on SCM awareness and sponsorship
- SCM Direction – tasks that provide the SCM organizational direction
- SCM Foundation – tasks that establish the infrastructure to move the SCM direction forward

Software Configuration Management: Implementation Roadmap   M. E. Moreira
© 2004 Mario E. Moreira   ISBN: 0-470-86264-5 (HB)

These phases generally occur in a sequence, although many of the tasks in the SCM Direction and SCM Foundation phases may occur in parallel. While these tasks follow a rough order, they can be done in any sequence and have few hard dependencies amongst them. In fact, many of these tasks may be done individually whenever the need arises within the organization. The process flow diagram below illustrates this point.

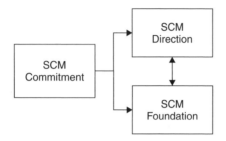

Figure 3.2   Organization Level Process Flow

1.2. How to Use this Chapter

It is important to walk through each phase in this chapter and review each task in each phase. Consider customizing the task name to one that best aligns with the terminology used within the workplace. Also, when reviewing a task, consider customizing it in a manner that may provide a better chance of implementation or adoption.

Determine which tasks will be undertaken for the particular effort according to the level of SCM maturity and how much the organization can adopt. Try not to take on more than an organization can handle. Consider performing the 'Raise Awareness of SCM' and 'Evaluate Management Support and Sponsorship' tasks first in order to get an understanding of how much support there is for an SCM effort at the organization level. Also, the SCM budget task will align with the organization's budgeting cycle so should be done in whichever timeframe this occurs. Certain tasks are believed to be important, but may not have organization level support. However, if they have application level support, then the tasks may be moved into one of the early phases at the application level (see Chapter 4).

Use the name of each task selected in this chapter to create an SCM work breakdown structure (WBS) or SCM organization level project plan.

2. SCM Commitment Phase

The SCM Commitment phase provides tasks that help in understanding the level of commitment there is (and will be) for SCM within the organization. Tasks in this section include: raising awareness of SCM; determining management support and sponsorship; and defining an SCM budget.

2.1. Raise Awareness of SCM

This task provides steps for raising awareness of SCM within an organization. The key to this task is to make the SCM function visible to management and staff.

Key Steps:

1. Identify an appropriate presentation template (if one exists).
2. Name the presentation file and title page, 'Overview of Software Configuration Management'. Within the presentation, document the following:
   - A definition of SCM for the organization. Consider reviewing the following sections as input to creating the definition:
     - Chapter 2 Section 1 for a general, short overview of SCM.
     - Chapter 2 Section 2 for a more extensive view of SCM and its component parts.
     - Chapter 2 Section 4 for various views of SCM from books, websites, and discussion groups.
   - The benefits of SCM. Consider reviewing Chapter 2 Section 3 for input.
   - A vision statement of how SCM may exist within the organization over the next one to three years.
     - For example this may include stating that all code will be in a version control technology, change control will be applied to the requirements baseline, and a release process and release engineering technology will be used to migrate deliverables into production.
   - The SCM roles and responsibilities which will be utilized within the organization (if known). Consider reviewing Section 3.2.2 in this chapter.
3. Review the presentation with the appropriate management level for approval of the content and agreement to present the materials.
4. Schedule an SCM awareness session with key staff members. This usually includes management and key development and QA/test staff.
5. Conduct the SCM awareness session. Ensure an opportunity for questions and answers is provided.
6. From the 'Overview of Software Configuration Management' materials, create a poster that can be placed on bulletin boards to provide additional awareness of SCM. Consider other channels (e.g., a website, lunch sessions, etc.) to provide visibility of the SCM function.
7. Store the materials in a readily accessible location.

Roles:

- SCM manager – task lead
- Senior management

Considerations:

- This activity establishes a common understanding of SCM within the organization.
- Consider terminology that may exist in the organization or can be more easily adopted.
- At this point, focus on just introducing SCM to the organization. While it may be appropriate to introduce all aspects of SCM, focus attention only on the areas that will be covered initially. For example, if there is no plan to support SCM audits, mention it as a function of SCM, but do not focus any level of detail on it.

- For more on the topic of defining SCM, consider reading 'Understanding the Many Views of Configuration Management' in *Configuration Management: The Missing Link in Web Engineering* [Dart 2000].
- This task may also be done at an application level.

Output:

- 'Overview of Software Configuration Management' presentation
- SCM poster
- SCM awareness sessions conducted

2.2. Perform an Organization-Level SCM Risk Assessment

This task provides steps for creating an SCM risk assessment template and performing an SCM risk assessment to identify risks that may impact the success of SCM as it relates to the organization. It then recommends reviewing the risks with appropriate management, determining appropriate mitigation actions, and adding the mitigation actions into the appropriate plan to minimize the impact of the risk or probability of the risk occurring. This task may help provide guidance on the priority order of the SCM tasks that may be undertaken.

It should be noted that there is a difference between a risk and a problem (or issue). A risk indicates that there is a chance or probability of a negative event happening, but it has not yet happened. A problem indicates that a negative event has happened. The value of managing risks is to avoid the negative event (e.g., problem) happening so it does not impact the organization.

Key Steps:

1. Create an SCM risk list template. Consider using:
   - Existing risk assessment processes and risk list templates within the organization.
   - The SCM risk list template found in Section 1 of the Appendix which includes a template, risk definitions, risk categories, and example risk conditions.
2. Perform the SCM Risk Assessment.
   - Schedule a meeting with key management. This may include senior management, heads of development, QA/test, and production staff.
   - Conduct the meeting. Identify the SCM risks and document them in the SCM risk list.
     - Introduce the risk categories (i.e., Personnel; Estimates; Scope; Technology; Management; Sponsorship; Policy; Schedule; Location) as guidance on what may be considered.
     - Document each risk including the description, suspected root cause, the impact on SCM or the application, the severity of the impact, probability of occurrence, and suggested mitigation action.

Note: should SCM problems be identified, consider capturing them using a problem management process and/or technology (should one exist).
3. Meet with management and review the SCM risk list. Agree on which mitigation actions should be initiated.
4. Prioritize and add the mitigation actions to the appropriate plan or tracking list.

Roles:

- SCM manager – task lead
- Senior management, heads of development, QA/test, and production

Considerations:

- Consider performing periodic organizational SCM risk assessments to help determine if risks are being mitigated and to identify new risks.
- It is recommended that you perform periodic SCM risk assessments at the application level and project level.
- For more on the topic of risk, consider reading Appendix 3 in [Dart 2000].

Output:

- SCM risk list template
- Identified SCM risks
- Review of SCM risks and agreement to initiate the mitigation of selected SCM risks
- Mitigation action of selected risks in plan or tracking list

2.3. Evaluate Management Support and Sponsorship

This task provides a method of taking the pulse of management to determine the level of commitment and support that exists for SCM. This may impact the ability of SCM to succeed.

Key Steps:

1. Identify questions that will assess management's level of commitment to SCM. Consider using the management commitment evaluation instrument (see Section 2.3.1).
2. Schedule a meeting with the appropriate level of management.
3. At the meeting, assess the level of commitment via the management commitment evaluation instrument or appropriate questions.
4. Increase management commitment, if necessary and if possible (see Section 2.3.2).

Roles:

- SCM manager – task lead
- Senior manager

Consideration:

- It is important to periodically check the level of management commitment during the establishment of an SCM function.

Output:

- Identified level of management commitment

2.3.1. Management Commitment Evaluation Instrument

As mentioned above, a high level of management commitment to an effort will have a positive impact. Below are several questions, in the form of a management commitment evaluation instrument that can be used to derive an appropriate level of management commitment. This is not intended to be a precise measurement instrument, but will provide an approximate level of management commitment by referring to the scale below.

Question	Range of Potential Answers	Points
Where is the sponsorship level of the SCM effort? Note: if you only need middle management level sponsorship, then that level would receive 10 points and line management level would receive 5 points.	• Senior management – 10 points • Middle management – 5 points • Line management – 3 points	
Is there appropriate and realistic budget/funding for the SCM effort? Funding may include: the ability to purchase tools, the permission to hire SCM personnel; the go-head to implement the SCM tools and processes for an application; and support for daily SCM activities on projects.	• Full funding – 10 points • Partial funding – 5 points • No funding – 0 points	
Are SCM objectives tied to the manager's performance objectives (i.e., to management's merit or base salary pay increases)?	• Major part of manager's performance objectives – 10 points • Minor part of manager's performance objectives – 5 points • Not on manager's performance objectives – 0 points	
	Total Score	

This scale provides only an approximate level of management commitment:

Score	Level of Management Commitment
21–30	High
11–20	Medium
0–10	Low

2.3.2. Ways to Improve Management Commitment

What do you do if the level of management commitment is low or is not clear? There are several possible suggestions for improving management commitment. They are:

- Identify one or more senior-level managers who may be willing to be the sponsor for the SCM effort or who can provide access and support to an appropriate sponsor.
- Identify champions who have established a reputation for implementing change. This can show management that there is credible support for the SCM idea.
- Identify SCM risks. By exposing risks, you can better justify the establishment of SCM in order to remove or reduce risks.
  - To identify risk at the organizational level, consider performing an organization-level SCM risk assessment (see Section 2.2).
- Perform a 'lessons learned' (post-mortem) session at the end of each project for the next six months to capture areas for improvement. If SCM related issues continually arise, prepare a report highlighting the more prevalent SCM issues and present it to management.
  - If a lessons learned template does not exist within the organization, consider using the template in Section 2 of the Appendix.
  - For more on the topic of lessons learned, consider reading:
    - 'Postmortem Planning' in *AntiPatterns and Patterns in Software Configuration Management* [Brown *et al.* 1999].
    - *Project Retrospectives: A Handbook for Team Reviews* [Kerth 2001].
- Brainstorm areas of SCM improvement with senior technical staff. Present outcome to management.
- Prepare a business case or return on investment (ROI) on the benefits of SCM (practices and technology) and how it can potentially save money and time in the long term. ROI information from SCM technology vendors may help especially if there are no SCM technologies currently in use or SCM technologies are used inconsistently.
- Advocate making SCM an organizational objective. If this can be achieved, ensure that the SCM objective is part of all levels of the management merit objectives and merit increases.

2.3.3. Ways for Management to Express Commitment for the SCM Objective

If there is adequate management commitment for an SCM effort, then it is important for this information to be communicated from senior management to the appropriate staff.

This will highlight the importance of SCM to the staff. Several suggestions for senior management include:

- Communicate SCM objectives with the group or organization in staff meetings or company meetings.
- Provide visible and continuous support. This can include requesting progress status of the SCM effort and periodically providing praise when milestones are completed.
- Stress the importance of teamwork among engineers, project management, SCM and QA/test personnel in meeting the SCM objectives.

2.3.4. Improve your Chances of a Successful Transition to SCM

There are several key factors to improving the chances of a successful SCM implementation. The biggest factor is to determine what level of change your organization can accept and also what level of change you are planning to introduce. This may require analysis. For example, an article entitled 'Adapting your Technological Base: The organizational challenge' [Adler and Shenhar 1990] suggests that as the level of learning is elevated, from skills, to processes, to structure, to strategy, to culture, the 'time to adjust' also increases. This indicates that adding a skill for a tool may have a small adjustment time, but adding processes and changing culture will have a large adjustment time due to the level of change.

What this implies is that if an organization already understands the importance of SCM or has some level of SCM technology and process in place, then the transition effort to better SCM will require a less extensive change to the organization. However, if the organization does not understand SCM, does not have SCM processes in place, or has not used SCM technology to manage code, then there is a significant change effort that must occur and this must be recognized and planned for a more successful SCM implementation. With this in mind, it is recommended that you involve SCM personnel, key technical staff, and champions in any SCM implementation effort or significant SCM task.

2.4. Define an SCM Budget

This task provides guidelines on defining and maintaining a budget to fund SCM. One of the best ways to determine management support for SCM is to ensure that a budget amount gets established for SCM and included in the budget process. It is important that money is budgeted for SCM needs, or the likelihood that SCM will be implemented effectively or in a timely manner will be greatly reduced.

Key Steps:

1. Focusing on a one year period (or the budget period within your organization), consider the number of SCM personnel and the cost of new SCM infrastructure items (software, hardware, etc.) that will be needed.
   - SCM personnel costs:
     - Determine the number of personnel that the SCM staff will support. Consider discussing this with application teams to derive a budget amount.

- Determine the number of SCM staff required to support the application personnel with respect to the support ratio (the number of personnel that an SCM staff member can support). See Section 4.1.1 for information on SCM staff support ratios.
- SCM infrastructure costs
  - If there is a cost for the SCM technology software, determine the number of licenses needed for the budget year and multiple by the cost per license. For example, 10 licenses at $1000 each may cost $10,000, depending on the license scheme and vendor discounts (see Section 4.2.2 in Chapter 4 for more on license schemes and estimating license costs).
  - If there is a cost for the SCM technology maintenance, determine the number of licenses and multiple by the cost of each license. Then multiple the result by the maintenance percentage. For example, 10 licenses were purchased for $1000 each. Maintenance is 15% of the cost of the license. Therefore, 10 licenses multiplied by $1000 equal $10,000, and then multiply this by 15%, which is $1500.
  - Determine if there are other technology costs peripheral to the SCM tool. For example, a tool may be needed to provide a connection between two operating systems. If there is a cost associated with this, multiply the cost per license (and or maintenance cost) with the number of licenses needed.
  - Determine if hardware (servers or workstations) are needed to support the SCM infrastructure. Calculate the cost by the number that is needed.
- Other SCM costs
  - If there are any organizational SCM drivers such as IEEE, ISO, or CMM requirements, then those costs should be included.
  - Include any SCM vendor training costs that the SCM group will absorb and any other materials (SCM books, etc.).

2. Using the budget process within the organization, add the SCM budget items into the budget spreadsheet or database (or whatever mechanism is used to enter budget data).
3. Prepare a justification for every SCM budget line item that is entered, to defend the budget costs (if necessary) and for historical purposes.
4. Monitor the budget approval process to ensure that the SCM items remain in the budget. Be ready to justify your SCM budget costs as necessary.

Roles:

- SCM manager – task lead
- Budget owner of SCM (if not the SCM manager)

Considerations:

- The assumption is that the SCM manager will talk to application teams concerning their SCM technology needs to help derive a budget amount.
- If costs for SCM (personnel and/or infrastructure) are charged at the application team level, then the application team creates the budget and SCM items are added to it.

If this is the case, ensure that the SCM budget items get added to the application team budget and approved.

Output:

- An approved budget that includes SCM items (personnel and infrastructure)

2.5. SCM Commitment Phase Completion Checklist

The items in this checklist may be used to determine if SCM tasks have been completed in this phase:

- Were SCM awareness sessions held within the organization?
  - Have the SCM awareness materials been placed in an easily visible and accessible location?
- Is there an appropriate level of management commitment and sponsorship within the organization?
- Have SCM needs been budgeted for?

3. SCM Direction Phase

The SCM Direction phase includes tasks that provide the direction for SCM within an organization. Tasks in this section include: creating an SCM policy and creating an SCM plan.

3.1. Create an SCM Policy

This task helps to create a simple policy at the organization level that shows there is management commitment and provides defined objectives for what to expect in the area of SCM. An SCM policy may be prepared at the organization level or application level.

Key Steps:

1. Identify a policy template. Consider using:
   - A copy of the policy template found within the organization (if it exists).
   - The SCM policy template in Section 4 of the Appendix, which parallels the key steps below. However, the policy may be written in an order that is more readily acceptable to an organization and items may be added or removed as appropriate.
2. Include the following sections (if they do not already exist):
   - **Objective** – identify the purpose of SCM for the organization. For example, 'This policy defines the doctrine for Software Configuration Management (SCM).'
   - **Scope** – identify the scope of SCM to be applied. For example, 'This policy applies to all applications and their respective projects within the organization.'
   - **Authority and Compliance** – indicate who authorizes the policy and who ensures compliance to the policy.

- **Policy Declaration** – indicate the specific SCM objectives that must be adhered to. They may include:
  - SCM Roles and Responsibilities – The objective is to ensure there are roles that include specific SCM responsibilities within the organization. Review the current SCM roles throughout the organization and consider identifying a role nomenclature that can be consistently applied (e.g., SCM Engineer for the personnel who support the SCM technology and perform the build and release tasks). For more on identifying SCM role names, consider Section 4.1.4.
  - SCM Processes – The objective is to ensure there are SCM processes used throughout the organization. Determine which SCM processes should be part of the standard set.
  - SCM Technology – The objective is that all application teams use the prescribed SCM technologies. Recommend the best SCM technology for the organization (consider Section 4.2.1 in Chapter 4).
3. Have the SCM policy reviewed and approved by the appropriate management.
4. Provide a presentation to appropriate staff to review and discuss the content of the SCM policy.
5. Place the SCM policy in an easily visible and accessible location such as the organization website and CM website.
6. Utilize SCM auditing processes and metrics to determine if the SCM policy is being adhered to (see Section 4.3).

Roles:

- SCM manager – task lead
- Senior management – approval

Consideration:

- An SCM policy may be created at the application level if it is not practical or possible to get it reviewed or approved at the senior management level.

Output:

- Approved SCM policy
- SCM policy that has been distributed and reviewed by organization or appropriate staff

3.2. Create an SCM Plan

An SCM plan provides the common structure for implementing consistent and effective SCM within an organization. If the organization would like to have a consistent level of SCM or an organization-level certification such as CMM, ISO, etc., consider establishing a standard organization-level SCM plan that can be used as the basis for performing SCM across the organization. An SCM plan may be created at the application level if it is too difficult to get organization-level support.

An SCM Plan will typically include: SCM terminology; reference documents (SCM policy, processes, templates, and related application/organization documents); SCM roles and responsibilities and organizational structure (relative to SCM), and SCM activities (a list of activities to be undertaken). In a nutshell, the SCM plan is the focal point for SCM.

This task provides guidelines for creating the SCM plan that can be used throughout the organization. It is written at a high level so that it may be customized to the needs of an application.

Key Steps:

1. Create an SCM plan. Consider using:
   - An SCM plan template found within the organization (if it exists)
   - SCM plan templates from professional organizations (e.g., IEEE)
   - The SCM plan template found in Section 5 of the Appendix. This template should be customized in a way that is more readily acceptable to the organization.
2. Include the following sections (if they do not already exist):
   - **Objective** – indicate the objective of SCM. For example, 'The objective of the SCM Plan is to provide details for establishing and managing SCM processes for the organization'.
   - **Scope** – identify the scope of where SCM may be applied. For example, 'This SCM Plan applies to all applications and their respective projects.
   - **SCM Terminology** – identify the SCM terminology and acronyms to be used within the organization. Consider reviewing Section 4.2 for more information on this topic.
   - **SCM and Related Documents** – list all documents that provide guidance and direction to the organization and which may have an impact on SCM. See Section 3.2.1 for more information on this topic. Consider grouping these documents into the following three categories and list the documents that would belong in each:
     - Reference documents
     - SCM policy and standards
     - SCM processes and templates
   - **SCM Organizational Structure** – indicate where in the organization the SCM personnel will report. See Section 4.1 for more information on this topic.
   - **SCM Roles and Responsibilities** (including CCB) – list the roles and the corresponding responsibilities of those who perform SCM tasks. Keep in mind, that even senior management has SCM responsibilities such as providing SCM sponsorship. See Sections 3.2.2 and 3.2.3 for more information on this topic.
   - **SCM Activities** – provide the type of tasks necessary to implement effective SCM. These may be represented in an SCM implementation plan, an SCM problem list, and a project plan (software development project release plan).
3. Get the SCM plan reviewed and approved by the appropriate personnel. If it is an organization-level SCM plan, the approval is needed at the senior management level. If it is an application-level SCM plan, the approval is needed at the application owner level.

4. Provide awareness of the customizable SCM plan to the appropriate audience in the form of a presentation. Ensure the application owner and project managers know it is available as an SCM plan template for their application development teams.
5. Place the customizable SCM plan in an easily visible and accessible area like the organization website and/or internal SCM website.

Roles:

- SCM manager – task lead
- Senior management – approval, if at the organization level
- Application owner – approval, if at the application level

Considerations:

- An SCM plan may be created at the application level if it is not practical or possible to get an it approved at an organizational level.
- For more information on CM Plans, review *CM Plans: The Beginning to your CM Solution* [Bounds and Dart 2001].

Output:

- Customizable SCM Plan that is reviewed and approved for use

3.2.1. Define SCM Documents and Related Documents

It is important to identify documents, both SCM and non-SCM, that provide guidance and direction for the organization, application development, and SCM. These may include organizational policies and standards, SCM processes, templates, guidelines, etc. used to provide guidance for SCM.

Document these items within the 'SCM and Related Documents' section of the SCM Plan (or similar document). Indicate the location of these documents (e.g., LAN drive, website, etc.). Consider identifying and documenting these documents in the following categories:

- **Reference Documents** – documents that provide standards, guidelines, and policy for the application that may be relevant to SCM but are not specifically SCM documents. This may include application coding standards, the application requirements list, etc.
- **SCM Policy and Standards** – documents that provide guidance and direction for SCM. The SCM policy states the SCM objectives that must be met to comply with SCM technologies and processes. The SCM standards provide direction for establishing SCM in a uniform manner.
- **SCM Processes and Templates** – documents that provide step-by-step guidance for performing SCM processes and tasks. Consider reviewing Chapter 4 Section 6 for discussion of SCM processes. Typically SCM processes include: Identification, Version Control, Build, Release, Problem Management, Change Control, Audit, and Review.

If any SCM documents do not exist yet, but are planned to exist in the future, include the name of the document and place a 'TBD' in the location column.

3.2.2. SCM Roles and Responsibilities

This section defines the key roles involved in SCM tasks. These are not always SCM specific roles, but include roles that have an SCM responsibility. Document these roles within the 'SCM Roles and Responsibilities' section of the SCM plan. Typical roles that participate in SCM activities at some level include:

- SCM Manager – responsible for overall SCM planning, design, budgeting, hiring, and guidance tasks.
- SCM Engineer – performs the SCM technical implementation and administrative tasks. This may include setting up and administering the SCM technologies, performing build and release functions, and supporting the users of the SCM system. This SCM role may also be known as SCM Administrator or Release Engineer, amongst other titles.
- SCM Coordinator – performs many of the procedural SCM tasks. This may include developing the SCM processes, supporting the CCB (as CCB coordinator) and problem management, and coordinating SCM audits and reviews.
- Senior Management – sponsors SCM at the organization level. Provides budgetary resources and funds for SCM activities at the organization level.
- Application Owner – Sponsors SCM at the application level. Actively participates in CCB and authorization tasks in relation to SCM resources, requirements, and product deliverables. Provides budgetary resources and funds for SCM activities at the application level. This role may also be known as Product Manager, Program Manager, or Application Manager, amongst other titles.
- Project Manager – ensures that SCM activities/tasks are in a project plan and enforces the use of SCM technologies and processes at the project level.
- Application/project team – follows SCM processes in the development of the application and utilizes the SCM technologies and processes.
- System Administrator – provides system support for implementing, maintaining and troubleshooting SCM technologies.
- Note: this section does not address the CCB roles and responsibilities (see the next section for that information).

Role names may be modified for the needs of the organization, application, or project. Provide a description of each role, which may include the expected SCM tasks that need to be completed. The roles of SCM Manager, SCM Engineer, and SCM Coordinator may be played by the same person or different people depending on the size of the organization.

3.2.3. Change Control Board Roles and Responsibilities

This section provides the key roles needed on a Change Control Board (CCB) and a description of the responsibilities. Consider customizing the roles and responsibilities for the organization's needs. The same person may play more than one role (e.g., the Project Manager may represent the Requestor, or the CCB Chairperson may play the CCB Coordinator role). Document the roles within the 'Change Control Board (CCB) Roles and Responsibilities' section of the SCM plan.

CCB members are the stakeholders of the application or project and are qualified to comprehend the scope and impact of a change. They are responsible for managing the critical baselines which may include requirements, environment, and production for an application and the various projects within an application lifecycle. Prior to a CCB becoming active, notify the people of the roles they will play and educate them as to their responsibilities. Section 8.4 in Chapter 4 discusses appropriate materials for educating and training CCB members. Recommended CCB members include:

- CCB Chairperson – leads the CCB meeting. Ensures that each change is objectively discussed and that costs, benefits, and risks are considered. Ultimately responsible for the success of a CCB meeting. Best played by a non-stakeholder for objectivity reasons. This position is considered mandatory.
- CCB Coordinator – manages the CCB materials and process. This includes organizing the change request forms (CRFs) and the change control log (CCL), preparing the agenda including which CRFs will be discussed in the meeting, preparing and sending the minutes of CCB meetings, and scheduling and inviting appropriate attendees to regular CCB meetings. This person may be the CCB Coordinator for multiple projects. The CCB Chairperson may play this role if staff is limited. This position is considered mandatory.
- Application Owner – manages the application lifecycle and is responsible for assessing the business impact of proposed changes to the past, current, and future releases in the application lifecycle. This position is considered mandatory.
- Project Manager(s) – manages a particular release of the application and is responsible for assessing the business and technical impact of proposed changes in relation to that release. This position is considered mandatory.
- QA/Test Representative – focuses on what impact the proposed changes will have on the quality of the release and the test schedule. If the QA and test functions represent two distinct areas, then a member from each group should attend the CCB. This position is considered mandatory.
- Requestor – submits a change request via a change request form (CRF), may attend the CCB when change is being discussed, and indicates the merits of the changes to the members of the CCB. May be a member of an internal division, an external customer, or a representative of the customer. This position is considered optional.
- SCM Engineer – focuses on what impact the change may have on the release needs (infrastructure changes, dates of release, etc.). This position is considered optional.
- Document Representative – focuses on what impact the change may have on the documentation deliverables that are associated with a release. This position is considered optional.
- Production Representative – focuses on what impact the change may have on the production aspects of the change. This position is considered optional.

3.3. SCM Direction Phase Completion Checklist

The items in this checklist may be used to determine if SCM tasks have been completed in this phase:

- Has an SCM policy been created?
  - Has the SCM policy been communicated to the staff?

- Has a customizable SCM plan been created?
  - Has the SCM plan been communicated to the appropriate staff?
- Have the SCM policy and SCM plan been placed in an easily visible and accessible location?

4. SCM Foundation Phase

The SCM Foundation phase provides tasks that begin building the SCM framework. Tasks in this section include: establishing an SCM personnel structure, consistent SCM terminology, and organizational SCM metrics.

4.1. Establish an SCM Personnel Structure

Due to the complex nature of many of today's application development environments and the SCM processes and technologies that are needed to maintain integrity of an application's assets, it is recommended that a more formal SCM personnel structure exists. SCM personnel can provide management with an established means of controlling the changes to the application, provide development staff with a structured environment in which to work, and provide the company with assurance that whatever is being released into the marketplace is re-creatable, traceable, and maintainable. By instituting SCM personnel, the developers and managers can concentrate on their work while SCM work is performed by SCM professionals. This typically establishes a better scenario where developers are happier focusing on their work and SCM personnel are more effectively focusing on SCM tasks. This 'super task' provides input to many aspects of establishing an SCM personnel structure.

Key Steps:

1. Determine the SCM staffing level needed (see Section 4.1.1 for more details on this topic).
2. Determine whether the SCM function should be centralized or decentralized (see Section 4.1.2 below for more details on this topic).
3. Determine where SCM personnel should report within the organization (see Section 4.1.3 for more details on this topic).
4. Create an SCM job family with titles and levels (see Section 4.1.4 below for more details on this topic).
5. Define required SCM skills and create an SCM job description for hiring SCM personnel (see Section 4.1.5 below for more details on this topic).
6. Interview and hire SCM staff as needed (see Section 4.1.6 below for more details on this topic).

Roles:

- SCM manager – task lead
- Recruitment and/or HR

- Senior management
- In-house interview team

Considerations:

- You may find personnel interested in SCM within an organization that have sufficient basic skills to move into the SCM role. However, it typically requires an experienced SCM person to effectively implement SCM technologies and processes.
- For more on the topic of SCM personnel, consider reading the "Software Configuration Management Expert" chapter in [Brown *et al.* 1999]

Output:

- SCM staffing levels
- SCM personnel reporting structure
- SCM job description
- SCM job family
- Offer extended to the best available SCM candidate

4.1.1. Determine SCM Staffing Level

The staffing level of SCM personnel is typically related to the number of personnel SCM can support. The SCM staffing level is derived from the number of personnel that require SCM support divided by the number of personnel one SCM staff member can support based on the type of work needing done. For example, if there are 150 engineers within the organization and each SCM staff member can support approximately 30 engineers based on the type of SCM work being requested (i.e., 30:1 ratio), then the appropriate SCM staffing level for the organization is five (i.e., 150 divided by 30). It should also be recognized that in many cases the number of SCM personnel is a decision made by senior management that may not understand SCM support levels. In this case, it is important to work with and educate management so the best staff levels are identified.

This task provides guidelines for determining support ratios and the number of SCM staff needed for an organization. It may be fair to say that this is an oversimplification of deriving support ratios. Consider establishing a support ratio matrix that better aligns to the organization being supported.

Key Steps:

1. Identify the number of personnel that will need support from SCM staff within the first year.
2. Document the type of SCM and other work that will be expected from SCM staff.
3. Compare the type of SCM work documented above with the ratio guidelines indicated below.

- High Ratio SCM work – 50:1 – The SCM staff may be involved with the common set of SCM tasks. They support and troubleshoot development and build and package the release. The environment is established and well automated.
- Medium Ratio SCM work – 30:1 – The SCM staff is involved with a common set of SCM tasks. They support and troubleshoot development, build and package the release, implement SCM systems, move new applications to SCM, establish SCM processes, and perform SCM training.
- Low Ratio SCM work – 15:1 – The SCM staff is involved with a common set of SCM tasks. They support and troubleshoot development, build and package the release, implement SCM systems, move new applications to SCM, establish SCM processes, and perform SCM training. This may also include managing the development tools and the makefiles, establishing and maintaining the integration between SCM and other tools, and managing the change control tasks, the audit tasks, and other SCM related tasks.

4. Calculate the staffing level. From the ratio identified, divide the number of personnel being supported by the first number in the ratio. For example, if there are 150 personnel that need SCM support and the ratio is 30:1, then 150 divided by 30 equals 5 SCM personnel needed to support the organization or application team based on the type of SCM work being requested.

5. With the above information, meet with the appropriate level of senior management and discuss the ratio and calculated SCM staffing level.

6. On-going: It is recommended that the SCM Manager review the SCM staff levels with their manager on a quarterly basis or when there are changes to the number of applications and/or development personnel that the SCM personnel will need to support.

Roles:

- SCM manager – task lead
- Senior management

Considerations:

- SCM may be asked to support groups across an organization, on several application teams, or just one application team. If SCM is required on more than one team, then the type of work required for SCM to perform may vary. This may add to the complexity of determining the staff ratios for SCM personnel.
- It is also important to note that if an application team or part of an organization claims they need no SCM staff, it can be certain that personnel within the team(s) are performing SCM functions whether they think so or not.
- After a ratio is agreed, it will be used as a measure to hire more SCM personnel as new application teams request SCM services. Ultimately, the staffing level needs to be constantly monitored so that an organization or application team has the appropriate number of SCM staff for a successful release of high quality deliverables. If the ratio is incorrect (and typically there are not enough SCM staff), this can lead to problems in the SCM system and build and release process. Also, if not enough

SCM staff are available, they may be overworked (which may cause the SCM staff to leave the organization).

Output:

- SCM staffing ratio
- SCM staffing level

4.1.2. Determine if SCM should be Centralized or Decentralized

If there is a need to standardize SCM technologies and processes across the organization, it may be feasible to have a centralized SCM organization to work on the various application teams. There may be cost-savings benefits because it may be easier to implement SCM using more of a cookie cutter approach or sharing an existing SCM system. Another benefit is that SCM engineers can be cross-trained on other SCM systems and application environments so single-points-of-failure (SPOF) risks are reduced.

Key Steps:

1. Identify and consider the factors that help determine if it is appropriate to centralize or not.

   The organization would derive benefit from centralization in the following situations:
   - The organization would like consistent technologies or processes across the workplace. It may be easier to implement this when there is a central SCM group that can help determine the consistent technology and process approach. If one of the SCM organizational policy statements supports a consistent technology and process, then centralization may help.
   - There are application teams that have similar needs. When development groups have similar development needs (e.g., similar platforms, development tools, etc.), they may benefit from having a central SCM group that can reuse implementation plans, share hardware and SCM personnel resources, and use existing experience in an environment.
   - There is a need to reduce single points of failure. A single SCM person in an application development team creates a single point of failure (SPOF). This can be eliminated if the SCM person is part of an SCM group whereby other SCM personnel can provide coverage should the primary SCM support be unavailable.
   - With a more common (and centralized) SCM approach, the SCM learning curve is reduced when application staff move from one application team to another.
   - There is a need to reduce cost. A centralized group can focus on negotiating SCM technology purchase agreements based on a potential or known volume for an organization over time. Also, a centralized group will better enable reuse of SCM technology so that divisions and application teams are not purchasing SCM technology licenses when they may already be available in other parts of

the organization. And finally, as mentioned above, a centralized SCM group that manages servers may place several projects on shared hardware, thus reducing hardware and support costs.

The organization would benefit from decentralization in the following situations
- When a centralized SCM group has a different focus on technologies and processes than what is required for an application team.
- The divisions within an organization are independent and do not have a common SCM understanding.

2. Determine if a centralized or decentralized approach is desired.
3. With the above information, meet with the appropriate level of senior management and discuss the approach being considered and why. Gain consensus on an approach.

Roles:
- SCM manager – task lead
- Senior management

Considerations:
- Another option that is used by some organizations is to have a centralized SCM organization for establishing technology and process standards and include decentralized yet cooperative SCM personnel that work directly for application teams for their builds and releases. This may be beneficial in an organization in that it allows divisions or application teams to retain a level of independence, but benefits from the experience, practices, and cost savings of the centralized SCM group.
- For more on the topic of centralized/decentralized SCM, consider reading the "Decentralize Configuration Management" chapter in [Brown *et al.* 1999].

Output:
- A centralized or decentralized approach for SCM personnel is determined

4.1.3. Determine the SCM Personnel Reporting Structure

One of the primary objectives of SCM is to ensure the integrity of the product and produce high-quality deliverables. Other groups within an organization may have similar or different objectives. For example, while one of the objectives of a development group is to produce high-quality deliverables, another of the objectives is to meet time-to-market goals which may take precedence over producing high-quality deliverables if there is a chance that they miss their delivery dates. However, the primary objective of a QA group is to perform verification tasks to ensure the deliverables are high quality. Therefore, this is aligned with SCM quality objectives.

Ideally, (if large enough) the head of SCM should be at the same level as the head of development and QA. If this cannot be achieved, then it is recommended that SCM report into the head of QA. This may be more reasonable when the number of SCM personnel is less than five. Other areas into which SCM personnel may report are Centers of Excellence (CoE) type groups and production support or operations groups. The least recommended approach is to have SCM report to the head of development (or within the development group). Due to a tendency for development to meet their time-to-market goals, it may override the quality goals, thereby reducing the potential quality of the deliverables.

This task provides guidelines for determining where in the organization SCM personnel should report.

Key Steps:

1. Acquire available information on the current personnel structure (e.g., organization charts).
2. Identify and rank the groups that are more closely aligned to the objectives of SCM (i.e., with the highest priority as quality and next highest as time-to-market goals).
3. With the above information, meet with the appropriate level of senior management and discuss and identify the best person for SCM personnel to report into. Attempt to focus on those groups that are more closely aligned with the objectives of SCM.

Roles:

- SCM manager – task lead
- Senior management

Considerations:

- Some organizations may have multiple QA/test and development groups and if SCM is decentralized, then SCM personnel may report into multiple groups.
- The reporting structure of SCM may depend on how committed an organization is to maintaining the balance between quality versus time-to-market. If the organization places a higher priority on time-to-market objectives (than on producing quality products), then SCM may be found in the development group. If the organization places a higher or equal priority on quality, then SCM may be found in a QA group.

Output:

- SCM personnel reporting structure

4.1.4. Establish an SCM Job Family with Titles and Levels

When an organization determines the need for SCM personnel, consideration should be given to establishing an SCM job family. In smaller organizations, SCM personnel may be assigned within the general developer/engineer or QA/test job family. However, when several SCM personnel exist, consideration should be given to creating an SCM job family with titles, levels, and descriptions. SCM titles may be challenging since SCM personnel are called various names in the industry today (e.g., configuration manager, SCM engineer, build engineer, release engineer, integration engineer, system engineer, source control engineer, librarian, etc.). The key is to identify a title that is general enough that it covers a range of the SCM work that those holding the title will perform. This task provides guidelines for creating an SCM job family.

Key Steps:

1. Identify a job family template or guidelines. If this exists, use it as a guideline for completing the remaining steps.
2. Determine a common SCM title that can be used throughout the organization. Consider a title that covers the range of work that will be performed (e.g., SCM Engineer).
3. Determine the number of SCM grade levels, where the grade levels align to the current job family grade levels within the organization, and titles that aligns with each grade level (e.g., junior SCM engineer, SCM engineer, senior SCM engineer, etc.).
4. Create an SCM job family matrix that includes the SCM title per level and a corresponding description. See the SCM job family example immediately following this task for an example of such a matrix.
5. With the draft SCM job family matrix, meet with the appropriate level of senior management. Review and gain consensus on the SCM job family. Update the matrix as appropriate.
6. Provide the SCM job family matrix to the group within the organization that establishes the job families for the organization. This may be HR or Recruiting. Request that a new SCM job family is created, based on the SCM job family matrix, to align with the current organization job family structure.

Roles:

- SCM manager – task lead
- Senior management
- HR/Recruiting

Consideration:

- While this is a recommended task, if senior management and/or HR/Recruiting are unwilling to create a job family for SCM at this time, wait until there are more SCM staff within the organization, then revisit this task.

Output:

- SCM job family within the organization

The following is an example of a five grade SCM job family. It uses the 'SCM Engineer' as the basis for all titles. Each grade level includes a corresponding title, years of expected SCM experience, and a description of the expected work experience.

Table 3.1 Example of an SCM Job Family Matrix

Grade	Grade Title	Years in SCM	Description
I	Junior SCM Engineer	0–2	This person has SCM build and release experience working with established SCM processes and SCM technologies.
II	SCM Engineer	2–5	This person has solid SCM process and technology administration and troubleshooting skills. The more advanced personnel in this space can establish and automate a build and release process. This person can also train users in the usage of the SCM tool.
III	Senior SCM Engineer	4–8	This person has senior level SCM process and technology administration and troubleshooting skills, can troubleshoot various SCM issues, has implemented an SCM system one or more times.
IV	Design SCM Engineer	7–12	This person has performed advanced SCM process and technology administration and troubleshooting, build and release skills, has implemented SCM technologies more than once, and can effectively design and automate a process on top of the SCM technology.
V	Architect SCM Engineer	10+	This person has guru level SCM process and technology administration, troubleshooting, build and release skills; has implemented SCM technologies several times; can design and automate a process on top of the SCM technology; and can engineer separate and unique functions for SCM.

4.1.5. Define SCM Skills and Create an SCM Job Description

Hiring good SCM personnel can be a challenging task. What skills must good SCM personnel have? Considering the vastness of the task of controlling complex environments, it is not recommended that you fill this position with a junior-level person, although this is commonly the case at many companies. The skills and experience needed in SCM personnel may include:

- SCM technology
- SCM process
- Build and release
- Scripting
- Development technology (e.g., IDEs, databases, makefiles, compilers, etc.)

- QA/Test (desirable)
- System administration (desirable)
- Project planning/management (desirable)
- Facilitation and training (desirable)
- Programming/coding language competency (desirable)

It will be difficult to find a person who meets all of the qualifications so identify which skills are the highest priorities for the needs of the organization or application team.

This task provides guidelines for identifying SCM skills and creating an SCM job description for the organization.

Key Steps:

1. Identify the skills needed for SCM personnel (see skills listed immediately above as an example).
2. Identify the SCM titles based on the level of SCM personnel desired (see Section 4.1.4).
3. Create an SCM job description. Consider using the job description template for the organization (if one exists) or the example of an SCM job description found immediately following this table as the basis for the job description.
4. Meet with the appropriate level of senior management and gain approval for the use of the SCM job description.
5. Provide the SCM job description to HR/Recruiting for use when additional SCM personnel are needed.

Roles:

- SCM manager – task lead
- Senior management
- Recruitment

Considerations:

- This job description may be used as the template for all SCM job descriptions in the future.
- For more on the topic of appropriate levels of SCM personnel, consider reading the "Software Configuration Management Expert" chapter in [Brown *et al.* 1999]

Output:

- SCM Job Description

The following is an example of an SCM job description. This job description does not differentiate between experience levels or skills. It should be modified with the appropriate level of experience (in years), platforms, and SCM technologies in mind.

SCM Job Description

Required Qualifications:

- 5 years of SCM technology experience on <Windows/UNIX/LINUX> platform
- Experience with build and release processes

- Experience with SCM standards, processes, and methods
- Skilled with shell/perl programming for automation and improvements
- Excellent communication skills
- Bachelors Degree or equivalent

Desired:

- System administration experience
- QA/Test experience
- Technical writing skill
- Production support/troubleshooting experience

Responsibilities:

- Maintain, improve, and automate the SCM system
- Establish and maintain the software build and release process
- Build and package deliverables and migrate code changes into test and production environments
- Support development personnel in any SCM need
- Perform SCM audits
- Troubleshoot SCM problems at any point in the application or project lifecycle
- Provide SCM technology and process training

4.1.6. Interview and Hire SCM Personnel

This task provides guidelines for interviewing (and hiring) SCM personnel.

Key Steps:
1. Determine the grade level and corresponding title of the SCM position. Consider reviewing the SCM job family if it exists within the organization. See Section 4.1.4 above for more details on this topic.
2. Create an SCM job description specific to this position. See Section 4.1.5 above for more details on this topic.
3. Working with Recruiting, post the SCM job description on all appropriate job posting sites.
4. Review and evaluate incoming resumes and identify the top 4–6 candidates that meet the job description requirements.
5. Identify an in-house interview team. This may be composed of SCM personnel, hiring manager, senior management, and application owner (of the application team where the candidate will be working).
6. Schedule interviews with each of the candidates and the in-house interview team.
7. Conduct interview sessions.
8. Evaluate each candidate. Consider preparing an interview evaluation form for each candidate. Each candidate should be rated on the following:
   - The 5 to 8 highest priority SCM skills required/desired, including SCM technology, SCM process (SCM plans, processes, etc.); build and release; programming

(Perl, shell, etc.); system administration; communication; and teamwork. Consider applying a 1–10 rating with 10 being the highest rating for each skill area.
- How quickly the candidate can come up to speed in the position being offered.
- Does the candidate fit the need of the group.

9. Tabulate results of all evaluations.
10. Identify the top two candidates from the tabulated results to determine which candidate has the highest average score to help in determining the best candidate.
11. Meet with the in-house interview team and gain consensus on identifying the best candidate.
12. Extend offer to the candidate.

Roles:

- SCM manager – task lead
- In-house interview team
- Recruiting

Considerations:

- While interviewing, evaluate based on the level into which the candidate is being hired.
- For more on the topic of the need for SCM personnel, consider reading the "Software Configuration Management Expert" chapter in [Brown *et al.* 1999]

Output:

- Completed interview evaluations
- Offer extended to the best available SCM candidate

4.2. Establish SCM Terminology

This task helps establish a common SCM language in order to increase SCM understanding and have more effective SCM discussions within an organization.

Key Steps:

1. Identify any commonly used terminology in the organization that describes an SCM practice or function within the organization. This may include acronyms such as 'SCM'.
2. Define and document a common set of SCM terminology that will help facilitate more effective SCM discussions and an understanding of SCM. As a starting point, consider reviewing the terminology in:
   - The SCM glossary example in Section 3 of the Appendix
   - SCM books and industry standard organizations (e.g., IEEE, SEI CMM, etc.)
3. If there are acronyms being used, ensure they are expanded to the words they represent and defined appropriately.

4. Identify events and places where the SCM glossary may receive visibility. For example, include SCM Terminology as part of the SCM training, hold meetings to discuss it, create posters, or send email with this information.

Roles:

- SCM manager – task lead

Considerations:

- Consider integrating commonly used SCM terminology within the organization into the SCM glossary. This makes it easier for users to adopt the SCM terminology.
- It is important to note that the term Software Configuration Management (SCM) has a number of aliases that are used interchangeably. It is important to align people to one standard name within an organization for this function to establish a common understanding.
- The output of this task (i.e., the SCM glossary) can be included in (or referenced by) the SCM plan (at the organization level) or SCM design specification (at the application level).

Output:

- Standard SCM glossary (SCM terminology and acronyms)

4.3. Establish Organization Level SCM Metrics

This task focuses on identifying and tracking SCM metrics at the organization level. If the organization is serious about SCM, it is suggested that appropriate organizational level metrics are identified and tracked to ensure SCM is occurring according to stated goals and objectives.

Key Steps:

1. Identify the SCM objectives for the organization. This may exist in an SCM policy (see Section 3.1 for more on this topic).
2. Consider the measure of success for each SCM objective as the basis for the SCM metrics. If organizational SCM metrics exist, ensure these are included. Examples of SCM metrics at the organization level include (but are not limited to):
   - The percentage of application teams using an SCM technology compared to the expected goal at that point in time (if the SCM technology implementation has just started, the goal for the first year may be that 25% of the application teams use the SCM technology).
   - The percentage of application items that are in the SCM technology repository. The goal should be 100%, but there may be some cases where this is not possible.
   - The percentage of application teams compliant with SCM processes. The goal should be 100%, but there may be a phased implementation of the SCM processes. This data may be captured via audits or assessments.

- How compliant an organization is compared to a standard like ISO, IEEE, SEI CMM, etc.
3. Communicate the SCM metrics that will be collected throughout the organization (so there are no surprises and so personnel know what is being measured).
4. Determine the frequency at which organizational level SCM metrics will be collected. Consider a frequency that minimizes effort and allows personnel to have time to improve from one reporting period to another.
5. Provide senior management with SCM metrics results and solicit their expected results and improvement requests.
6. Prepare and implement a plan to address the senior management improvement requests and other areas that may be improved.
7. Publish periodic metric reports (at the determined frequency) and place metrics in appropriate places (e.g., websites, bulletin boards, etc.).

Roles:

- SCM manager – task lead
- Senior management

Considerations:

- It is important to communicate the SCM metrics to the organization. This provides awareness, allows the groups to proactively plan for appropriate actions to meet the SCM metrics objectives, and reduces concern.
- It is important that metrics do not get misused for punishment purposes by senior management. It this occurs, then the metrics will be looked on with suspicion and distrust.

Output:

- Periodic SCM metrics that are published in an appropriate location
- SCM improvement plans

4.4. SCM Foundation Phase Completion Checklist

The items in this checklist may be used to determine if SCM tasks have been completed in this phase:

- Have general SCM roles and responsibilities been defined?
- Has it been determined if the SCM function will be centralized or decentralized?
- Has an SCM personnel reporting structure been defined?
- Has an SCM job description been created?
- If applicable, has an SCM job family been created?
- Has SCM terminology been defined?
    - Has SCM terminology been communicated to the staff? If so, how?
- Have organizational level SCM metrics been established?
    - Are the SCM metrics being collected and used to improve SCM or the organization?

4

Establish an SCM Infrastructure for an Application

1. Focusing on the Application Level

This chapter focuses on SCM tasks that should be considered for establishing an SCM system at the application level. In order to benefit from technology, an application must have well-defined and repeatable processes. Establishing a common infrastructure supported by SCM processes and technologies will provide integrity to the development of the application.

An application typically has an extensive lifecycle and may 'live' several years (provided that the application is successful). For example, there have been many releases of word processing and spreadsheet programs that have been on the market for a number of years and numerous incremental releases have been available over time. For this discussion, a word processing program is equivalent to an application. There may be multiple releases of an application while it is viable. It is this time period from first inception of the application until the last release, which constitutes the application lifecycle.

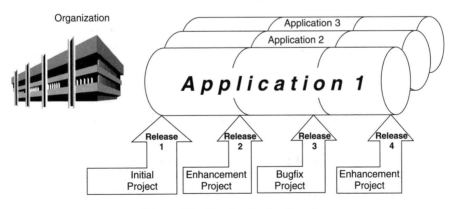

Figure 4.1   The Application Level

Software Configuration Management: Implementation Roadmap   M. E. Moreira
© 2004 Mario E. Moreira   ISBN: 0-470-86264-5 (HB)

1.1. Application Level Phases

This chapter is divided into phases constructed in a particular order to establish an SCM system at the application level. The phases include:

- SCM Analysis – tasks focused on analyzing the state of SCM and assessing SCM risks
- SCM Implementation Planning – tasks focused on planning for the SCM implementation effort
- SCM Technology Selection – tasks focused on evaluating SCM technology
- SCM Design – tasks focused on designing the SCM infrastructure
- SCM Process – tasks focused on preparing SCM processes
- SCM Technology Implementation – tasks focused on establishing the SCM infrastructure
- SCM Training – tasks focused on providing SCM training to personnel
- SCM System Testing – tasks focused on validating the readiness of the SCM system
- SCM System Transition – tasks focused on moving users to the new SCM system

Many of the phases occur in sequence, but some phases will occur in parallel with others. The process flow diagram below illustrates this point. After the SCM analysis phase and toward the end of the SCM implementation planning phase, the SCM design, SCM technology selection, and SCM process phases may begin at roughly the same time. The SCM process phase may continue through the SCM system testing phase. The SCM training phase must begin after the selection of the SCM technology due to the need for the SCM engineer to be trained in implementing and administering the technology and may continue through the SCM system transition phase due to the need for 'just-in-time' SCM technology user training during the cut-over to a live SCM system.

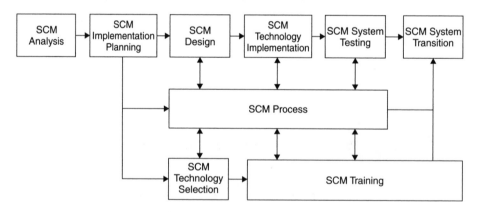

Figure 4.2   Application Level Process Flow

1.2. How to use this Chapter

It is important to walk through each phase in this chapter and review each task in each phase. Consider customizing the task name to one that best aligns with the terminology used with the workplace. Also, when reviewing a task, consider customizing it in a manner that may provide a better chance of implementation or adoption.

Determine which tasks will be undertaken for the particular effort according to the level of maturity of the application team. Select the task and include the name of the task in the SCM implementation plan. Try not to take on more than an organization or application team can handle. Consider performing the SCM analysis task in order to get a picture of the state of SCM for the application.

At this point in the book, it is assumed that resources (e.g., people and funding for the SCM technology) are available. If this is not case, go back to Chapter 3 and work through the management commitment, budgeting, and hiring tasks. Having SCM resources available will have a major impact on the success of an SCM implementation.

2. SCM Analysis Phase

The SCM analysis phase provides tasks that help in understanding the current state of SCM for the application. These tasks include assessing the implementation readiness, preparing high-level estimates for the SCM project, performing an SCM analysis, and performing an application level SCM risk assessment.

2.1. Assess the Implementation Readiness

This task includes steps to help assess the readiness of an SCM implementation effort and identify resistance within an application team. This section will also provide ways to improve implementation readiness that may have a tremendous impact on improving the chance of success of the SCM implementation effort.

Key Steps:

1. Identify questions that can help assess the state of readiness of an application team that is beginning a technology and process transition. Consider using the following questions as a starting point:
   - Are there SCM technology and processes in place? No SCM technology may highlight a more crucial need. However, if an SCM technology exists, expect some resistance from those who feel the current technology is adequate.
   - Are other technology and process changes occurring at the same time? Note: Change refers to an introduction of significant technology and process (new requirements, tools, and process, new test suite and test process, etc.)
   - Is there resistance to using new SCM technology and processes? Determine this based on discussion with application personnel who will be the target users of the technology and processes. If there does appear to be resistance, ask the personnel for ways that may reduce the resistance.
2. Identify personnel on the application team that are in leadership and influential positions (e.g., application owner, project managers, leads, etc.) who will be surveyed.
3. Meet with the identified personnel and ask the questions above.
4. Analyze the responses from the meeting.
5. If the implementation readiness appears low or resistance appears high, then determine ways to increase readiness and reduce resistance for a more successful implementation and adoption of the technology.

- Review the feedback from the meeting and consider ways to reduce resistance.
- Read Section 2.1.1 for ways to improve readiness.
6. Put a plan in place to increase the state of readiness and reduce resistance based on the ideas considered.
7. Implement the plan.
8. Evaluate results periodically.

Roles:

- SCM manager – task lead

Consideration:

- Identify implementation transition readiness materials that may provide more ideas for improving readiness by searching the web using the following key words: technology adoption, technology transition, and change management.

Output:

- Identified level of implementation readiness
- Identified level of resistance
- Plan prepared and enacted to improve implementation readiness and reduce resistance.

2.1.1. Ways to Improve Implementation Readiness and Reduce Resistance

What do you do if the state of implementation readiness is not as high as desired? A key suggestion is to investigate the type of resistance that may exist by talking with several key employees who will be using the SCM technology and processes. [Myers *et al*. 1990] say that there may be a number of reasons for resistance and give corresponding suggestions to improve the chances of making a successful implementation:

- Lack of understanding of the technology or process. What to do: Ensure there are the appropriate presentations or meetings to discuss the technology and processes. Also, consider explaining the benefits to the users of SCM. In general, ensure there is sufficient information communicated to the users and that questions are appropriately addressed.
- Adjustment problems. Transition will upset the status quo. Many people simply do not like change and prefer the system the way it is, even with the problems. What to do: Explain the benefits of the change, air all concerns, and ensure the staff understand there will be support throughout the implementation effort.
- Impact of power base. This change may reduce a person's role. What to do: Provide awareness of what the new roles will be. Ensure there is support and training for any transition of roles.
- Covert resistance. What to do: Provide multiple opportunities to express resistance and create an atmosphere of trust. Remove any retribution associated with expressing diverse opinions.

- Concern over success. What to do: Ensure the success criteria are clear. Ensure a reward system is in place to promote a successful transition. Avoid any retribution for missing milestones.
- Improper time in the release cycle. The middle of a long release lifecycle, in many cases, is simply not the appropriate time to introduce a technology and/or process change and resistance may stem from the timing. What to do: Indicate that while the implementation may start, the transition to the new technology/process will not occur until after the end of the release.
- Too many changes are already occurring. What to do: Wait until there are fewer technology changes occurring. Ideally, only the SCM implementation transition occurs, but this may not be realistic. However, the less change occurring, the better the chance of successfully moving to the SCM technology and processes.

2.2. Prepare High-Level Estimates for the SCM Project

Prior to detailed planning, this task helps estimate the approximate effort and duration of an SCM implementation project. The SCM technology being specified in this task is the SCM version control/build management type. The estimates should be based on the known complexity of application development. For example, is the SCM technology being implemented on one platform or two platforms? Is the application you are placing under SCM small, medium, or large? Is there one or more applications being imported into the SCM system? Is the application dependent on another application's code during compile or run-time? This estimate can then be used to prepare the application owner and others for a realistic timeframe of establishing an adequate SCM infrastructure.

Key Steps:

1. Determine the list of key characteristics that will indicate the complexity of the SCM implementation effort. They typically include (but are not limited to):
   - the number of applications to import and support
   - the size of applications
   - build and run-time dependencies
   - the number of platforms
   - the number of users
   - the automation level desired
2. Identify how this SCM implementation aligns to the characteristics. For example, identify the number of applications to convert, the size of applications, the number of developers, etc.
3. Determine the complexity of this SCM implementation by comparing the application characteristics with those found in the SCM infrastructure complexity matrix (see Section 2.2.1 below).
4. Identify the high level effort and duration estimates for this SCM infrastructure implementation project.

Roles:

- SCM manager – task lead

Considerations:

- This is just a high level estimate and it is expected that proper planning should occur to provide a more accurate estimation of effort and duration. For more on this topic, see Section 3.1 in this chapter.
- The estimates assume that this is a full SCM Implementation (from planning through release).

Output:

- High-level estimate of effort and duration for implementing an SCM infrastructure

2.2.1. High Level Estimates using an SCM Infrastructure Complexity Matrix

The following table is an SCM infrastructure complexity matrix that provides high level estimates of effort and duration for an SCM infrastructure implementation based on application characteristics. This is not a precise measure and will vary depending on the resources available (i.e., personnel, equipment, and technology), expertise of the personnel, and how robust the SCM system is expected to be.

It is important to understand that the duration of an SCM infrastructure project is dependent on many factors such as hardware availability, resource availability for the project, etc. For example, having to wait for hardware or having SCM resources pulled from this project to support a release will increase the duration.

Also, there may be characteristics of an SCM infrastructure project that reside in more than one complexity level. Identify where the majority of the characteristics live to determine the complexity of the SCM infrastructure project. Note: all complexity levels include the creation of SCM processes.

Table 4.1 SCM Infrastructure Complexity Matrix

Complexity Level	Characteristics	Effort/hrs	Duration
Low	• 1 small application (or less than 500 files) • No code to import • No build dependencies to other applications • 1 platform (i.e., operating system) • Basic implementation • 5 or fewer users of the SCM system • No automation • No IDE integration(s)	100–300 hrs	1–3 months
Medium	• 1 medium application (or 500–1500 files) or 2–3 small applications • May import latest code release	250–600 hrs	3–6 months

Table 4.1   (*continued*)

Complexity Level	Characteristics	Effort/hrs	Duration
	• Few build dependencies to other applications • 2 platforms • Basic implementation • Small amount of automation • No IDE integration(s)		
High	• 1 large application (or 1500–5000 files) or more than 3 small/medium applications • Import full code base including history • Build dependencies to other applications • 2 platforms • Medium amount of automation • Integration with IDE	500–1000 hrs	5–9 months
Very High	• 1 very large application (or 5000+ files) or more than 5 small/medium/large applications • Import of full code base including history • Build dependencies to other applications • 2+ platforms • Development at multiple sites sharing the code base • Medium/high amount of automation • Integration with IDE	900–2500 hrs	7–18 months

2.3. Perform an SCM Analysis

This task provides steps for performing an SCM analysis to get a picture of the current state of the SCM environment in which the application lives. This will also help identify tasks to establish a solid SCM infrastructure.

While there are many ways to perform an SCM analysis, there are typically two conditions that help define the SCM analysis approach: whether the application has no SCM infrastructure; or whether there is an SCM infrastructure in place that must be replaced or improved upon.

For the first condition, a more straightforward approach can be applied, focusing on what the development environment is or is expected to be (e.g., what the development platform is, etc.). In the second condition, more consideration must be given to investigating the way the current technologies are used and the processes in which SCM occurs. It is important to know how technologies and processes are currently working so that the current process does not "break" when the replacement SCM system or SCM improvements are implemented (e.g., typically, releases of an application must continue for revenue reasons so you must work around the current process).

Key Steps:

1. Schedule a meeting with key application personnel.
2. In the meeting, identify what SCM infrastructure is in place. Essentially, attempt to determine the state of the SCM environment. Consider using the SCM analysis investigator template in Section 6 of the Appendix, which can be used as a guideline for this analysis task. Consider identifying information in the following areas:
   - Process overview:
     - SCM plan or design specification
     - SCM roles and responsibilities
     - SCM problem management process and technology
     - SCM change control process and technology
     - Other SCM processes
     - Release migration path (how does code get from the developer to production)
     - SCM training available
   - Technology overview:
     - Development and production platform(s)
     - Coding language and development tool(s)
     - Number of developers
     - Size of application(s)
     - Build and run-time application dependencies
     - Current SCM version control technology (if it exists)
     - Location of code repository
     - SCM release engineering technology
3. Summarize the results of the analysis. An SCM analysis summary template is available in Section 7 of the Appendix. The results should include:
   - Strengths – attempt to list at least five SCM strengths within the application team even if they are not directly related to SCM (this may be difficult if SCM is weak on the application). The objective is to positively motivate the team and show that there is potential for good SCM practices.
   - Opportunities for improvement – limit this to the three biggest areas of SCM improvement for the application team. If too many are presented, this may reduce the level of enthusiasm for SCM.
4. Meet with the key application personnel and application owner and review the summary.

Roles:

- SCM manager – task lead
- SCM coordinator
- Key application personnel
- Application owner

Considerations:

- If there is no SCM infrastructure, then the time it takes to complete this task will be reduced.

- The recommendations from the summary become inputs to the SCM implementation plan.

Output:

- SCM analysis summary

2.4. Perform an Application-Level SCM Risk Assessment

This task provides steps for creating an SCM risk assessment template and performing an SCM risk assessment in order to identify the risks that may impact the success of SCM as it relates to the application. It recommends reviewing the risks with the application owner, determining the appropriate mitigation actions, and including the mitigation actions into the appropriate plan to minimize the impact of the risk or possibility of the risk occurring.

It should be noted that there is a difference between a risk and a problem (or issue). A risk indicates that there is a possibility of something negative happening, but it has not yet happened. A problem indicates that something negative has happened. The value of managing risks is to avoid the negative event (i.e. problem) happening so it does not impact SCM or application development effort.

Key Steps:

1. Identify an SCM risk list template. Consider using:
    - Existing risk list templates found within the organization.
    - The SCM risk list template found in Section 1 of the Appendix, which includes template definitions, risk categories, and risk conditions.
2. Perform the SCM risk assessment.
    - Schedule a meeting with key application personnel.
    - Conduct the meeting. Identify the SCM risks and document them in the SCM risk list.
        - Introduce the risk categories (e.g., Personnel; Estimates; Scope; Technology; Management; Sponsorship; Policy; Schedule; Location) as guidance on what may be considered.
        - Document each risk including the description, suspected root cause, the impact to SCM or the application, the severity of the impact, probability of occurrence, and suggested mitigation action.
    Note: should SCM issues (negative events currently impacting SCM or the application) be identified, consider capturing them using a problem management process and/or technology (should one exist).
3. Meet with the application owner and project manager(s) and review the SCM risk list.
    - Agree on which mitigation actions should be initiated.
4. Add the mitigation actions to the appropriate plan (e.g., SCM implementation plan or development project plan).

Roles:

- SCM manager – task lead
- Key application personnel
- Application owner and project manager(s)

Considerations:

- Consider performing periodic SCM risk assessments throughout the implementation effort.
- For more on the topic of risk categories, read Appendix A.3 in [Dart 2000].

Output:

- SCM risk list template
- Identified SCM risks, reviewed by application owner
- Mitigation action for selected SCM risks added to a plan or tracking list

2.5. SCM Analysis Phase Completion Checklist

The items in this checklist may be used to determine if SCM tasks have been completed in this phase:

- Has the implementation readiness of the application team been assessed?
  - If readiness is inadequate, have ways to improve technology readiness been tried?
- Has a high level estimate of the effort and duration of the SCM infrastructure complexity been prepared?
- Has an SCM analysis of the current state of the application occurred?
  - Has an SCM analysis summary been created and reviewed with the appropriate personnel?
- Has an SCM risk assessment occurred?
  - Were the SCM risks reviewed with the application owner and appropriate mitigation actions defined?
  - Were mitigation actions added to the appropriate plan or tracking list?

3. SCM Implementation Planning Phase

The SCM Implementation Planning phase provides tasks that help establish a roadmap for an SCM infrastructure implementation. These tasks include developing an SCM implementation project plan; setting up an application document repository including a version numbering convention; and establishing application level SCM metrics.

3.1. Develop an SCM Implementation Project Plan

This task provides steps to help prepare the SCM implementation project plan, effectively the project plan for establishing an SCM system.

This SCM implementation project plan should not be confused with the traditional CM Plan advocated by the IEEE organization or the SCM Plan advocated by the Software Engineering Institute (SEI) Capability Maturity Model (CMM). The latter types of plans (CM Plan and SCM Plan) provide the framework for SCM (i.e., processes, roles and responsibilities, SCM activities at a high level). The SCM implementation project plan is a work breakdown structure (WBS) or task list, with dates, role assignments, dependencies, and timelines. As mentioned before, this is effectively the roadmap for the SCM infrastructure implementation effort.

Key Steps:

1. Identify and acquire the standard project plan template within the organization or group. If one does not exist, consider using the customizable SCM implementation project plan template found in Section 8 of the Appendix.
   - Ensure the plan template includes at least the following columns or fields: Phase; Task; Task Owner; Dependency; Start Date; End Date; and Estimated Effort
   - At a high level, consider including the following phases: Analysis; Planning; Design; Technology Selection; Implementation; Process; Training; Test; and Transition.
   - This becomes the basis of the SCM implementation project plan.
2. Identify and document the tasks needed to establish an SCM system in the Task column within the plan. It should cover the typical tasks needed to establish SCM for an application team.
   - As guidance for determining the tasks needed, review each task in this chapter.
   - Select and document the SCM tasks to create the type of SCM implementation plan needed.
   - Also review the SCM analysis summary (the output from task 2.3 in this chapter), provides specific areas that need attention. Ensure tasks that improve these areas get included in the SCM implementation plan.
3. Establish dependencies between tasks in the Dependency column.
4. Assign an owner to each task in the Task Owner column.
5. Assign an estimated effort for each task in the Estimated Effort column. This will be helpful when identifying the critical path tasks to ensure they are getting the appropriate focus.
6. Determine the start and end date for each task in the Start Date and End Date column.
7. The duration of an SCM implementation effort is typically longer than expected due to the many dependencies (e.g., hardware availability, resource availability from project team, etc.). For example, waiting for hardware or pulling an SCM resource from the project to support a release will increase the duration of the SCM implementation.
8. Review the SCM implementation project plan with all appropriate personnel (those that will work on and will be impacted by the effort).

9. On-going: Utilize a project planning process to properly manage to the plan. As a minimum, perform the following:
   - Update plan based on progress and impacts
   - Review plan on a regular basis with impacted personnel

Roles:

- SCM manager – task lead
- SCM engineer and SCM coordinator – contributors
- Impacted personnel – application owner, project managers, etc. (as reviewers)

Consideration:

- The expectation is that the SCM implementation plan will be managed with project planning processes.

Output:

- SCM implementation project plan

3.2. Establish a Document Infrastructure

This task ensures that early in the application lifecycle there is an infrastructure to support the numerous documents that will be produced. Two key components of a document infrastructure are the document repository and the document version numbering convention.

A document repository should be created to capture and store the various application and project-related documents, including project plans, project charters, requirements documents, design documents, test plans, SCM documents, and numerous other lists, templates, training materials, and processes. Documents may be stored in an SCM version control repository, a document management tool, or in a well-structured common directory on a file system that is readily available to the appropriate personnel. Once the SCM technology selection phase begins, a more formal evaluation of a document repository technology may be warranted if the initial repository is not satisfactory. As more documents are produced and staff numbers increase, access to shared documents becomes critical.

A version numbering convention for documents consists of a numbering scheme which increments when changes occur in a document. The version number is included on all publicly available documents. When new versions of the same document are created, the older versions of the document continue to exist. People often become unclear whether they are looking at a new version or an older version. This is especially confusing when two people are discussing the 'same' document and realize the content is, in fact, different.

Key Steps:

1. Establish a version numbering convention. Consider using:
   - A version numbering convention used within the organization (if it exists).

- A version numbering convention that includes a major version indicator, a minor version indicator, and a draft version indicator (e.g., **a.bc**). For more details on the suggested version numbering convention, see Section 3.2.1 below.
- Document the version numbering convention as a standard, guideline, or process guide.
- Communicate the version numbering convention to the application personnel. This may take the form of brief training or an awareness session.

2. Establish a document repository for the application. Identify the variety of document repositories that are in use within the organization.

- Investigate if a document repository standard exists or identify the most commonly used document repository within the organization (LAN directory, document management technology, SCM version control technology, etc.).
- Select a document repository. Consider choosing the document repository that is already in use with the application, within the organization, or which may be the easiest to set up. Validate the choice with the application owner and project manager(s). For a more robust evaluation, see Section 4.2.1.
- Establish a structure in which the documents will reside.
  - Consider a 'release' level directory structure or field to differentiate between different releases of the application. For example, if using a LAN directory, then consider the following directory structure:
    '<application name>/Release 1', then '<application name>/Release 2'
  - Consider maturity level directory structures or fields. For example, a 'Prod' directory is created for all released documents and a 'Draft' directory is created for all draft documents. For example:
    '<application name>/Release 1/prod' and '<application name>/Release 1/draft'
  - Also consider fields for version number, title, and category (process, plan, etc).
- Set up the document repository. If it is a vendor product, then install the product as per the installation instructions, identify an administrator to support the technology and ensure the administrator of the document repository technology receives appropriate training or learning opportunities to support the technology.
- Identify all who need access to the document repository and provide access to all appropriate application personnel.
- Prepare a process for using the document repository, particularly for modifying documents. This may include a Version Control Process (see Section 6.4).
- Communicate the information on the document repository to application personnel. This may take the form of brief training or an awareness session.

Roles:

- SCM engineer – task lead
- SCM manager
- Application owner

Considerations:

- The easier and more accessible the document repository, the more likely it will be used.
- It is recommended that you identify a robust and automated document repository technology from a document management or SCM technology vendor. These provide a more automated way of managing documents, searching for information, and tracking changes.
- Every project that passes into the planning and requirements phase should begin using a document repository for managing the changes to the items.
- Version numbers do not have to be used on all documents, only those publicly shared.
- A version number should be applied to a document, even if it is stored in SCM version control technology. This is because the version numbering convention reflects the versions of the released documents and the SCM technology simply increments the version number without any intelligence about whether the document is ready to be released or whether it is still draft and being checked in for security and back up reasons.

Output:

- Established version numbering convention
- Established document repository
- Application personnel aware of (and/or trained in) the version numbering convention and the document repository
- Optional SCM version control process for document management

3.2.1. Version Numbering Convention Details

A recommended version numbering convention uses a minimum of three places for the numbers: one digit to the left of the decimal point and two digits to the right of the decimal point (e.g., **a.bc**).

- The digit before the decimal point (**a**.bc) is the *major* version indicator for a released or production-ready document. The first time a document is released for public consumption, it becomes 'version 1.0'.
- The first digit after the decimal point (a.**b**c) is the *minor* version indicator for a released document. After a document released to the public (version 1.0) has a minor modification, it becomes 'version 1.1'.
- The second digit after the decimal point (a.b**c**) is the *draft* version indicator for a document in a draft state. If a document has not yet been released (and is not ready for public consumption) but is made available for review, then it becomes 'version 0.01'.

Consider the extent of the changes when revising released documents (e.g., major or minor). Is the scope changing or are simple comments being added? The extent of the changes will determine the change (or increment) of the version number. Below are suggestions for the two categories of changes.

- Major changes – scope, direction, major changes/additions to subject, adding new sections.
- Minor changes – adding new information to existing sections, updating existing sections, formatting and typos.

It is important to understand the distinction between *release* and *draft* documents. Release documents are documents that have been completed with respect to the deliverables for which they have been designed (i.e., they meet the requirements) and are available to the public (either internal or external) as if they are in production. A draft document refers to a document in the making. Due to the need to acquire and deliver information on a high volume and speedy basis, many documents are delivered in a draft state. The reason to give a version number to release-ready documents may be obvious, but it is also important to give a version number to the draft documents before they are distributed since there may be several iterations of the draft before it is release-ready.

3.3. Establish Application-Level SCM Metrics

This task focuses on identifying and tracking SCM metrics at the application level. Consider tracking application-level SCM metrics in conjunction with organization-level SCM metrics. This provides a robust view of the level and performance of SCM being applied.

Key Steps:

1. Identify and review existing SCM metrics being collected on the application (if any) or metrics deployed on other applications.
2. Identify SCM metrics that can be collected which can improve application development, help in improving SCM processes, and meet SCM objectives.
   - Consider investigating what metrics other professionals in the SCM field may be deploying (check websites, e-groups, etc.).
   - Consider reviewing and collecting at least the following SCM metrics that may get captured at the application level but would be applied from project to project:
     - Percentage of Files Changed (from Release to Release) – requires baseline data of the current number of files and a way to identify changed files. This identifies risk in relation to how much of the code baseline has changed, therefore helping identify what needs to be tested and how thorough testing should be.
     - Most Frequently Changed (within a release or from release to release) – requires a way to identify changed files over time. This identifies high volatility files which may require focused testing or consideration of dividing the file into two or more files.
     - Build Times (if compiling code) – requires known start time and end time, then calculating build time. Track over time (trend). Can be used to improve build times and therefore help support time-to-market goals.
     - Build Success Rate (if compiling code) – requires definition of successful build. Track over time (trend). Can identify common build failures for improvement.

- Defect Density – requires lines of code or some sizing measure and defect tracking counts. Track over time (trend). Can be used to determine stability of product.
- If no organization-level SCM metrics are being tracked, consider reviewing and collecting the following SCM metrics as they relate to SCM usage for the application:
  - Percentage of application configuration items that are in the SCM technology repository. The goal should be 100%, but there may be cases where this is not possible.
  - Percentage of application teams compliant with (i.e., using) SCM processes. The goal should be 100% but there may be a phased implementation of the SCM processes.
  - See Section 4.3 in Chapter 3 to review other organization-level metrics.
3. Select and prepare a list of proposed SCM metrics.
  - For each SCM metric under consideration, identify the respective benefit of the metrics compared to the ease (or difficulty) of setting up and implementing the process for periodic collection of the measurement data. With this in mind, for each proposed metric, document the following:
    - the benefit of each metric (how the metric can be used to improve the application processes, quality, and time-to-market or to reduce risk, etc.)
    - who would benefit from the collection of the metrics
    - how frequently the metrics should be collected
    - how the metrics will help the application team and/or SCM
    - the effort that is required to collect the metrics
  - Review the proposed metrics with the application owner discussing the above information and select the initial set of SCM metrics that will be identified, collected, and tracked.
4. Establish a metrics collection process, the more automated the better. This may involve scripting/coding a metric collection solution or acquiring a metrics collection technology.
5. Determine what will be reported for the SCM metrics. Ensure the metrics graphs and charts are easy to interpret by others, particularly application owners and senior management.
6. Establish a periodic SCM metrics reporting cycle. Ensure the application owner, project manager(s), and senior management (as appropriate) receive the metrics.
7. Consider communicating the SCM metrics to application personnel (via email, posted on a bulletin board, or published on a website).
8. Periodically, review SCM metrics, identify opportunities for improvement, and prepare action plans to carry out improvement efforts.
9. Long-term: Once you have tracked the metric for at least 5–10 periods or cycles, consider identifying the acceptable data range (or norm) within each metric. For example, if build times are being collected for five consecutive weeks and the average build time is 30 minutes per week, then the acceptable range for build times may be 25 to 35 minutes. Anything outside that range should be investigated.

Roles:

- SCM manager – task lead
- application owner

Considerations:

- SCM metrics at the application level should ultimately be used to improve the development and release processes for the application team. For example, if an objective of an SCM metric is to get all developers trained, then the training will enable developers to utilize the SCM technologies effectively and ensure all CIs are in the SCM version control repository.
- It is very critical to communicate the SCM metrics to the application team. This provides awareness, reduces concern, and allows the team to proactively plan for appropriate actions to meet the SCM metrics objectives.
- It is important that the application owner and/or senior management do not mis-use metrics for punishment purposes, otherwise SCM will always be looked on with suspicion.

Output:

- Identified SCM metrics
- An efficient process of collecting the measures that make up the SCM metrics
- Periodic reviews of SCM metrics with management and published in an appropriate location
- Action planning to improve SCM processes are established and managed

3.4. SCM Implementation Planning Phase Completion Checklist

The items in this checklist may be used to determine if SCM tasks have been completed in this phase:

- Has an SCM implementation project plan been created?
  - Has the SCM implementation project plan been reviewed by the appropriate personnel?
- Has a version numbering convention for documents been established?
  - Has the version numbering convention been communicated to application personnel?
- Has a document repository been established for the application?
  - Have application personnel been informed of the document repository and the process to add/change/delete documents?
- Have application level SCM metrics been defined and established?

4. SCM Technology Selection Phase

The SCM technology selection phase provides tasks that help in the process of evaluating, selecting, and acquiring SCM technology.

4.1. SCM Technology Types

There is no single technology that handles all SCM functions. Some people believe that since a tool is called an SCM technology, whatever the tool 'does' becomes 'SCM'. For example, if the SCM technology performs version control functions, then version control becomes what they believe is SCM. However SCM, as shown in this book, is very broad and represents a wide array of functions and tasks that span an organization, applications, and projects.

This book covers five types of SCM technologies. This does not imply that these are the only SCM technologies, but they are the most common.

4.1.1. SCM Version Control/Build Management Technology

This technology provides version control and build/compile functions. It includes a version control repository into which configuration items are placed. Some version control technologies do not provide build management functionality while others include process management functionality. It is not uncommon for SCM technologies that have version control and build management functionality to be referred to as simply version control or source management tools, or expansively as SCM (or CM) tools. However, the term version control is too simplistic since most first-tier SCM technologies contain much more than just version control functionality and conversely, the term SCM (or CM) tools is too expansive since no SCM tool handles all SCM functions. When selecting a version control/build management technology, ensure it can support version control and applicable build processes.

4.1.2. SCM Problem Management Technology

This technology provides problem tracking and management capabilities. This technology type is synonymous with defect tracking, incident tracking/management, and bug tracking technology. The importance of having a problem management technology is to have a place to identify and track problems related to the application, the application environment, and projects that produce application deliverables. During an application's lifecycle, various types of problems may be encountered. Problems may be divided into three distinct types: defects, issues, and non-compliances. When selecting a problem management technology, ensure it can support the application's problem management process, should one exist.

4.1.3. SCM Change Control Technology

This technology provides change management capabilities to manage changes to baselines that require change control. This technology type may be associated with a requirements engineering technology since requirements baselines are typically managed with change control processes. For basic change control capabilities, a problem management technology may be sufficient. However, managing changes to established baselines require the ability to capture change history. When selecting a change control technology, ensure it can support the application's change control process, should one exist.

4.1.4. SCM Release Engineering Technology

This technology provides migration and installation capabilities. This technology type is synonymous with deployment, installation, and migration technology. It is important to have a consistent and reliable technology that will ensure the integrity of the production baseline as it approaches and enters production. When selecting a release engineering technology, ensure it can support the application's release process, should one exist.

4.1.5. SCM Distributed Access Technology

This technology provides capabilities of accessing code from distributed sites where changes to an application code baseline may occur from local and remote sites. This may include technology solutions such as remote logon, terminal services, remote client snapshot, or remote server repository replication. Some options are not specifically SCM technologies (e.g., remote logon and terminal services). Remote server repository replication and remote client snapshot may be a feature (or add-on) to an SCM version control/build management technology.

Since technologies that provide distributed development go beyond specific SCM technologies, consideration must be given to the global SCM/development strategy and the best technology approach that fits the application characteristics under development. For more on this topic, see Section 5.3. When selecting a distributed access technology, ensure it can support the application's branch/merge process, should one exist.

4.2. Select an SCM Technology

This 'super-task' provides steps to ensure there is a methodical process for evaluating and selecting an SCM technology that meets the needs of an application. This is effectively a high-level task that includes subtasks that must occur to select the SCM technology. It will include subtasks of evaluating and selecting SCM technologies; identifying the number of SCM technology licenses needed; preparing a justification for purchasing SCM technology; and purchasing and acquiring the SCM technology.

Key Steps:

Note: Replace 'SCM technology' with the SCM technology type that is being evaluated and selected (e.g., 'SCM technology' becomes 'SCM version control/build management technology').

1. Identify if a standard for the SCM technology exists within the organization.
   - If a standard for the SCM technology exists within the organization and it meets the basic needs of this application (at a high level), consider selecting this technology (and go to step 5).
   - If no organization standard exists, identify existing SCM technology used by related application teams that are dependent on this application (or vice versa). If one meets the basic needs of this application (at a high level), consider:
     - selecting this existing technology (and go to step 3).
     - including it as a candidate for evaluation

- If no organization SCM technology standard exists and none of the existing technologies used by related applications meet the basic needs, then proceed to the next step for evaluating and selecting an SCM technology for the needs of the application.

2. Evaluate and select an SCM technology. Go to subtask 4.2.1 to perform this activity. Review any existing SCM processes relevant to this SCM technology to help establish functional requirements from a process perspective. See Section 6 in this chapter for more on SCM processes.
3. Determine the number of SCM technology licenses needed (see Section 4.2.2).
4. Prepare a purchase justification for the SCM technology, if needed (see Section 4.2.3).
5. Obtain approval and acquire the SCM technology selected and number of licenses needed (see Section 4.2.4).

Roles:

- SCM manager – task lead
- Application owner
- SCM engineer
- Key lead developers
- Test/QA manager
- Senior management
- Finance/purchasing personnel
- Anyone else that may have a vested interest in the selection and/or purchase of the technology

Consideration:

- For more on the topic of SCM technology evaluation, consider reading the 'Configuration Management Tool Selection and Deployment' chapter in [Dart 2000].

Output:

- Completed SCM technology evaluation requirements list (whether research and demonstration evaluation or full evaluation)
- Completed SCM technology evaluation summary (for all evaluation levels)
- A selected SCM technology
- Number of SCM licenses to be purchased
- Purchase Justification for SCM Technology
- Purchase has been approved (or not)
- Acquired SCM technology (if approved)

4.2.1. Evaluate and Select an SCM Technology

This task includes steps to ensure there is a methodical process used in evaluating and selecting an SCM technology that meets the needs of the application. Typically, very little time is spent evaluating an SCM technology, even though it will be one of the more highly used technologies in the development lifecycle.

There are several levels of technology evaluation that may be performed. The evaluation levels include:

- Research Evaluation. This constitutes an evaluation based on reviewing the evaluations published in trade magazines, journal and evaluation documents and selecting a technology from this information.
- Research and Demonstration Evaluation. It would include the above, but instead of ending with a technology selection, two or three of the top candidates would be brought in-house for a demonstration by the vendor. Also, a set of SCM technology requirements for the needs of the application will be prepared. During the demonstrations and after they are concluded, an assessment on how the technologies met the requirements would be performed. Then a selection would be made. A Request for Proposal (RfP) from each technology vendor may be requested as part of this evaluation.
- Full Evaluation. It would include the Research and Demonstration evaluation, and the top two to three tools (or as many as desired) would be brought in-house for a 3–6 month evaluation that would exercise and test the technology against the SCM technology requirements specified. A Request for Proposal (RfP) from each technology vendor may be reviewed as part of the evaluation criteria.

Overall, a Full evaluation is ideal, but a Research and Demonstration evaluation should be the minimum effort if possible, recognizing that some application teams may have limited time in evaluating an SCM technology. The following provides the steps for a full SCM technology evaluation (including a Research evaluation and a Research and Demonstration evaluation). These steps may be customized or scaled-down according to the needs and type of evaluation that is performed.

Key Steps:

1. Identify which evaluation level (Research, Research and Demonstration, or Full) will be performed.
2. For all evaluation levels (Research, Research and Demo, or Full), review SCM technology evaluations found in trade magazines and journal and evaluation documents. This will provide an insight into the strengths and weaknesses of current SCM technology. Specifically, identify which SCM technology will operate on the platforms (operating systems) being used and identify if the cost is within the price range under consideration.
3. For Research evaluation (only), select the top SCM technology from step 2.
   - Write up the reason(s) it was selected, including any known benefits and risks, and summarize the results in an SCM technology evaluation summary (see Section 9.1 of the Appendix). The subtotal and total score sections do not have to be completed since none were derived.
   - Review the SCM technology evaluation summary with the appropriate level of management who can authorize the acquisition of the SCM technology and any associated costs.

- Store the SCM technology evaluation summary in a readily accessible location for future reference.
4. For Research and Demo evaluation or Full evaluation, select the top 3–5 SCM technologies from Step 2. Create an SCM technology evaluation requirements list (see Section 9 of the Appendix) that will be used to compare the technologies in more detail.
   - Establish an SCM technology evaluation team. This may include (but is not limited to) SCM personnel, the application owner, key project personnel, and QA/test personnel.
   - Define and document the requirements in the SCM technology evaluation requirements list. This may consist of several requirements areas:
     - Functional requirements of the SCM technology (e.g., version control, build function, workspace management, integration with problem management tool, etc.). Review existing SCM processes relevant to the SCM technology being evaluated. This may help derive functional requirements for the SCM technology. See Section 6 for more on SCM processes.
     - Implementation and integration requirements (e.g., expertise required for implementation, ease of implementation; other tools integrated with this product, etc.).
     - Customer support requirements based on vendor offerings (e.g., available 7×24, website information, 1–800 number, etc.).
     - Cost requirements (e.g., price per license, discount available, etc.).
   - Define the weight range (e.g., 1 through 5 with 5 being the most important) for the requirements in the SCM technology evaluation requirements list (e.g., an important requirement may receive a weight of 4, a critical requirement may receive a weight of 5, and a nice-to-have requirement may receive a weight of 1). This becomes the multiplier for the evaluation score for each requirement.
   - Request a demonstration from the vendors of the 3–5 SCM technologies selected. During the demonstrations, ask questions specifically on how the SCM technology meets each requirement.
   - In the 'Score' column, rate the capability of the SCM technology in relation to the requirements in the SCM technology evaluation requirements list. Note: this is a preliminary scoring for a Full evaluation.
   - Multiply each score by the weight of the requirement to derive the weighted score. Add weighted scores to determine which technology has the highest total score at the end of the evaluation.
   - After the demonstrations, in a Research and Demo evaluation, select the top SCM technology based on the total score and proceed to step 6 below. In a Full evaluation, narrow down the SCM technologies to the top two (or three at most) based on the total score and proceed to step 5. Note: If one of the SCM technologies is a clear winner, there may be no need to proceed to the full evaluation (step 5).
5. For Full evaluation of the top two SCM technologies, request a 3 or 6 month in-house evaluation copy and license of the SCM technology from the vendor.

- Create a prototype environment similar to the working development environment. This would include installing the SCM technology and importing any items.
- Exercise and test the SCM technologies to determine if they meet the requirements. Re-score the capability of each SCM technology in relation to the requirements in the SCM technology evaluation requirements list (see Section 9 of the Appendix).
- Multiply each updated score by the weight of the requirement to derive the weighted score. Add the weighted scores to determine which tool has the highest total score at the end of the evaluation.

6. To complete the evaluation:
   - Prepare an SCM technology evaluation summary. This is where the selected technology is documented (see Section 9.1 of the Appendix).
     - In the Benefits/Risks section, document any known benefits and risks of the SCM technology. Indicating known risks may help in risk mitigation planning.
     - In the Requirements Summary section, for each specific requirement area, provide the top reason(s) why the first choice technology was selected over the second choice. Also document the subtotal scores of each requirements area.
     - In the SCM Technology Selection section, document the total score of each SCM technology.
     Note: This summary may become the basis for preparing a justification and requesting authorization for purchasing the tool.
   - Review the SCM technology evaluation summary with the appropriate level of management who may authorize the acquisition of the SCM technology and any associated costs.
   - Store the SCM technology evaluation requirements list and SCM technology evaluation summary in a readily accessible location for future reference.

Roles:

- SCM manager – task lead
- SCM technology evaluation team (e.g., the application owner, SCM engineer, key project leads, test/QA manager)

Considerations:

- It is important to store the evaluation materials in a readily accessible location so that you have an objective trail on why a particular technology was selected. This information may be useful six months to a year later when others ask why the SCM technology was selected.
- In some cases, an SCM technology request for proposal (RfP) may be created. If so, consider including the following questions:
  - How are releases and enhancements versioned and delivered to the customer?
  - How are customers made aware of new releases and patches?
  - What is the best price the vendor will offer for purchasing a range of licenses?

- What other vendor items may be purchased to improve the SCM technology or the implementation of the SCM technology?
- Note: Add any questions that are thought to be important to the quality and cost. Since vendors receive numerous requests for proposals, attempt to keep the questions concise and provide a reason why you are asking them.

Output:

- Completed SCM technology evaluation requirements list (if Research and Demonstration evaluation or Full evaluation)
- Completed SCM technology evaluation summary
- A selected SCM technology

4.2.2. Determine Number of SCM Technology Licenses Needed

This task provides steps to help estimate the number of licenses that may be needed to ensure users have adequate access to the SCM technology. The specific number of licenses will depend on the license scheme that the SCM vendor uses.

Key Steps:

1. For the technology selected (from Section 4.2.1 above) identify the license scheme that the SCM vendor uses. Typical license schemes include (and not limited too): a dedicated license (per user); a floating license (shared by users); per server license (access by all users on a server).
2. Identify the number of personnel or servers that will use the SCM technology.
3. Calculate the number of licenses by the number of personnel or servers using the licenses according to the license scheme:
   - If the license scheme is for a dedicated license per user, then the number of licenses needed is equal to the number of users (i.e., 20 users = 20 licenses needed).
   - If the license scheme is for a floating license, then consider the percentage of time all users will be using the licenses concurrently. If that percentage is 75%, then multiply the number of users by 75% (i.e. 20 users $\times$ .75=15 licenses needed).
   - If the license is based on a server, determine how many servers there are, then the number of licenses is equal to the number of servers utilizing the technology. Note, however some per-server license schemes limit the number of users per server so this must be taken into consideration.

Roles:

- SCM manager – task lead

Considerations:

- There are other license schemes as well so keep this in mind when calculating the number of licenses.
- If the scores from evaluating two SCM technologies are similar, then consider identifying the number of licenses needed for each. The total cost of these licenses may have an impact on which SCM technology is selected.

Output:

- License scheme used by the SCM vendor
- Number of SCM licenses needed

4.2.3. Prepare Purchase Justification for SCM Technology

This task provides steps to prepare a justification, which may be needed for purchasing the SCM technology. Once an SCM technology has been selected and the number of SCM licenses has been determined, a purchase justification and possibly a Return on Investment (ROI) may be needed in order to get management approval for purchasing the product.

Key Steps:

1. Identify the guidelines for purchasing a product within the organization. Look for existing formats on how to write justifications.
2. Prepare a purchase justification in the proper format (if it exists) using the materials from the SCM technology evaluation. This may provide senior management with a consolidated overview of the reasons to purchase this particular SCM technology.
   - Establish the reason for acquiring the SCM technology. Include the benefits of the SCM technology and the risks it will reduce. See Section 3 of Chapter 2 for more on this topic.
   - Establish why this particular SCM technology was selected by reviewing the SCM technology evaluation summary (see Section 4.2.1).
   - Provide the estimated cost of the SCM technology based on the number of SCM licenses indicated (see Section 4.2.2).
   - Identify any quantifiable Return on Investment (ROI) information. Examples of potential cost savings by utilizing an SCM technology:
     - For an SCM version control technology, identify the number of times code is lost and the effort associated with finding and rebuilding that code. Multiply the effort (in hours) with an hourly rate and this may be considered a cost saving if the technology is purchased and implemented.
     - For any technology, estimate the potential savings from automating the build, migration, and installation processes. This can equate to a reduction in effort or an increase in productivity for developers and SCM personnel. Significant automation can lead to a reduction in personnel.

3. Review the purchase justification with members of the SCM technology evaluation team. Update as appropriate.
4. Store the purchase justification in a readily accessible location for future reference.

Roles:

- SCM manager – task lead
- Application owner

Considerations:

- ROI for technology requires a strong process component to accompany the technology. Otherwise, the application team can fail as badly with an excellent technology as without.
- It may be very difficult to collect concrete ROI data since much of it is estimated and it may require baseline data from prior years.
- It is advisable to prepare a justification to accompany any purchase requisition over a certain cost (in line with the guidelines within the organization).

Output:

- Purchase justification for the SCM technology
- Optional – return on investment (ROI)

4.2.4. Acquire the Selected SCM Technology

This task provides steps to acquire the SCM technology once the approval to purchase it is received. In many cases, the approval process requires buy-in to the purchase prior to placing the order.

Key Steps:

1. Deliver the purchase justification (from Section 4.2.3) and SCM technology evaluation summary (from Section 4.2.1) to the appropriate manager who has authority to sign for the requested purchase of the SCM technology.
   - Request approval to move forward and acquire the technology.
   - If approved, prepare a purchase order for the number of licenses indicated (see Section 4.2.2), the cost, and any pertinent information as per the organization's purchase order process.
2. Route the purchase order to the appropriate personnel for approval. The purchase justification and supporting SCM technology evaluation items may be needed.
3. Once approved, send the purchase order to the appropriate SCM vendor.
4. When SCM technology is received, verify all items are delivered:
   - Media
   - Books (software user guide, installation guide, etc.)
   - License string (or similar) for the number of licenses that have been requested

Roles:

- SCM manager – task lead
- Management
- Purchasing

Considerations:

- The purchase order/requisition process may be automated so steps 1 and 2 above may be handled in an automated online manner.
- In some cases, the SCM technology selected may not be purchased due to cost reasons. You may have to go back to the SCM requirements evaluation spreadsheet (see Section 4.2.1) and revise (e.g., increase) the weight of the cost requirements. Cost may have a higher weight than previously indicated.
- The amount of money spent on SCM technologies may be an indication of how committed senior management is to quality SCM. See Section 2.3 of Chapter 3 for more on this topic.

Output:

- Purchase has been approved (or not)
- Purchase order is created and submitted
- SCM technology is acquired

4.3. SCM Technology Selection Phase Completion Checklist

The items in this checklist can be used to determine if SCM tasks have been completed in this phase:

- Was the selection of SCM technology made using an evaluation process?
  - Did the evaluation process include identifying requirements (even at a high level), identifying benefits and risks of that tool, and preparing a summary of the results?
  - Has a summary of why the technology was selected been documented and stored in a readily accessible location?
  - Was the license scheme identified and has the number of licenses that are needed been determined?
  - Was a purchase justification for the SCM technology prepared?
  - Was the SCM technology purchased and acquired?

5. SCM Design Phase

The SCM design phase provides tasks that help establish the design aspects prior to implementing an SCM system. The tasks include creating an SCM design specification, establishing a master application inventory, and if applicable, defining a global SCM/development strategy.

5.1. Create an SCM Design Specification

This section lists the steps to prepare a design for implementing an SCM system. The SCM design specification works in conjunction with the SCM plan and focuses on the SCM technical and process design aspects for implementing SCM in an application environment.

An SCM design specification adds to an existing SCM plan (see Section 3.2 of Chapter 3). If an SCM plan does not exist, the SCM design specification document may substitute for it because an SCM design specification includes key elements of an SCM plan.

To implement an SCM system successfully, the SCM design specification requires thought in the following areas: SCM terminology, SCM roles and responsibilities, application environment details, application environment change policy, SCM system details, label and branch naming conventions, SCM activity management documents (SCM implementation plan, problem list, and risk list), SCM training, and SCM processes. In a nutshell, in the absence of an SCM plan, the SCM design specification becomes the focal point document for SCM within an application team.

Key Steps:

1. Identify if an SCM plan exists.
   - If an SCM plan exists for the application, go to Step 3.
   - If an SCM plan does not exist, create an SCM design specification document. Use the template from Section 10 of the Appendix. This template includes many elements of an SCM plan.
2. Complete the initial sections:
   - **Objectives** – Define the objectives. For example, 'The objective of the SCM Design Specification is to provide details for establishing and managing SCM for <the organization name> <or the <application/product name> team>. It also provides direction for preparing, designing, implementing, and maintaining an SCM environment'.
   - **Scope** – Define the scope. For example, 'This SCM Design Specification applies to all projects of a respective application'.
3. Include the following sections if they do not already exist:
   - **SCM Roles and Responsibilities** – These are SCM (including CCB) roles and responsibilities for the application team, including the personnel assigned to each role. For more details, go to Sections 3.2.2 and 3.2.3 of Chapter 3.
   - **SCM Terminology** – This is a list of SCM terminology and acronyms that are used (or that should be used) by the application team. For more details, see Section 4.2 of Chapter 3.
   - **SCM and Related Documents** – These are documents that provide guidance for the application team (e.g., policy, standards, processes, templates, and reference documents). For more details, go to Section 3.2.1 of Chapter 3.
4. If you are preparing an SCM design specification, include the following sections. Note: if it is an SCM plan, add and complete these sections as an 'SCM Design' chapter within the SCM plan.

- **SCM Activity Management Documents** – includes any SCM activity based documents such as plans, problem lists, and risk lists that are used to manage SCM. Place this section near the 'SCM & Related Documents' section. See Section 5.1.1 below for more details.
- **Application Environment Change Policy** – includes the guidelines for upgrading the environment (technology and servers) in which the SCM system lives. This is used to minimize or prevent dependency impacts on the application and improve the integrity of the environment. See Section 5.1.2 below for more details.
- **Application Environment Details** – includes information about the server environment in which the application will be developed and tested. See Section 5.1.3 below for more details.
- **SCM System Details** – includes the details of where the SCM technologies will live for the application(s), system(s) involved, and accounts needed. See Section 5.1.4 below for more details.
- **Label Naming Convention** – includes the label naming convention guidelines for placing tag attributes on baselines of code within a version control repository. See Section 5.1.5 below for more details.
- **Branch Types and Branch Naming Convention** – includes guidelines for branching types, naming conventions, and a branch/merge process flow. See Section 5.1.6 below for more details.
- **SCM Training** – includes a list of SCM courses offered either in-house or by a vendor that can be delivered to application personnel and lists those who have taken SCM courses. See Section 5.1.7 below for more details.

5. Once the preliminary SCM design specification is defined and documented (whether in the SCM plan or the SCM design specification document), perform the following:
   - Set up a meeting with the application owner and key stakeholders associated with the application.
   - Conduct the meeting and review the sections of the SCM design specification.
   - Get buy-in to the SCM design specification.
6. Provide awareness of the SCM design specification to members of the application team (either in a meeting forum or via email) and what it means to them.
7. Place the customizable SCM design specification in an easily accessible area like the application website or document repository.

Roles:

- SCM manager – task lead
- SCM engineer
- SCM coordinator
- Application owner
- Stakeholders

Considerations:

- For CMM compliance, if an SCM Plan does not exist, then an SCM design specification document may be adequate as long as it includes the key sections of an SCM plan.

- The SCM design specification provides a central place where auditors can go for SCM information on the application.

Output:

- SCM design specification (either as a separate document or a chapter in the SCM plan)
- Awareness of the SCM design specification provided to application personnel

5.1.1. Identify the SCM Activity Management Documents

This task provides steps to identify SCM activity and task based documents such as plans, problem lists, and risk lists that are used to manage SCM.

Key Steps:

1. Identify and list the documents (and their locations) that are used to manage SCM activities and tasks in the 'SCM Activity Management Documents' subsection of the SCM design specification or SCM plan. Typically the subsections include the following:
   - SCM implementation plans – typically refers to implementation plans that are focused on establishing and/or improving an SCM system for an application.
   - SCM problem lists – typically refers to any SCM related issues, defects, and non-compliance lists. Problems may be captured and managed in a number of ways (spreadsheet, technology, website, etc.).
   - SCM risk list – refers to SCM related risk lists associated with the application.
2. Review for completeness.

Roles:

- SCM manager – task lead

Consideration:

- SCM related problems may be intermingled with the problem list(s) of the application team.

Output:

- 'SCM Activity Management Documents' section in the SCM design specification or SCM plan document.

5.1.2. Define the Application Environment Change Policy

This task provides steps to prepare guidelines for authorizing and managing changes to any part of the application environment (including the SCM system) that may impact the integrity of the application. It is recommended that a customized Change Control Process should be followed in relation to making decisions on changes to the application environment. The application environment (including the SCM system) may be considered an environment baseline that should be managed from a change perspective. Managing changes to environment items such as the operating system, hardware, network, and technology may impact the integrity of the application and are therefore considered critical to the success of an application.

Key Steps:

1. Define the elements of an application environment change policy in the SCM design specification or SCM plan document. This includes defining the following:
   - A policy statement that includes what must happen before changing any part of the application environment baseline (including the SCM system).
   - A change control process that is used to evaluate changes to the application environment baseline (see Section 6.2).
   - The items that should be managed in the environment. Consider including: server operating system changes; server hardware changes; changes to technology used for application development and testing; changes to SCM related technology; and network changes that impact the server(s) in which the application items reside.
   - Who authorizes environment changes. This is typically the application owner (or representative) and the SCM manager and may include others such as the system administration personnel. Combined, these people act as a CCB.

Roles:

- SCM manager – task lead
- SCM engineer
- Application owner or technical representative
- System administration personnel

Consideration:

- The information defined here will be used throughout the application lifecycle, therefore consider putting appropriate thought into this task.

Output:

- Application environment change policy (in the SCM design specification or SCM plan)
- Application environment change control process

5.1.3. Define the Application Environment Details

This task provides steps to establish an understanding of the technical environment in which the application and the SCM system will live. This information helps determine if the environment is adequate in establishing a robust SCM infrastructure and provides input to designing an effective SCM system.

Key Steps:

1. Define the application and SCM server environment information in the 'Application Environment Details' subsection of the SCM design specification or SCM plan document. This includes defining the following:
   - Application information. This provides a basic understanding of application logistics and dependencies. Identify the following:
     - Name of application
     - Organization in which the application lives
     - Estimated size of application code base (including all documents)
     - Estimated size of application installation base
     - Build-time dependencies with other applications
     - Run-time dependencies with other applications
   - Server information. For each server within the application environment that is used as part of the SCM system, document the specifications and file systems. This provides an overview for determining where items may be placed or where items already exist. Identify the following for each server:
     - Server Function: SCM technology installation, repository, build, licenses, etc.
     - Machine Type: manufacturer and model
     - OS Version: operating system and release number
     - Location: location of server – city/site, area of the building, floor, etc.
     - IP Address: network address for system
     - RAM: amount of RAM on server
     - Domain: name of domain in which the system is in
     - Data on disk: identify how the SCM related data on the server is or may be segmented (e.g., install area, repository area, workspace area, etc). Include the size and map or mount point (and any directories)
2. After the current specifications are identified, consider the desired specification. For example, the SCM server has 1 GB RAM, but the desired amount may be 2 GB RAM.
3. Place a request for the desired improvements to the application owner or personnel who can authorize the request.

Roles:

- SCM engineer – task lead
- SCM manager
- System administrator
- Application owner or technical representative

Consideration:

- Ensure there is due consideration given to the desired specifications of the servers or components of the servers. Starting with an appropriately sized server may prevent down time in the future which may impact the time-to-market goals of a project release.

Output:

- Application environment details section (in the SCM design specification or SCM plan)
- Request(s) for improvements of server(s)

5.1.4. Define the SCM System Details

This task provides steps to design and define the details of the installation aspects of an SCM technology. This allows for a more thought-out approach.

Key Steps:

1. Design, define, and document the details of the installation aspects of the SCM technology in the SCM system details subsection of the SCM design specification or SCM plan document. This includes defining the following:
   - SCM Technology and Release Number – the SCM technology and the release being installed and used.
   - SCM technology installation location – where the SCM technology is installed on the device. This may be the specific location on the server or client.
   - SCM technology repository location – where the code repository associated with the SCM technology will reside. The top level of the repository is adequate.
   - SCM technology run-time location – from where the technology operates or executes (may be the same as the installation location specified above). Users of the SCM technology may have to map drives to this location to run the technology.
   - Build Server(s) and Build Location(s) (if applicable) – the location where official builds and packaging occur.
   - SCM technology license location and amount – the license facility location and the number of existing licenses (consider including the license string if it exists).
   - SCM technology administrator account – the account used to administer the SCM technology. If there is a system administrator who manages accounts and groups, request consultation on account and group standards.
   - SCM technology build engineer account (if applicable) – the account used to perform the official builds and packaging for the application. If there is a system administrator who manages accounts and groups, request consultation on account and group standards.
   - User workspace location(s) – where the users control versions of their code. Consider standardizing the location using a common directory path across clients and/or on a central server (e.g., all user workspaces are found in /usr/dev/<userid>). This allows for easier identification of user work areas for troubleshooting and automation.
   - Workspace naming convention – the naming convention for workspaces. Consider the user id, application name, release number, and type of work being performed (latest, bugfix, etc.). This allows for easier identification of who owns

which workspace and for easier troubleshooting and automation. The convention should align with the branch naming convention since all workspaces are derived from a branch.

2. Review the items for accuracy. Include a review with system administration personnel. Update as appropriate.

Roles:

- SCM engineer – task lead
- SCM manager
- System administration personnel

Consideration:

- Complete one SCM system details table for each SCM technology used.

Output:

- SCM system details (in the SCM design specification or SCM plan)

5.1.5. Define the Label Naming Convention

This task provides steps to help define the label naming convention guidelines for placing tag attributes on baselines of application code that reside within an SCM version control repository.

Label attributes may be placed on a baseline of versioned items in an SCM version control repository. Typically labels are needed for various types of builds (nightly, milestone, etc.) and creation of release packages for pre-release and release (major, minor, patch, etc.). Thought should be given to the build and package levels that are used and the types of release that are likely to occur.

Key Steps:

1. Define the label naming convention in the SCM design specification or SCM plan document. Consider these or similar labels:
    - Development release baseline – an internal label used to define the starting point of development for a new release. This label (e.g., 'application name-DR#') may be used as the basis for the project release branch (see Section 5.1.6 below).
    - Nightly build – an internal label used to identify the development code baseline used in a regular periodic build/compile of an application. A nightly build label (e.g., 'application name-NB') gets reused at each build. It can be considered a throw-away label because, if the output does get used, it will receive an engineering build label placed on the source and deliverables (if the deliverables are checked in).

- Engineering build – an internal label used to identify a development baseline from a non-error build that gets used for packaging and testing at some level, therefore the baseline must be identified. This label will have a number at the end which is incremented by one each time a non-error build is used for packaging and testing (e.g., 'application name-EB#'>.
- Pre-release – an internal label used to identify a package of deliverables targeted for testing and the corresponding development code baseline. This label will have a number at the end which is incremented by one each time a package of deliverables is prepared for testing (e.g., 'application name-PR#'>.
- Release – an internal label that may align with the external release name and number used to identify the release package of deliverables heading for (or in) production. This label may use the external release name and number each time a package of deliverables is prepared for release into production (e.g., 'application name-R#'>. It may have a major and a minor number to designate the type of release (e.g., R1.0 or R1.1).
  - There are many times when the internal release label name and the external release name are completely different. This may be a result of the fact that a group like marketing or sales which is separate from the application team may name the release of the application (i.e., the product). If this is common, then define an internal release label that is understood by the application team.
  - For more on pre-release and release (major and minor) numbering conventions, see Section 3.2.1 of the chapter.
- Bugfix release – an internal label used to identify the bug fixes needed to correct release deliverables that are in production. This label will have a number at the end which is incremented by one each time a bugfix set of deliverables is prepared for production (e.g., application name-R#-Bug#>.
2. Review the label naming convention for accuracy.
3. Consider sharing the label naming convention information with the application owner and key technical leads for understanding. Update as appropriate.

Roles:

- SCM engineer – task lead
- SCM manager
- Application owner and key technical leads – reviewers

Considerations:

- Build labels may not be applicable if no compile/builds occur for the application.
- The information defined here will be used throughout the application lifecycle, therefore consider putting appropriate thought into this task.
- The application of standard labels becomes important if SCM baseline audits occur. This allows for easier identification of development and production baselines.
- For more on the topic of label naming conventions, consider reading the 'Product Release Classifications and Numbering' chapter in [Bays 1999] and the 'Active Development Line' and 'Codeline Policy' chapters in [Berczuk 2002].

Output:

- Label naming convention (in the SCM design specification or SCM plan)

5.1.6. Define the Branch Design

This task provides steps to help define the branch design used by the application team and within an SCM version control repository. A branch design is expressed in three areas: branch types, branch naming convention guidelines, and a branch/merge process flow.

A branch type is a baseline of code that is one or more levels away from the main branch (or trunk) with each branch type in that branch system sharing a common ancestor main branch. This implies that the branch may be merged into or out to an ancestor branch. Typically branch naming conventions are needed for branch types to easily understand where in the ancestor chain it belongs. It is important that the branch naming convention identifies the parent branch a user workspace is backed by, to increase ease of troubleshooting, and promote more effective automation.

Key Steps:

1. Define the branch types and the corresponding branch naming conventions in the SCM design specification or SCM plan document. Consider the following as guidelines for branch type and naming conventions:

   - Main branch – a branch referred to as the mainline and trunk. It may be the final destination of the release deliverables. This branch may simply be called the main branch, for example: </main>.
     - Note: A Release label or Bugfix Release label may be attached to code baselines at this level.
   - Project Release branch – a branch where the code is put when it has been fully tested and is awaiting the installation into production. This allows continued work on the Integration branch. In some cases a Project Release branch is not used and the Integration branch serves as the Project Release branch (i.e., the production ready release deliverables come directly from the Integration branch into the Main branch). In other cases, the Project Release branch is the final destination for the release deliverables. This branch may simply be called the release number of what is being worked on, for example: </main/rel#>.
     - Note: A Pre-Release label may be attached to code baselines at this level.
   - Integration branch – the main project branch used by all of the project team to promote (checkin and/or merge) their changes (from their private branch or similar) for an integrated view of the project changes. This ensures that all of the changes work as a unit (i.e., they can be built, packaged, and tested together). It may be created from the Project Release branch or Main branch. Once changes are complete in the Integration branch, they are merged into the Project Release branch. This branch name may include the release number and an 'integration' identifier, for example: </main/rel#/int>.

- Note: An Engineering Build or Pre-Release label may be attached to code baselines at this level.
- Shared branch – similar to an Integration branch but used by a subset of personnel, who want to share new or volatile changes, to reduce impact on others until these changes are stable. It is created from an Integration branch. Once changes are complete and tested in the Shared branch, they are 'promoted' (i.e., merged and checked in as required) into the Integration branch. This branch name may include the release number, the integration branch, and the shared branch identifier, for example: </main/rel#/int/shared-id>.
  - Note: An Engineering or Pre-Release label would be attached to code baselines at this level.
- Private branch – a branch used by only one person. It is created from a Shared or Integration branch. Within this branch, the person may make multiple changes and checkin unfinished code without impacting others. Once changes are complete in the private branch, they are merged (including the checkin step) into a Shared or Integration branch. This branch name may include the release number, the integration branch and possibly a shared branch identifier. It will also include the user id to distinguish it from other user private branches, for example: </main/rel#/int/userid_private> or </main/rel#/int/shared-id/userid_private>.
- Bugfix branch – a branch used to address defects found in a release. It is typically created from the Main branch or where the previous release is baselined and labeled. A Bugfix branch is effectively a limited use branch (for one or a small set of defects). Once changes are complete in the Bugfix branch, they are merged into a Main branch (and possibly to an Integration branch of the new/next project release to ensure the fix gets into the next release). This branch name may include the main branch with the appropriate release and the bugfix identifier either for a set of bugfixes or for a specific bugfix, for example: </main/rel#-bugfix> or </main/rel#-bugfix#>.
- Site branch (optional) – if development is occurring at multiple sites, then give consideration to a branch that allows different sites to develop independently. This branch is best created from an Integration or Shared branch so that changes can be managed and merged from each site separately. See Section 5.3 if this is occurring or may occur in the future. This branch name may include the release number and the site branch identifier, for example: </main/rel#/int/site-id> or </main/rel#/int/shared-id/site-id>.

2. Create an accompanying branch and merge process flow diagram. From the branch types and branch naming conventions defined above, create a diagram showing how the branches relate to each other and how merging may occur. This would include the relationship of a parent branch to the child branch (branching out) and the merge back from the child to the parent branch until a release package is merged into the last branch in the process flow. As an example, see the Branch and Merge Process Flow Diagram in Section 10 of the Appendix.

3. Review the branch types, branch naming convention, and branch and merge process flow diagram with the application owner and key technical leads for accuracy, understanding, and buy-in.

4. Communicate the branch types, branch naming convention, and branch and merge process flow diagram to the application team. Consider adding this to the in-house SCM user training course if it exists.

Roles:

- SCM engineer – task lead
- SCM manager
- Application owners, key technical leads, system administrator(s) – as reviewers

Considerations:

- There may be variations of branch types, branch naming conventions, and branch and merge process flows. Customize as appropriate.
- The information defined here will be used throughout the application lifecycle. Therefore, consider putting appropriate thought into these areas.
- For more on approaches to branch patterns, consider reading the 'Patterns', 'Mainline', 'Private Workspace', 'Active Development Line', 'Codeline Policy', 'Private Versions', 'Release Line', 'Release-Prep Code Line', and 'Task Branch' chapters of [Berczuk 2002].

Output:

- Defined branch types, branch naming convention, branch and merge process flow diagram in the SCM design specification or SCM plan
- Awareness of the branch design information communicated to appropriate personnel and added to the SCM user training materials

5.1.7. Define SCM Training

This task provides steps to help define a list of SCM courses offered either in-house or by an external vendor that can be delivered to the application and SCM personnel. It also keeps track of those who have taken SCM courses.

Key Steps:

1. Define and document SCM training to be made available to application and SCM personnel in the SCM Training section in the SCM design specification or SCM plan document.
2. Identify the types of SCM courses desired and document this information in the 'List of SCM courses available' subsection of the SCM Training section.
   - For SCM personnel, consider SCM technology user training; SCM technology administration training; and SCM certification training.
   - For application personnel, consider SCM technology user training and SCM process training (Change Control, etc.).

Include the expected length of the course, a course description, who should attend the course, and how to register for the course.

3. Create a list (or table) to capture who has taken SCM training courses. It is important to ensure that users are trained because it implies better usage and understanding of SCM processes and technology and it reduces user problems. See the 'Who has taken SCM Training' subsection of Section 10 in the Appendix.

4. Review the list of SCM courses available with the application owner and project manager(s) to provide awareness of potential training available, get buy-in, and increase expectation of who should take SCM training.

5. Communicate the SCM course offering with a draft schedule of which courses will be offered and who should attend.

Roles:

- SCM manager – task lead
- SCM coordinator, SCM engineer
- Application owner, project manager(s)

Consideration:

- For CMM compliance, a review of the SCM training should occur at least once during each project lifecycle.

Output:

- A list of SCM training courses offered
- A list to track who has taken SCM training
- Awareness of and buy-in to SCM training courses from the application owner and project manager(s)
- Communication of SCM training course offering, draft schedule of when training will occur, and an expectation of who should take specified SCM training courses

5.2. Establish a Master Application Inventory

This 'super task' provides steps to help an application team define application baselines, the level of SCM rigor applied to a baseline, and the configuration items found within a baseline. Ultimately, this produces a centralized master inventory of baselines and their items which make up the application and application environment.

The reason for performing this task is that it is very important to be aware of the configuration items (CIs) needed for an application and application environment; to group the configuration items into categories (baselines); and to specify a level of rigor in which the CIs within baselines should be managed. The overall objective of creating a Master Application Inventory is that once all application items are identified, the application infrastructure (requirements, plans, environment, technology, code, etc.) may be recreated at another location for disaster recovery purposes or for additional site replication.

Key Steps:

1. Create a master application inventory document. Consider using the template found in Section 11 of the Appendix. This document includes sections for general application information; defined application baselines with their SCM rigor and CI types aligned with the baseline and; an inventory of the CIs within each baseline.
   - The Application Information section (or similar) includes the application name, organization, application owner, SCM manager for the application, version number of this document, and last updated date.
   - The Application Baseline Definition table defines the baseline categories, SCM rigor (applied to each baseline), and the categories of items found within each baseline. Consider using the Application Baseline Definition table within Section 11 of the Appendix to document this information:
     - To define baseline categories, see Section 5.2.1 below.
     - To define the level of SCM rigor applied to each baseline, see Section 5.2.2 below. Enter the selected level of SCM rigor against the appropriate application baseline type.
   - Set up a meeting with the application owner, project manager(s), and test manager(s) to review the baselines and the SCM rigors associated with them.
     - Get buy-in to the application baseline types and SCM rigor for each baseline. In particular, focus on the level of SCM rigor applied to the baselines and CIs therein, because this is the area that will impact the day-to-day work of the application team.
   - Create an Application Inventory List table. Identify and document the CIs within each baseline. Consider using the Application Inventory List table discussed in Section 5.2.3 below using the example in Section 11 of the Appendix.
2. Review the master application inventory with SCM personnel for accuracy.
3. Provide an overview of the master application inventory (in a meeting forum or via email) to members of the application team. Include a walk-through explaining the baselines, the level of SCM rigor applied to the baselines, and what this means to the application team.

Roles:

- SCM manager – task lead
- Application owner, project manager(s), test manager(s) – reviewers

Considerations:

- This master application inventory may be completed in conjunction with the SCM Identification Process (see Section 6.3).
- All baselines are subject to SCM audit and SCM report at some level. The baselines (and CIs therein) may be audited to ensure the integrity of baselines and to verify if application personnel are following the appropriate level of SCM rigor.

Output:

- Completed master application inventory document:
  - Baseline types and levels of SCM rigor applied to baselines
  - Application inventory list
- Overview of the master application inventory to application team members

5.2.1. Define Application Baselines

This task provides steps to identify the application baselines relevant to an application. A baseline can be described as a collection of similar configuration items at a specific point in time during the lifecycle, for example requirements, development, and production baselines. It is important to identify and group the CIs into appropriate baselines because it may provide a structure to better track the changes to the CIs in the baseline (e.g., the baseline in January can be compared with the same baseline in March to determine changes). Typically, along with identifying each CI, the version number of the CI is identified. This allows for further recognition when an item has changed.

Key Steps:

1. Define the baseline categories for an application. A baseline is a collection of similar configuration items. Examples of baseline categories include (but are not limited to):
   - Functional baseline – CIs that provide direction to the project (plans, requirements and design documents, etc.). In many cases, people separate the project requirements into its own baseline (called the Requirements baseline).
   - Requirements baseline – CIs that represent requirements that capture the needs of the customer in relation to the application or product.
   - Development baseline – CIs used in the development phase of a project (internal and third party code, etc.).
   - Test baseline – CIs used during the test phase of a project (test cases, plans, etc.)
   - Environment baseline – CIs that make up the application environment (operating system, hardware, network, and technology, etc.)
   - Production baseline – CIs released (release deliverables) to the customer and which are considered in production.
2. Document the application baseline categories in an application baseline definition table (see Section 11 of the Appendix).

Roles:

- SCM manager – task lead
- Application owner

Consideration:

- Consider investigating if baseline categories already exist at the organization level.

Output:

- Defined and documented baseline categories for the application in an application baseline definition table (or similar)

5.2.2. Specify SCM Rigor per Application Baseline

This task provides steps to establish a level of SCM rigor for the baseline categories. Various levels of SCM rigor may be applied to a baseline. The levels of SCM rigor include (but are not limited to) identification, version control, and change control.

Each baseline may have more than one level of SCM rigor applied to it. For example, a CI in the production baseline must be identified before it can be version controlled and change controlled. While it may be beneficial to identify, version control, and change control all items in each baseline, it may not be cost-effective or may not be the priority of an organization to do so at the time.

Key Steps:

1. For each baseline category identified in Section 5.2.1 above, specify the level of SCM rigor to be applied. The levels of SCM rigor include:
   - **Identification** of a CI in a baseline (name of the document or technology and its version/release number). The implication is that it is not only important to identify the item name, but also to identify the version or release of that item, since the current item may be considerably different from the previous version or release of that item. This is the lowest level of SCM rigor that may be applied to a CI or baseline.
   - **Version control** of a CI in a baseline in an automated manner (typically using an SCM version control technology) that tracks the change of each item by the version number and therefore tracks the history of changes to the CI. If version control is applied to a baseline, it implies identification.
   - **Change control** of a CI that demands an approval of the change prior to the change occurring to understand the impact of the change and to track the change until closure. The most rigorous level of SCM applied to a CI. If you apply change control to a baseline, it implies identification and version control (although there are exceptions).
2. Document the specified level of SCM rigor to be applied to each baseline in an SCM Rigor column within the application baseline definition table. Suggestions of what level of SCM rigor to apply to baselines include (customize as appropriate):
   - Functional baseline – identification and version control
   - Requirements baseline – identification, version control, and change control
   - Development baseline – identification and version control
   - Test baseline – identification, version control, and change control
   - Environment baseline – identification and change control
   - Production baseline – identification, version control, and change control

Roles:

- SCM manager – task lead
- Project manager

Consideration:

- Some baselines may be tracked by a technology that can automatically determine changes. For example, a requirements baseline may be stored in a requirements management technology provided that the technology includes versioning of the requirements and can track changes to the requirements baseline.

Output:

- Defined and documented level of SCM rigor for each baseline in an application baseline definition table (or similar)

5.2.3. Prepare an Application Inventory List

This task provides steps to create a list of CIs for each application baseline. The output is placed into an Application Inventory List. The overall objective of the application inventory list is to capture all items of the application so that the application infrastructure (e.g., requirements, plans, environment, code, etc.) can be recreated if necessary. It is also useful to perform this task so the location of items such as code can be identified to make it easier to import code into the SCM technology repository. By capturing this information, application team members may get a better understanding of all of the elements needed to create, operate, utilize, and maintain an application infrastructure.

Key Steps:

1. Create an application inventory list that includes the following columns. Consider using the table in Section 11 of the Appendix, which includes the following fields:
   - **Baseline** – to which the CI belongs. See Section 5.2.1 where baseline categories are established.
   - **Name** – the name of the configuration item.
   - **Version/Release Number** – the version or release number of a configuration item.
   - **Description** – a description of the configuration item: what it is used for; what it works in conjunction with; when it should be used, etc. If the item is part of the environment baseline such as a development technology or server hardware, consider including information such as the vendor name, etc.
   - **Location** – where the CI resides (it may be an SCM technology, a LAN directory, the web, a document repository, etc.). Enter TBD in the Location column for CIs that will be needed, but have not yet been created. It may also include where installation media resides.

2. Define how the CIs will be sorted (i.e., the sorting method). Options include organizing CIs by baseline or by the phase in which they get created/used in a project lifecycle.
3. Identify and document all CIs (or the more important CIs) for the application by sorting method in the application inventory list.
4. Review the list with key technical personnel from the application team for accuracy.

Roles:

- SCM coordinator – task lead
- SCM manager, SCM engineer
- Key personnel – reviewers

Considerations:

- The application inventory list may be one table with all baselines and CIs or may exist as separate tables, one per baseline.
- The application inventory list must be continually updated as changed (added, modified, or deleted) information is collected that may impact the application.
- For the Development baseline, each piece of code does not have to be listed separately. However, you should document the location of the SCM version control technology repository where the code resides. This assumes that a list of the code (and its version numbers) can be readily generated from the SCM version control technology.
- A decision should be made about which CIs will not have a level of SCM applied to them. For example, minor items like memos, agendas, minutes, and messages, may not have to be included in the inventory list. However if an item includes a decision concerning or impacting the application, then consideration should be given to identifying it.

Output:

- Completed application inventory list

5.3. Define a Global SCM/Development Strategy

This task provides steps to prepare a strategy for establishing a global SCM/development infrastructure for an application. It is applicable to global distributed development efforts (i.e., using two or more sites). Today, many development organizations have an application being developed in multiple locations. It is important to define a strategy that includes an appropriate global SCM/development technology, an applicable code branching and merging process, and effective roles and responsibilities. The steps in this task focus on the areas for consideration when establishing a global SCM/development strategy.

Key Steps:

1. Create a global SCM/development strategy document. Consider using the template found in Section 12 of the Appendix.

2. Define the objectives. For example, 'The purpose of the global SCM/development strategy is to identify and evaluate the best approach to performing development across distributed locations'.

3. Perform a distributed analysis to identify the characteristics of each application that may be developed from distributed sites. Analyze and document the following areas:

   - Name of application(s) that may be developed across different sites (in an 'Application Name' column).
   - Number of development personnel at each site who may work on the application (in the '# at Site X' columns). Note: Add more site columns as appropriate.
   - When in a project lifecycle additional sites begin and end their work (e.g., somewhere between the Design and Test phases), in the 'Lifecycle' column.
   - Identify the complexity of the current technology used to develop the application (in the 'Complexity' column). The level of complexity may be derived by how much RAM the development technology requires, how network intensive it is, and whether it is ASCII text-based or object-based. Consider establishing a technology complexity classification. The following are examples of technology complexity.
     - Low complexity development technology: low RAM requirements, low network dependency or few network transactions, and ASCII text-based development. Examples include C, C++, Perl, Cobol.
     - High complexity development technology: high RAM requirements, high network dependency or constant network transactions, and object-based development. Examples include development technologies driven by IDEs.

4. Determine the distributed direction. This section uses the application characteristics defined in the distributed analysis section above to determine the distributed access technology, code availability, and branch/merge approaches. Consider and document the following:

   - **Distributed Access Technology** – Identify the approach to technology by which code will be retrieved from the remote sites for development, in the distributed access technology column. The approach selected becomes the requirement for a technology that will support that approach. There are two primary categories of distributed technology. They include:
     - **Distributed Site** – this is when the code physically resides in two or more locations. This is applicable for development technologies of all complexity (i.e., low to high) and recommended for medium to high complexity. This can be implemented in two ways:
       - **Remote Client Snapshot** – this is when the application code is populated (checked out or retrieved) directly from the local server to the client at the remote site. The initial population of the code baseline to the remote client may take time and varies according to the network performance across sites. But once a snapshot of the full baseline is on the client, single or multiple checkouts/checkins of code may be relatively quick (pending any network performance issues).

- This method requires low setup effort, has low network dependency (unless interacting with the server at the local site for version control or retrieval operations), and has the client working on its own without continuous reliance on the WAN or LAN. It may be recommended for projects where a small to medium number of people from remote sites are working with the local site.
- **Remote Server Repository** – this is when the application code is populated (replicated or retrieved) from the local server to a central server at the remote site and the clients at the remote site retrieve code from this central remote server. The initial population (or retrieval) of the code baseline to the remote server may take time and varies according to the network performance between sites. But once the full baseline is on the remote server, periodic updates of the changed code (from each site) are replicated/retrieved relatively quickly (pending network performance). The clients at the remote site use the server at the remote site to version control or retrieve the code baseline with no WAN dependency.
  - This method requires medium setup effort, has low to medium network dependency unless the code repositories are being updated by each other, and has the client working on its own without continuous reliance on the WAN. It may be recommended for projects where a medium to high number of people from remote sites are working with a local site.
- **Single Site with Distributed Site Access** – this is when the code resides at only one site and all remote sites use the resources of the local server and/or clients where the code resides. This is applicable for low to medium complexity development technologies and recommended for low complexity development technologies depending on network performance. This can be implemented in two ways:
  - **Terminal Emulation** – this is when remote personnel remotely logon to the local systems to perform development work. The remote personnel perform version control on the local server or client in a similar way to the local personnel. This allows personnel to remotely log on directly to a local system where the code resides and is worked on.
    - This method requires low setup effort but has high network (WAN) dependency. The number of personnel at remote sites that may work in this setup is directly proportional to the network bandwidth and performance to the local site, but is typically a low number of personnel. This method is only recommended for low complexity development technologies.
  - **Terminal Services** – this is when remote personnel use a local terminal services server or client to host the development technology and application code which comes directly from the local server. The activity from the local server or client is viewed via the remote client with low network utilization. The remote personnel perform version control on the local server or client as if it were their own client. This technology minimizes network bandwidth

challenges and allows personnel to remotely utilize local systems to access and work on the code on a local system.

- This method requires medium setup effort and has medium network (WAN) dependency. It may be applicable for a small to medium number of personnel at remote sites working with the local site. It is only recommended for low to medium complexity development technologies.

- **Code Availability** – Document the code availability approach. Will personnel at all sites have access to modify all code or will personnel from specific sites have only certain sections of code available for modification? The advantage of having only one site modify a unique set of code CIs is that this may reduce or eliminate the need for merging and reduce the need for constant communication with another site when the same area of code is being changed. Note: This is effectively an application owner (or project management) decision, but has a direct impact on SCM processes.

- **Branch/Merge Approach** – Document the branch types and branch naming convention used in the Branch/Merge column. See Section 5.1.6 for more on branch types and branch naming conventions.

  - When following a remote client snapshot approach, it is recommended that each user works from a private branch that may be backed by a site or integration branch, depending on the comfort level of the changes from the remote site (if there is a high comfort level then use the local site integration branch, otherwise use a site branch from the integration branch).

  - When following a remote server repository approach, it is recommended that each user works from a private branch that is backed by a unique site branch. This allows each site to work independently from each other. The remote site personnel promote code into the site branch. This effectively becomes a 'site integration' branch for the remote site.

  - When following either of the single site with distributed site access approaches it is recommended that each user works from a private branch that may be backed by a site or integration branch depending on the comfort level of the changes from the remote site (if there is a high comfort level then use the local site integration branch, otherwise use a site branch from the integration branch).

  - Note: When using a branch for each site, identify a code integrator at each site who validates the code in the site branch before merging the code from the site branch to the integration branch. For more on merging, see Section 6.5.

5. Identify the **Distributed Roles and Responsibilities.** Identify the roles needed for effective distributed site development and identify personnel at appropriate sites that are responsible for playing these roles. The following are suggested roles and responsibilities:

  - Code Integrator
    - Establishes the site branch (as needed) following the branch naming convention.
    - Merges code from the site branch to a local shared branch or integration branch.
      - Note: Application personnel who are very familiar with the code may play this role.

- Project Manager
  - Identifies how many developers will work on the application at each site.
  - Determines when, in a project lifecycle, the additional sites begin and end their work.
  - Identifies the complexity of the development technology used for application development (in conjunction with the SCM Manager).
  - Identifies the code availability approach.
  - Ensures there is a well-defined communication and collaboration process that supports distributed development (in conjunction with the application owner).
- Application Owner
  - Determines the most appropriate distributed access technology (in conjunction with the SCM Manager).
  - Ensures there is a well-defined communication and collaboration process across sites (in conjunction with the Project Manager(s)).
- SCM Manager
  - Identifies the complexity of the development technology used for application development (in conjunction with the Project Manager).
  - Determines the most appropriate distributed access technology (in conjunction with the Application Owner).
  - Determines the branch types and branch naming convention.
6. If a distributed access technology approach is identified, but a specific technology is not selected, then consider evaluating those technologies that are in this category (using the technology evaluation process described in Section 4.2).

Roles:

- SCM manager and SCM engineer – task leads
- Application owner
- Project manager(s)

Considerations:

- There are other distributed access approaches that may be considered. Ensure they support the processes being used. For example, using an SCM Version Control Technology web interface may allow other sites to access the local code baseline. However, ensure that this approach supports the branching/merging process used.
- Network performance may be a significant factor in the distributed access technology approach that is selected. If network performance is poor, then selecting a technology that has low network dependencies is recommended.
- SCM personnel at each site should determine how to best keep each other informed of events, tasks, and changes that may impact application development and SCM functions across sites.
- Developing an application from distributed sites implies that there is project management, trained at managing distributed and parallel development efforts, which plans for the impact of branching and merging activities and, most importantly, who

understands the importance of communication and collaboration in a challenging global environment.

Output:

- Global SCM/development strategy which includes:
  - Distributed analysis
  - Distributed direction
    - Distributed access technology
    - Code availability approach
    - Branch approach
  - Distributed roles and responsibilities

5.4. SCM Design Phase Completion Checklist

The items in this checklist may be used to determine if SCM tasks have been completed in this phase:

- Has an SCM design specification been prepared and reviewed by appropriate staff?
  - Has an application environment change policy been established?
  - Has an SCM system details section been prepared?
  - Has the label naming convention been defined?
  - Has a branch design been defined (i.e., have branch types, branch naming conventions, and a branch and merge process flow diagram been developed)?
  - Has appropriate SCM training been identified for the application team personnel?
- Has a master application inventory been prepared?
  - Have baseline categories been established for the application?
  - Has a level of SCM rigor (i.e., identification, version control, change control) been defined for each baseline?
  - Has an application inventory list been prepared for the application?
- Has a global SCM/development strategy been prepared, if distributed development is expected to occur for an application?

6. SCM Process Phase

The SCM Process phase focuses on SCM processes and associated templates that may be used by the application team during a project lifecycle.

6.1. Develop an SCM Problem Management Process

This task includes steps to develop a repeatable process for documenting, tracking and resolving problems to closure.

A problem refers to something that is causing a negative impact on the application. The term 'problem' in this context is a superset term and may be divided into (but is not limited to) types such an issue, defect, and non-compliance. An issue may be defined as an unanswered question, disagreement, or shortage of resources that impede progress. A defect can be defined as a deviation in code that does not meet requirements or function as expected. A non-compliance can be defined as a deviation from applicable policies, standards, processes, or methods.

Key Steps:

1. Create an SCM problem management process document for the application. Consider using one of the following approaches:
   - Identify if a successfully used problem management process exists. If so, consider using it. However, review the remainder of the steps in this task to ensure the process includes key elements of a problem management process.
   - Use the template found in Section 13 of the Appendix.
2. Define and document the objectives of this process. For example, 'To provide a repeatable process for documenting, tracking and resolving problems'.
3. Define and document the scope of this process. For example, 'This process applies to all projects related to this application'.
4. Define and document the problem types (e.g., defects, issues, non-compliance, etc.) that are managed by this process. For example, "This process applies to defects and issues'.
5. Define and document severity levels within the organization. A simple example includes:
   - Severity 1 = Critical with no workaround
   - Severity 2 = Critical with workaround
   - Severity 3 = Major with workaround
   - Severity 4 = Minor with workaround
6. Define and document the state transitions that represent the problem lifecycle. State transitions are the stages a problem will go through until it is closed. An example of state transitions for a problem include:
   - New – a problem is identified and problem request is open (also called 'Opened')
   - Assigned – the problem has been reviewed by the appropriate management and assigned to an application staff member (change agent)
   - Fixed – the change agent completed the activities involved with resolving the problem
   - Tested – a test staff member verified that the problem is resolved
   - Closed – management reviewed problem status and closed the problem.
7. Identify and document the steps of the process. As a starting point, consider using the customizable steps found in Section 13 of the Appendix. Suggested steps for this process include:
   - Submit a problem request into an automated problem management technology or on a manual form.
   - Review new problem requests. This includes analyzing the problem, assessing the severity level, and estimating the cost/effort of correcting the problem.
   - Determine if action is required. If it is, then assign a change agent to the problem. If not, then close the problem request.

- Resolve the problem.
- Validate that the resolution was successful. If it was not, send the problem request back to the change agent to implement a corrective solution.
- Close the problem request.
8. Create a Problem Request Form template (see Section 13.1 of the Appendix) and customize it to support the process. This template should include a section for the requestor to open the problem and a section for the manager and change agent to review the problem and update the request. This can be in the form of a template or the creation of fields within an automated problem management technology.
9. Once the process and PRF template are documented, review the items with the application owner and key staff. Update as appropriate.
10. For awareness and training, provide an overview of the process and PRF template to staff who will use the process.
11. Place this process in the application team document repository, advising personnel of the location.

Roles:

- SCM coordinator – task lead
- SCM manager
- Application owner
- Test manager

Considerations:

- Within the process steps, consider documenting the role(s) that would perform each step.
- To establish an overall problem management infrastructure, see Section 7.2.
- Problem management is synonymous with defect tracking, incident tracking, or bug tracking, and can be used to track any type of problem.
- This task is important for SEI CMM compliance.
- While this task is created at the application level, it will be used at the project level.
- For more on the topic of problem management, consider reading the 'Defect Tracking' chapter in [Bays 1999].

Output:

- Customized SCM problem management process
- Customized problem request form template
- Defined problem types
- Defined severity levels
- Defined state transitions

6.2. Develop an SCM Change Control Process

This task includes steps to develop a repeatable process for controlling changes from the initial submission of the change to closure on items in a critical application baseline that may have significant impact to the application. Changes may be additions, deletions, or modifications to a baseline.

Consider completing this task concurrently with task 6.2.1 below, (Prepare Change Control Conduct Guidelines). These two tasks work together to provide a more solid change control process.

Key Steps:

1. Create an SCM Change Control Process document for the application. Consider the following approaches:
   - Identify if a successfully used change control process exists. If so, consider using it. However, review the remainder of the steps in this task to ensure the process includes the key elements of a change control process.
   - Use the template found in Section 14 of the Appendix.
2. Define and document the objectives of this process. For example, 'To provide a repeatable process for controlling changes to items in important baselines of an application'.
3. Define and document the scope of this process. For example, 'This process applies to all projects related to this application'.
4. Define and document the baselines that are managed by this process. For example, 'This process applies to the requirements, environment, and production baselines'.
5. Define and document the priority levels (if none exist within the organization). A simple example includes:
   - Priority 1 = must do, significant benefit
   - Priority 2 = great benefit
   - Priority 3 = some benefit
   - Priority 4 = minor benefit
   Note: Priority definitions may be based on (but are not limited by) the expected revenue of a change (the higher the revenue, the higher the priority) and the scope of the change (the more customers requesting the change, the higher the priority).
6. Define and document the state transitions (if none exist within the organization) that represent the change lifecycle. State transitions are the stages a change will go through until it is closed. An example of state transitions for a change include:
   - New – a change is identified and a change request is opened (this transition may also be called 'Opened').
   - Analyzed – the change has been analyzed for clarification of the change request and estimated effort.
   - Reviewed – the change has been reviewed by the Change Control Board (CCB) and a decision has been made:
     - If accepted, the state remains at 'Reviewed' in preparation for assigning the change to the appropriate personnel.
     - If rejected, the state changes to 'Closed'.
     - If more information is needed, the state changes to 'New' for further analysis.
   - Assigned – the change is assigned to the appropriate personnel (change agent).
   - Completed – the change agent has completed the activities involved.

- Tested – a test staff member has verified that the change is completed as requested.
- Closed – the CCB has reviewed the change status and closed the change.

7. Identify and document the process steps. As a starting point, consider using the customizable steps found in Section 14 of the Appendix. Suggested steps for this process include:
    - Submit change request (CRF) into an automated tool or on a manual form
    - Perform analysis of change request (determine impact, estimate effort, and prioritize)
    - Distribute CCB agenda and new CRFs for review
    - Determine status of change request(s)
    - Update CRF(s) and distribute CCB minutes
    - Assign change request and re-estimate effort
    - Implement change
    - Verify change
    - Close change request

8. Create a change request form (CRF) template that includes a section for the requestor to request the change, a section for the analyst to review the change, and a section for the CCB to indicate their ruling on the change.
    - A CRF may be in the form of a document template or the creation of fields within an automated change request technology (see Section 14.1 of the Appendix).

9. Once the process, the CRF template, and all other items are documented, review the items with the application owner and key staff. Update as appropriate.

10. Provide training on the process with the proposed CCB members. Consider performing training in conjunction with the review of the change control conduct guidelines (see Section 6.2.1 below). For more on Change Control Board Training, see Section 8.4.

11. Place this process in the application team document repository, advising personnel of the location.

Roles:

- SCM manager – task lead
- SCM coordinator
- Application owner
- Project manager(s)
- Test manager

Considerations:

- Within the process steps, consider documenting the role(s) that would perform each step.
- To establish an overall change control infrastructure, see Section 7.3.
- This task is important for SEI CMM compliance.
- For more on the topic of change control, read the 'Change Control' chapter in [Bays 1999].

Output:

- Customized SCM change control process
- Customized change request form template

- Defined priority levels and definitions
- Defined state transitions and definitions
- Change Control Board training

6.2.1. Prepare Change Control Board (CCB) Conduct Guidelines

This task provides steps to establish guidelines for the way in which the CCB will be conducted. The rules help objectify the CCB process in order to more effectively and efficiently rule on each change request.

Key Steps:

1. Create a change control conduct guidelines appendix to the SCM change control process or a separate CCB conduct guidelines document. As a starting point, consider using the customizable template found in Section 14.2 of the Appendix.
2. Document the following CCB-related items:
   - CCB Overview – Define and document the CCB span of control. This includes:
     - Which application(s) are managed by this CCB.
     - Which baseline(s) are managed – requirements, production, environment, etc.
   - CCB Meeting Logistics – Identify meeting patterns with the following information:
     - Frequency of meetings – how often the CCB meets
     - Meeting time/day – when the CCB meets
     - Length of CCB meeting – how long a CCB meeting should last
     - Length of time needed to discuss each CRF
     - Time period prior to CCB meeting when CRFs must be submitted to CCB Coordinator in order to ensure that they get added to the agenda.
     - Time period before CCB meeting that the CRF(s) and the agenda are sent out. They must be sent out at least one day before the meeting in order for CCB members to have adequate time to review the CRFs and agenda.
     - Method for prioritizing the CRFs during the meeting, e.g., by stated priority, by function, etc.
   - CCB Meeting Process – Determine the standard agenda for each CCB meeting. For example:
     - Review minutes from last CCB meeting
     - Review emergency CRFs (if any)
     - Discuss new and pending CRFs and determine a decision (e.g., approve, reject, pending, etc.)
     - Assign newly approved CRFs to change agents
     - Review CRFs closed since the last meeting. CCB members have the opportunity to reopen the CRF
     - Review the change metrics from the meeting to determine if there is too much volatility in the baseline; the project may want to stop or slow the baseline rate of change for more stability
     - Review all documented action items resulting from the CCB meeting

- CCB Voting Privileges – Determine who has CCB voting rights; in many cases there is a subset of CCB members whose vote matters.
- Voting Approval Method – Determine how many votes are needed to accept a Change Request; it may be a specified majority, consensus, quorum, or some other method.
- Waiving Policy – Determine if certain types of changes can be automatically approved. This may include correcting spelling mistakes. In all cases, a waived change should be captured in a CRF and brought to the attention of the CCB.
- CCB Technology – Indicate the CCB technology or repository where CCB work products are stored.
- Escalation – Determine the path of escalation including the roles that would participate.
- CCB Meeting Closure – Determine closure method from a CCB meeting:
  - Time period between approval of CRF and the notification sent to the change agents.
  - Time period between the end of the CCB meeting and the distribution of the minutes.
3. Review the change control conduct guidelines with the application owner.
4. Provide CCB conduct guidelines training to the proposed CCB members. Consider performing this in conjunction with the training of the SCM change control process (see Section 6.2 above). For more on Change Control Board training, see Section 8.4.
5. Place this process in the application team's document repository, advising personnel of the location.

Roles:

- SCM manager – task lead
- SCM coordinator
- Application owner

Considerations:

- CCB members must have the appropriate skills to understand the change requests and the authority to rule on them.
- CCB members must commit the time and effort for performing the CCB role.
- This task is important for SEI CMM compliance.

Output:

- Customized change control board conduct guidelines
- Change Control Board training

6.3. Develop an SCM Identification Process

This task includes steps to develop a repeatable process of identifying CIs and establishing baselines which enable management of the CIs.

Key Steps:

1. Create an SCM identification process document for the application. Consider one of the following approaches:
   - Identify if a successfully used Identification Process exists. If so, consider using it. However, review the remainder of the steps in this task to ensure the process includes the key elements of an identification process.
   - Use the template found in Section 15 of the Appendix.
2. Define and document the objectives of this process. For example, 'To provide a repeatable process of identifying CIs to establish baselines which enable management of the CIs'.
3. Define and document the scope of this process. For example, 'This process applies to all projects related to this application'.
4. Identify and document the steps. As a starting point, consider using the customizable steps found in Section 15 of the Appendix. Suggested steps for this process include:
   - Identify configuration items (CIs) for the application. For each CI used by the application, list it in an application inventory along with the level of SCM rigor applied to it. For more guidance on this, see Section 5.2 found earlier in this chapter.
   - Align CI Name with naming conventions (optional), if naming conventions exist.
   - Place CI into the baseline. This requires a process for placing the CIs into the baseline and assumes the existence of one of the following:
     - An SCM version control process for development baselines and a corresponding repository where CIs are stored (see Section 6.4).
     - An SCM release process for managing production baselines (see Section 6.7).
     - An SCM change control process for managing requirements and production baselines (see Section 6.2).
5. Review the process and all other elements with the application owner and key staff. Update as appropriate.
6. Provide awareness of the SCM identification process to the appropriate staff.
7. Place this process in the application team's document repository, advising personnel of the location.

Roles:

- SCM coordinator – task lead
- SCM manager
- SCM engineer
- Application owner

Considerations:

- Within the process steps, consider documenting the role(s) that would perform each process step.
- An appropriate SCM version control, SCM change control, or SCM release process may need to be created depending on the CI baseline being managed.
- This task is important for SEI CMM compliance.

Output:

- Customized SCM identification process
- Optional – updated master application inventory

6.4. *Develop an SCM Version Control Process*

This task includes steps to develop a repeatable process of checking out an item, modifying it, checking it back into baseline, and appropriately incrementing the version number. When using an SCM version control technology, the version number is incremented automatically.

Key Steps:

1. Create an SCM version control process document for the application. Consider one of the following approaches:
   - Identify if a successfully used version control process exists. If so, consider using it. However, review the remainder of the steps in this task to ensure the process includes the key elements of a version control process.
   - Use the template found in Section 16 of the Appendix.
2. Define and document the objectives of this process. For example, 'To provide a repeatable process for version controlled changes to any baseline'.
3. Define and document the scope of this process. For example, 'This process applies to all projects related to this application'.
4. Identify and document the process steps. As a starting point, consider using the customizable steps found in the template in Section 16 of the Appendix. Suggested steps for this process include:
   - Checkout Item – Transfer a copy of a configuration item (CI) from the appropriate repository to the work area.
   - Change Item – Change the CI using the standard editing tool to satisfy the change or problem request. Perform the appropriate level of testing to meet the checkin criteria (the CI may require one or more of the following testing actions):
     - Successful build (if applicable)
     - Successful unit test
     - Completed code or peer review
       - Note: The level of testing should be defined by the QA/test manager, project manager, and application owner.
   - Checkin Item – Place a modified version of the CI into the appropriate baseline.
   - Increment the version number for this item providing it a unique version identifier.
     - Automated – This is handled automatically if an SCM version control technology is used.
     - Manual – For a manual system, consider a convention which includes a major version indicator, a minor version indicator, and a draft version indicator.

For example, in **a.bc**, the digit to the left of the decimal point (is the major version indicator) and the digits to the right of the decimal point are the minor version indicator and the draft version indicator. Note: The draft version indicator is only used when the document is being reviewed in a draft state. For more details on the suggested manual version numbering convention, see Section 3.2.1.

- Note: Consider indicating specific commands and examples where possible.

5. Review the process and all other elements with the application owner and key staff. Update as appropriate.
6. Provide training on the process with the appropriate staff or include it as part of the overall SCM technology user training. For more on this topic, see Section 8.3.
7. Place this process in the application team's document repository, advising personnel of the location.

Roles:

- SCM engineer – task lead
- SCM manager

Considerations:

- Within the process step, consider documenting the role(s) that would perform each step.
- There may be more than one version control process if the version control commands vary with the specific SCM version control technology used.
- An SCM version control process may apply to a document management technology.
- The steps of the SCM version control process may be included in a package of user procedures.
- This task is important for SEI CMM compliance.

Output:

- Customized SCM version control process

6.5. Develop an SCM Merge Process

This task includes steps to develop a repeatable process that provides a consistent method of integrating a version of a configuration item from one branch to another, provided that they have the same ancestry. Merging implies that branches exist. For more on the topic of branching, see Section 5.1.6. Merging also implies that there is adequate project management, both directing the appropriate parallel and/or concurrent development activity and ensuring that merging activities are planned.

Key Steps:

1. Create an SCM merge process document for the application. Consider one of the following approaches:

- Identify if a successfully used merge process exists. If so, consider using it. However, review the remainder of the steps in this task to ensure the process includes the key elements of a merge process.
- Use the template found in Section 17 of the Appendix.

2. Define and document the objectives of this process. For example, 'To provide a repeatable process for merging a version of a configuration item from one branch to another, provided that they have the same ancestry'.

3. Define and document the scope of this process. For example, 'This process applies to all projects related to this application'.

4. Identify and document the process steps. As a starting point, consider using the customizable steps found in Section 17 of the Appendix. This process should support the branch and merge process flow and branch type and branch naming convention discussed in Section 5.1.6. Suggested steps for this process include:
   - Identify the target branch you will move to (this should be an ancestor of your current branch). Note: This assumes a checkout of CI has already occurred.
   - Merge from the target branch to your branch. Consider indicating specific commands and examples. Note: Merging it to your branch allows for more time to resolve conflicts (if any).
   - Resolve any logical lines of conflict (if appropriate) with the person that made the change to the prior version of the configuration item.
   - Compile/build (if appropriate)
   - Test
   - Checkin
   - Merge from your branch to the target branch
   - Checkin to target branch (some SCM technologies consolidate the functions of merge and checkin) Note: Consider including specific commands and examples where possible.

5. Review the process and all other elements with the application owner and key staff. Update as appropriate.

6. Provide training on the process with the appropriate staff or include as part of an overall SCM technology user training. For more on this topic, see Section 8.3.

7. Place this process in the application team's document repository, advising personnel of the location.

Roles:

- SCM engineer – task lead
- SCM manager

Considerations:

- With in the process step, consider documenting the role(s) that would perform each step.
- Typically, it is best to assign the task of merging to the personnel who are most familiar with the items being merged. They have the most knowledge about selecting the appropriate sections of code to merge and what to test.

- It is very important to make the merge process as understandable and streamlined for those using it as possible to reduce the effort it takes to perform this task.
- As per Section 4.2 in Chapter 5, ensure a merge activity is added to all project plans that require merging.
- The merge task may be more involved than first thought since it will not only include merging, but recompiling, and retesting of the CIs.
- The steps of the SCM merge process may be included in a package of user procedures.

Output:

- Customized SCM merge process

6.6. Develop an SCM Build Process

This task includes steps to develop a repeatable process for generating deliverables from CIs for potential migration to test and production. This process applies to CIs that produce separate deliverables (programs, binaries, executables, etc.).

Key Steps:

1. Create an SCM build process document for the application. Consider one of the following approaches:
   - Identify if a successfully used build process exists. If so, consider using it. However, review the remainder of the steps in this task to ensure the process includes the key elements of a build process.
   - Use the template found in Section 18 of the Appendix.
2. Define and document the objectives of this process. For example, 'To provide a repeatable process for generating deliverables from code'. There may be different audiences for a build process. These audiences include:
   - Build or release engineer (SCM engineer) who compiles all deliverables that will be used in the release package. This is often called the 'integration build'.
   - Application personnel who compile code in their workspaces after modifications.
3. Define and document the scope of this process. For example, 'This process applies to all projects related to this application'.
4. Identify and document the process steps. As a starting point, consider using the customizable steps found in Section 18 of the Appendix. Suggested steps for this process include:
   - Identify a specific workspace. Verify that it is a clean room workspace (i.e., that there are no items in the workspace, other than what belongs there).
   - Acquire the code for the build. This may involve a checkout of the versioned code or establishing a virtual workspace that displays the code.
   - Build code. Perform compile/build process using the specified compilers and tools.

- Validate deliverables and results. Identify that the build was successful. Determine if expected deliverables were built (compare with expected deliverables). Correct as needed.
- Capture the deliverables. This involves a means of easily identifying and extracting the deliverables. This may include checking in (see Section 6.4) and labeling (see Section 5.1.5) the deliverables into the SCM version control system.
- Summarize and send a build summary:
  - Create a summary of the results of the build. This may include:
    - The number of build errors (if any)
    - One line extract for each build error
    - A list of all CIs that have changed from the previous build/compile
  - Send the build summary to the appropriate personnel (project manager, application owner, QA personnel, etc).
- Note: Consider including specific commands and examples where possible.
5. Review the process and all other elements with the application owner and key staff. Update as appropriate.
6. Provide training on the process to the appropriate staff or include it as part of the overall SCM user training (see Section 8.3).
7. Place this process in the application team's document repository, advising personnel of the location.

Roles:

- SCM engineer – task lead

Considerations:

- Within each process step, consider documenting the role(s) that would perform each step.
- Consider automating the build process.
- This task is optional if no compile/build is needed to produce deliverables. Some development technologies do not compile a deliverable in this traditional manner.
- This task is important for SEI CMM compliance.
- For more on the topic of builds, consider reading the 'Builds' chapter in [Bays 1999].

Output:

- Customized SCM build process

6.7. Develop an SCM Release Process

This task includes steps to develop a repeatable process for managing changes into the production baseline.

Key Steps:

1. Create an SCM release process document for the application. Consider one of the following approaches:

- Identify if a successfully used Release Process exists. If so, consider using it. However, review the remainder of the steps in this task to ensure the process includes the key elements of a Release Process.
- Use the template found in Section 19 of the Appendix.
2. Define and document the objectives of this process. For example, 'To provide a repeatable process for managing changes into the production baseline'.
3. Define and document the scope of this process. For example, 'This process applies to all projects related to this application'.
4. Identify and document the process steps. As a starting point, consider using the customizable process steps found in Section 19 of the Appendix. Suggested steps for this process include:
   - Identify deliverables that make up the release package. This would include a list of names and locations of code, documents, installation scripts, etc. This may be based on labels found within the SCM version control repository. Output of this step may create a release inventory package.
   - Prepare release notes (see Section 6.7.1 below). This document accompanies the release package.
   - Submit a Change Request that documents this proposed change (i.e., release) to the production baseline. Collect documents that support the Change Request and the readiness of the release should the CCB want to review them with the change request. This may include a release package inventory, test report(s), an installation plan, and a backout and restore plan.
   - Determine status of Change Request. The CCB that authorizes the requirements baseline for this release should be the same group that rules on the corresponding release package. Consider using the SCM change control process (see Section 6.2). A suggested process to determine if the package is release ready is as follows:
     - The CCB reviews the Change Request and ensures the Release Criteria have been met. Effectively, determine if the release package includes:
       - The specified requirements (e.g., 100% of priority 1 and 2 and 50% of priority 3 requirements from the requirements baseline of this release).
       - Only the number of defects allowed in the release criteria (e.g., 0 severity 1 defects and no more than 10 severity 2 defects).
     - The CCB determines the decision. This will be either an approval, or a rejection that leads to a discussion on what needs to be corrected for approval to occur.
   - Migrate the approved release package into a staging area. This is a secure location where the release package waits until it is ready for installation into production.
   - Install the release package into the production baseline. Depending on the target of the release package, the installation plans may include one of the following approaches:
     - If the release target is media (such as a CD), then copy the release package onto the target media.
     - If the release target is a production system, then copy the current production baseline to a backout and restore area that may be used to quickly re-install

the current release back into production (for recovery purposes). Then copy the release package into the specified location in the production baseline.
- Finally notify appropriate personnel that the release package is in the production baseline.
- Validate the release package in production. Depending on the target of the release package, the verification steps may include one of the following approaches:
  - If the release target is media (such as a CD), then:
    - Validate that all release deliverables are on the media.
    - Perform an installation test (from the installation plan, if it exists) to ensure the new release of the application installs properly on a target system.
    - Perform test(s) to ensure the new release functions as expected.
  - If the release target is a production system, then:
    - Validate that all release deliverables are in Production.
    - Perform test(s) to ensure the new release functions operate as expected.
    - Note: If minor changes are made to the release deliverables, ensure the CCB are notified. If severe problems occur, notify stakeholders to discuss potential resolutions or begin the backout and restore of the previous release.
- Notify stakeholders and project team that the release package has been successfully installed and tested. Consider placing the release notes into the application team's document repository.
- Note: Consider including specific commands and examples where possible.
5. Review the process and template with the application owner and key staff. Update as appropriate.
6. Provide an overview or training on the SCM release process to the CCB and those involved with the release installation and verification steps.
7. Place this process in the application team's document repository, advising personnel of the location.

Roles:

- SCM manager – task lead
- Application owner
- SCM engineer

Considerations:

- Within each process step, consider documenting the role(s) that would perform each step.
- Consider using an automated technology to install a release into the production baseline.
- A release package may consist of (but is not limited to) a project release or bug fix release.
- This task is important for SEI CMM compliance.

Output:

- Customized SCM release process
- Customized release notes template

6.7.1. Prepare a Release Notes Template

This task provides steps to prepare a standard release notes template for an application with a consistent format for documenting the important information about a release that is given to customer(s).

Key Steps:

1. Create a release notes template. Consider using the template found in Section 19.1 of the Appendix as a starting point. Modify the format and style so that it represents the 'look' of the company. The following fields may be included:
   - Name of the company
   - Product/application name
   - Release number
   - Generally available (GA) release date
   - New features of this release
   - Defects corrected in this release
   - Installation plan (instructions)
2. Review the release notes template with the application owner, stakeholders, and any person required to add to release notes. Update as appropriate.
3. Place this process in the application team's document repository, advising personnel of the location.

Roles:

- SCM manager – task lead
- Application owner

Considerations:

- If many of the fields suggested above are found in a change control or defect tracking technology, then it may be possible to generate part of the release notes from the reporting function of these technologies.
- Consider investigating whether a release notes template(s) already exists within the organization and use this or a customized version of it as you review the key steps above.
- This task is important for SEI CMM compliance.

Output:

- Customized release notes template

6.8. Develop an SCM Audit Process

This task includes the steps to develop a repeatable process for assessing compliance with SCM processes and technology and determining the integrity of application baselines.

An SCM audit process may include audit checklists. Audit checklists include questions or areas of focus that help determine if the users of the SCM system are following the SCM processes (and their corresponding roles) and if the deliverables being developed can be identified in the development (and production) baselines and traced to the requirements to verify the traceability and integrity of the release deliverables.

Key Steps:

1. Create an SCM audit process document for the application. Consider one of the following approaches:
   - Identify if a successfully used SCM audit process exists. If so, consider using it. However, review the remainder of the steps in this task to ensure the process includes the key elements of an audit process.
   - Use the template found in Section 20 of the Appendix.
2. Define and document the objectives of this process. For example, 'To provide a repeatable process for assessing compliance with SCM processes and technology and determining the integrity of application baselines'.
3. Define and document the scope of this process. For example, 'This process applies to all projects related to this application'.
4. Prepare an SCM process audit checklist and an SCM baseline audit checklist. Consider using the templates in the appendix as starting points (see Sections 20.1 and 20.2).
   - Modify the checklists to be either more or less rigorous depending on the SCM maturity level of the organization (i.e., if immature, make it less rigorous; if more mature, make it more rigorous).
   - Place these checklists in an appendix of the SCM audit process for easy access.
5. Identify and document the process steps. As a starting point, consider using the customizable steps found in Section 20 of the Appendix. Suggested steps for this process include:
   - Determine what to Audit and when
     - Copy the SCM process audit checklist and/or the SCM software baseline audit checklist into a separate file with a unique name that includes the date of the audit.
     - Select audit questions based on the area in focus (it may be all items on a checklist or selected checklist items)
     - Determine a specific date for the audit
   - Select the audit team
     - Select personnel for the audit team from the project personnel
     - Assign roles to audit team members (i.e. decide who will audit what)
   - Prepare for audit
     - Schedule meeting times with project team members as appropriate
     - Notify project manager and application owner that the audit has been scheduled
   - Perform audit. Discuss selected audit questions with project personnel, document the results, indicate if the area is passed or failed, and include a recommended action if improvement is needed.

- Report results
    - Document results in the SCM status report template (see Section 21.1 of the Appendix) or similar. The results should include what was being done well, areas of improvement, and recommended actions.
    - Report results to the project manager and application owner (in line with the SCM oversight process if applicable).
    - Open problem requests for any audit improvement items and track them to closure.
    - Place a copy of the audit results in the application team's document repository.
6. Review the process and checklist templates with the application owner and key staff. Update as appropriate.
7. Place these items in the application team's document repository, advising personnel of the location.

Roles:

- SCM coordinator – task lead
- SCM manager
- SCM engineer
- Application owner

Considerations:

- Within the process step, consider documenting the role(s) that would perform each step.
- It is recommended that you limit the reporting distribution of the SCM audit report to only the project manager and the application owner. This allows them to resolve any problems or mitigate risks without the pressure of addressing senior management concerns. However, if no improvements are made after two audits, then consider reporting the results to the senior management level (to motivate improvements).
- This task is important for SEI CMM compliance.

Output:

- Customized SCM audit process
- Customized SCM process audit checklist and SCM baseline audit checklist

6.9. Develop an SCM Oversight Process

This task includes steps to develop a repeatable process for summarizing and discussing SCM activity and status with management.

Key Steps:

1. Create an SCM oversight process document for the application. Consider one of the following approaches:

- Identify if a successfully used SCM oversight process exists. If so, consider using it. However, review the remainder of the steps in this task to ensure the process includes the key elements of an oversight process.
  - Use the template found in Section 21 of the Appendix.
2. Define and document the objectives of this process. For example, 'To provide a repeatable process for summarizing and discussing SCM activity'.
3. Define and document the scope of this process. For example, 'This process applies to all projects related to this application'.
4. Identify and document the process steps. As a starting point, consider using the customizable steps found in Section 21 of the Appendix. Suggested steps for this process include:
   - Schedule an SCM oversight session with appropriate management. These may be on a periodic basis (e.g., 1st Tuesday of the month) or the end of each project lifecycle phase.
   - Prepare the SCM status report (consider using the example in Section 21.1 of the Appendix. Document all SCM status since the last review. Consider including: accomplishments, significant issues and risks, budgetary and staffing needs, training completed, audit results, etc. Provide supporting SCM reports and materials.
   - Conduct SCM oversight session. Review the current status of SCM activities, plans, milestones, and resources (budgetary and staffing items). Address issues, risks, and improvements.
   - Open actions to track to closure. An Action may be an issue, a risk mitigation, or an improvement task:
     - If it is an issue, add it to the problem list using the SCM problem management process and support technology (if one exists).
     - If it is a risk, add a mitigation action to the project plan or action list.
     - If it is an improvement, add it to the SCM plan or action list.
   - Store the SCM status report in the application's document repository. Utilize a naming convention that distinguishes it from other status reports – consider a date convention.
5. Review the process and status report template with the application owner and SCM staff. Update as appropriate.
6. Place these items in the application team's document repository, advising appropriate personnel of the location.

Roles:

- SCM coordinator – task lead
- SCM manager

Considerations:

- Within the process step, consider documenting the role(s) that would perform each step.
- It is recommended that the SCM manager limit the distribution of SCM status reports to the project and application owner.

- This task is important for SEI CMM compliance.

Output:

- Customized SCM oversight process
- Optional – Customized SCM status report template

6.10. Develop an SCM Report Process

This task includes steps to develop a repeatable process for reporting SCM data relating to an organization, application, or project that can be acted upon to promote continuous improvement. Data from the reports may be used for comparing past data and producing SCM metrics. SCM reports may be an output of other SCM processes.

Key Steps:

1. Create an SCM report process document for the application. Consider one of the following approaches:
   - Identify if a successfully used SCM Report Process exists. If so, consider using it as the basis for this process. However, review the remainder of the steps in this task to ensure the process includes key elements of a Report Process.
   - Use the template found in Section 22 of the Appendix.
2. Define and document the objectives of this process. For example, 'To provide a repeatable process for reporting SCM data relating to an organization, application, or project that can be acted upon to promote continuous improvement'.
3. Define and document the scope of this process. For example, 'This process applies to all projects related to this application'.
4. Identify and document the process steps. As a starting point, consider using the customizable steps found in Section 22 of the Appendix. Suggested steps for this process include:
   - Identify SCM data for generating reports. This may include data from processes, audits, measures, training, etc. For suggested measures, see Section 3.3.
   - Generate SCM reports. For each data type, identify and prepare a standard report template. Determine a repeatable process to collect the data. Place the collected data into the specific SCM report template. For example:
     - SCM audit data gets placed into SCM audit reports
     - SCM build data gets placed into SCM build logs and metrics reports
     - SCM change control data gets placed into SCM change request logs and metrics reports
     - SCM problem management data gets placed into SCM problem request logs and metrics reports
     - SCM review data gets placed into SCM status reports
     - SCM release data gets placed into SCM release notes
     - Other SCM measures get placed into SCM metrics reports

- Distribute SCM reports:
  - Determine the appropriate personnel distribution for each report
  - Determine the frequency for distributing the reports
  - Distribute reports to the appropriate personnel at the appropriate frequency
- Store SCM reports Store the SCM reports in the application team's repository.
5. Review the process with the application owner. Update as appropriate.
6. Provide awareness of the process to the application team.
7. Place this process in the application team's document repository, advising application personnel of the location.

Roles:

- SCM coordinator – task lead
- SCM manager
- Application owner

Considerations:

- Within the process step, consider documenting the role that would perform each step.
- Consider automating all or part of the data collection, report generation, and distribution of the SCM reports.
- If reports are too difficult to collect and generate, then the report process will not be sustainable over time. If this is the case, consider another approach or do not collect and generate that particular data.
- Consider the value of each report and ensure it is useful (e.g., can it be used to validate that processes are running well or to make improvement decisions). Otherwise, it may not be cost effective to produce the report.
- This task is important for SEI CMM compliance.

Output:

- Customized SCM reporting process

6.11. SCM Process Phase Completion Checklist

The items in this checklist may be used to determine if SCM tasks have been completed in this phase:

- Has an SCM problem management process been developed?
  - Have problem types been defined?
  - Have severity levels been defined?
  - Have state transitions been defined?
  - Has a problem request form been developed?
- Has an SCM change control process been developed?
  - Have baselines been identified which this process will manage?
  - Have priority levels been defined?

- Have state transitions been defined?
- Has a change request form been developed?
- Have change control conduct guidelines been created?
- Has change control process training occurred for the CCB members?
- Has an SCM identification process been developed?
- Has an SCM version control process been developed?
  - Has version control process training occurred (either separately or included as part of the overall SCM user training)?
- Has an SCM merge process been developed?
  - Has merge process training occurred (either separately or included as part of the overall SCM user training)?
- Has an SCM build process been developed?
- Has an SCM release process been developed?
  - Has a release notes template been developed?
  - Has a release sign-off form template been developed?
- Has an SCM audit process been developed?
  - Has an SCM process audit checklist been developed?
  - Has an SCM baseline audit checklist been developed?
- Has an SCM oversight process been developed?
- Has an SCM status report template been developed?
- Has an SCM report process been developed?
- Have all the SCM processes been placed in the application team's document repository?

7. SCM Technology Implementation Phase

The SCM technology implementation phase focuses on the implementation of the SCM infrastructure. While the primary focus is on the SCM version control/build management infrastructure, it also includes the high-level tasks for establishing problem management, change control, release engineering, and global SCM/development infrastructures.

7.1. Establish the SCM Version Control/Build Management Infrastructure

This 'super task' provides high-level steps to establish an effective SCM version control/build management infrastructure. By infrastructure, this is meant to include technology, processes, and training. The importance of this task is to establish an environment that can be used by the application team for the version control of application software items.

Key Steps:

1. Determine the transition order of candidate applications into the SCM version control technology repository. See Section 7.1.1 for details on implementing this task. This subtask helps select which application will be the first to transition into the SCM technology repository. Note: this task is not needed if there is only one application in question.

2. Optional – Restructure and/or refine the application code structure. See Section 7.1.2 for details on implementing this task.
3. Assign an SCM version control/build management technology administrator and train them in the appropriate SCM skills, roles, and responsibilities (i.e., version control technology and the associated process tasks). See Section 8.1 for more on providing technology administrator training. This responsibility may be separated into two roles: SCM version control technology administrator and build engineer
4. Review the selected SCM technology. This assumes that an SCM technology has been evaluated and selected. If it has not, then do so (see Section 4.2).
5. Install the SCM technology. See Section 7.1.3 for details on implementing this task.
6. Import the code into the SCM technology repository and baseline the code versions for continued development. See Section 7.1.4 for details on implementing this task. This includes the optional steps of compiling/building the application code outside of the SCM technology repository prior to the import and a compile/build after the import into the SCM technology to compare results (e.g., compare the build logs).
7. Create appropriate workspaces for the application team (for development work) and SCM staff (for builds and releases to occur). See Section 7.1.5 for details on implementing this task.

Roles:

- SCM engineer – task lead
- SCM manager
- Application owner(s)
- Project manager(s)

Considerations:

- Once the SCM version control/build management infrastructure is established, it is expected that personnel will be trained in the user commands of that technology and any corresponding processes. See Section 8.3 for more on providing appropriate user training.
- This super task combines all SCM version control/build management tasks and may be completed separately from the other tasks in this book if the focus of the effort is on SCM version control/build management infrastructure.

Output:

- An established and operationally-ready SCM version control/build management infrastructure
- Trained technology administrator(s)
- Installed SCM version control/build management technology
- At least one application has been imported into the SCM version control repository
- User workspaces
- Tested version control and build processes

7.1.1. Determine Transition Order of Applications into the SCM Technology

This task provides steps to help select which application will be the first to transition into the SCM version control repository. If there is only one application that needs to go into the SCM version control repository, then this becomes the first application and this task is complete. If you have several applications that need to go into the SCM technology repository, consider selecting an application that has the best chance of a successful import and transition for the pilot effort. What is learned from the pilot effort can reduce the time and difficulty of subsequent application transitions.

Key Steps:

1. Create a list of applications that can be moved to the new SCM environment. Document the application names in an Application column. Note: If there is only one application, then this task is complete and you do not need to visit the remaining steps.
2. For each application, identify the development platform(s) and the complexity of the application in separate Platform and Complexity columns. As a guideline, consider using the complexity matrix found in Section 2.2.1.
3. Identify and sort the list into low, medium and high complexity level applications.
4. Of those applications on the list that have low and medium level complexity determine:
   - The stage of the project lifecycle (e.g., requirements, design, development, test, on release) that the current project release of that application is in. Indicate this in a separate Lifecycle stage column.
   - The readiness of the project team to transition into the SCM environment in a separate Implementation readiness column. Indicate if the readiness is high, medium, or low. To assess readiness, see Section 2.1.
5. Analyze this information and select which application is most likely to succeed in the transition into the SCM infrastructure. Also, select a tentative order for the remaining candidate applications.
6. For the initial application, get buy-in from the application owner and the project manager(s).

Roles:

- SCM manager – task lead
- Application owners
- Project manager(s)

Considerations:

- When considering which application may move first into the SCM technology, select an application that is representative of the other applications (i.e. that has common code types and platform). In general, you are looking for an easy win or a success story that will make it easier to implement SCM for the remaining applications.

Output:

- Initial application is selected for pilot
- Tentative order for remaining applications

7.1.2. Restructure/Refine the Application Code Structure

This optional task includes steps that provide an opportunity for the application team to restructure or refine the application code structure prior to placing the code into the SCM version control technology repository. It may be beneficial to reorganize the code into a more modular or component basis to promote more effective parallel and distributed development.

Key Steps:

1. Review the code directory structure of the application selected for transition.
   - Identify all dependencies with other applications.
2. Identify a redesign approach to make the code structure more component-based and modular. It is critical that architecture personnel participate.
3. Copy the current application code into the prototype area.
4. Restructure the code as specified by the design approach selected. Modify until the application structure is working properly (this may require modifying files due to hard-coded paths, dependencies, and compile/build needs).
5. Once the design and restructuring has been completed, rebuild and/or test the functionality until it builds and operates as expected. Modify as appropriate.

Roles:

- Architects – task lead
- Application owner
- SCM engineer

Considerations:

- The advantages of restructuring may include creating a more modular and component based code structure that will allow for easier segmentation of work when parallel and/or distributed development occurs. This can reduce the amount of difficult merging that may occur.
- If code is reorganized, it is critical that a compilation of code is attempted afterwards.

Output:

- Modified code structure

7.1.3. Install the SCM Technology

This task includes steps that focus on the installation of an SCM technology (SCM technology and repository). This task assumes that an SCM technology has been selected. If this is not the case, see Section 4.2.

Key Steps:

1. Review the SCM System Details and Application Environment Details sections in the SCM Design Specification. If these sections have not been completed then see Sections 5.1.3 and 5.1.4. They will provide direction into the installation process (e.g., where the technology should be installed, where the SCM repository will live, etc.)
2. Identify the server and directory location where the SCM Technology will be installed. This information is found in the SCM system details in the design specification.
3. Identify personnel that will be needed to install the SCM technology. For example, the system administrator may be needed to install the technology due to the super-user privileges needed for the installation process.
4. Install the SCM technology as per the installation instructions into the installation location defined in SCM System Details in the SCM Design Specification.
   - If it is a vendor SCM technology, then installation instructions should come with the purchased technology.
   - If it is freeware SCM technology, then installation instructions may be found on the website from where the technology is downloaded.
5. Verify the installation occurred successfully and exercise the tool functionality.

Roles:

- SCM engineer – task lead
- System administrator

Consideration:

- It is highly recommended that the SCM engineer receives SCM technology administrator training prior to performing this task, (see Section 8.1).

Output:

- Operationally-ready SCM technology installation base

7.1.4. Import and Baseline Application into the SCM Technology

This task includes steps to ensure that all appropriate application code items are imported into the SCM version control repository. This task assumes that an SCM technology has been installed; if not see Section 7.1.3.

Key Steps:

1. Optional – If this application has a build component, build the code in its current state (outside of the SCM technology). Record the exact output of the compile/build even if it does not build correctly. It can be compared to the build results (e.g., the build log) once the code is imported into the new SCM version control technology repository.
2. Import the application code items.
   - Identify the current location of the pilot application. If a pilot application has not been selected, see Section 7.1.1 if more than one application is under consideration.
   - Identify all items of the application that must be placed into the SCM version control repository. Note: pieces of the application may exist in user directories, common directories, or other SCM version control technologies. If an application inventory list has been prepared for this application, then use it as the basis for identifying the code. To prepare an application inventory list, go to Section 5.2.3.
   - Determine if all current and past versions must go into the SCM technology repository or only the current (i.e., latest) versions. The import process will occur more quickly if only the current versions are imported. However, for history of the application and if older releases must continue to be supported, consider importing all versions of the code.
   - Using either the automated import feature of the SCM technology (if it exists) or a manual process, import all identified code (and targeted versions) into the SCM version control repository.
   - Verify that the identified items have been imported.
3. Baseline the application items
   - Upon completion of the import step, baseline the items by attaching a label to the specified versions. Consider using the label naming convention defined in Section 5.1.5.
4. Optional – If this application has a build component, build the code now that it has been imported into the SCM technology.
   - Create an official clean room build workspace using the instructions or commands of the new SCM version control technology. See Section 7.1.5 for more on creating workspaces.
   - Review the previous compile/build process for the application (if it exists).
   - Establish an updated/new build process as appropriate.
   - Perform a compile/build of the baseline of code using the build process and capture the output of the compile/build in a build log.
   - Compare the compile/build log against the compile/build log from the build outside of the SCM technology from Step 1. Identify and resolve any differences.
5. Establish a periodic backup of the SCM repository. Work with system administration to develop a backup process. If there is a standard backup and recovery process within the organization, consider using it. Once the backup process is in

place, it is important to perform a recovery step to verify the data. Consider the following steps:

- Determine what should be backed up. This should include the SCM repository, but may include other items within the SCM system.
- Determine the type of media to be used for backups relative to the amount of data to be backed up.
- Determine frequency of backups (e.g., daily, weekly, etc.). Note: Typically, back-ups should occur during the night.
- Determine whether full or incremental backups will occur and how often. It is recommended that you perform a full backup once a week with incremental backups daily. If it is an active project, consider full backups daily.
- Determine the storage location of the backup media.
- Determine the backup label naming convention (i.e., physical tag placed on the media).
- Develop a backup and recovery process. Suggested steps include:
  - Perform backup – Identify data to be backed up; backup data; label the backup; store the backup in an appropriate location.
  - Place a request for recovery of data – Include the data needed and the date from when the data should be recovered (when the data was last known to be valid).
  - Perform recovery – Backup media is identified and loaded on system; recover data; verify the data for correctness; report results to requestor.
- Determine how regularly a recovery test should occur. It is important to test the recovery to ensure accuracy of the backup and recovery process.

Roles:

- SCM engineer – task lead

Considerations:

- It is recommended that you automate this task as much as possible due to the complex nature of the import. Many SCM technologies have an automated import mechanism. This may reduce the chance of forgetting pieces of the application if done manually.
- If no build process exists, consider completing the task in Section 6.6 to establish a build process for the application.

Output:

- Application code items imported into the SCM version control repository
- Established development baseline
- Established and tested backup and recovery process
- Optional – Comparison of the compile/build log with the compile/build log from the build outside the SCM technology
- Optional – Customized SCM build process (new or updated)

7.1.5. Establish User Workspaces

This task provides steps to prepare the appropriate workspaces for development work and for builds and releases to occur. This task assumes that application code has been imported into the SCM technology repository. If it has not, complete the activity in Section 7.1.4.

Key Steps:

1. Determine the various workspace types that are needed and what branch the user workspaces should be created from. This may include (but is not limited to):
   - Latest (on the current/new release) – on an integration branch from the project release branch.
   - Bugfix (of previous release) – on a bugfix branch that is off the specific release baseline (label) on the main branch.
   - Note: Align the workspace types with the workspace branch types, the branch naming convention, and the branch and merge process flow diagram from Section 5.1.6.
2. Determine which application team members require which workspace baselines.
3. Ensure there is appropriate disk space for all workspaces if workspaces will reside on a central server. Assume the worst case scenario where all code from that baseline is needed in each workspace. This can be calculated by the number of workspaces that are needed multiplied by the size of the baseline which includes all source and if applicable, built items.
   - For example, 10 developers require a 'latest' baseline which is 500 megabytes, therefore 5 gigabytes of diskspace are needed. Also, 5 developers require the 'bugfix' baseline which is 400 megabytes, therefore 2 gigabytes are needed. Overall, a total of 7 gigabytes are needed.
   - Note: The amount of disk space needed will vary according to the way each SCM technology makes code accessible.
4. Determine the process for creating workspaces. This may include commands for creating a workspace, the naming convention of the workspaces, and the location(s) of workspaces. See the SCM System Details in the SCM Design Specification for more on workspace locations and naming conventions (see Section 5.1.4).
5. Create the required workspaces, as defined above. This task may be done by the SCM engineer or application personnel.
   - If users create workspaces, then the SCM engineer should document brief instructions for creating workspaces.
   - If the SCM engineer creates workspaces, he should notify users of their new workspaces.
   - Note: This step may be left until just prior to transitioning into the new SCM system.
6. Test an actual workspace to ensure the SCM system functions as expected. This involves developing an SCM version control process (see Section 6.4) to validate that checkouts and checkins of code can be processed from the workspaces.

Roles:

- SCM engineer – task lead
- Application personnel (if they create their own workspaces)

Consideration:

- If there is not enough disk space for the workspaces, order more as soon as possible.

Output:

- Defined workspace types
- Estimated size of disk space needed for workspaces
- Created workspaces
- Optional – Customized SCM version control process (new or updated)

7.2. Establish the SCM Problem Management Infrastructure

This 'super-task' provides the high-level steps to establish an effective problem management infrastructure. Infrastructure includes processes, technology, and training. The importance of this task is to establish an environment that can be used by the application team to open problems and track them to closure.

Key Steps:

1. Review the selected SCM problem management technology (from Section 4.2). If a technology has not been chosen, then complete this task.
2. Assign and train a problem management technology administrator on the appropriate SCM skills, roles, and responsibilities (e.g., problem management technology functionality and the problem management process tasks). See Section 8.1 for more on providing the appropriate administrator training.
3. Set up the problem management technology.
   - Install the technology as per the installation instructions from the vendor.
   - Configure the technology to meet the process needs as defined in Section 6.1. This includes (but is not limited to) defining the problem types, severity levels, and state transitions.
   - Test the problem management technology functionality. This should include testing the commands of the technology.
   - Validate the steps in the SCM problem management process that utilizes the technology functionality as stated. Update the process as appropriate.
4. Import any existing problems into the problem management technology. Identify where problems are being managed and ensure they are imported into this new system.
5. Train the user on the SCM problem management process and commands of the technology. See Section 8.3 for more on providing appropriate user training.

Roles:

- SCM engineer – task lead
- SCM manager
- Application owner

Considerations:

- Problem management is synonymous with defect tracking, incident tracking, and bug tracking, and can be used to track any type of problem.
- This problem management super-task combines all problem management tasks and may be completed separately from other tasks in this book if the focus is problem management.
- The problem management technology and the change control technology may be based on the same technology and have fields that differentiate them (e.g., a 'change' field versus a 'problem' field).
- For more on the topic of problem management, consider reading the 'Defect Tracking' chapter in [Bays 1999].

Output:

- Robust and operationally-ready problem management infrastructure:
  - Installed problem management technology
  - Tested problem management commands, functionality, and applicable process steps
  - Personnel assigned and trained to utilize the problem management technology and process and provide administrative support

7.3. Establish the SCM Change Control Infrastructure

This 'super-task' provides the high-level steps to establish an effective change control infrastructure. Infrastructure includes processes, conduct guidelines, roles and responsibilities, technology, and training. The importance of this task is to establish an environment to authorize and track changes to baselines that require a high degree of SCM rigor due to their potentially high impact on an application. For example, requirements are typically defined for each project release and requirements change throughout a project lifecycle. These changes need to be identified and tracked in order to determine the cost and schedule impact on the current release and future releases of an application.

Key Steps:

1. Review the selected SCM change control technology (from Section 4.2). If a technology has been chosen, then complete this task.
2. Assign and train a change control technology administrator on the roles and responsibilities (e.g., change control technology functionality and the change control

process tasks). See Section 8.1 for more on providing the appropriate administrator training.

3. Set up the change control technology.
   - Install the technology as per the installation instructions from the vendor.
   - Configure the technology to meet the process needs as defined in Section 6.2. This includes (but is not limited to) defining the baselines, priority levels, and state transitions.
   - Test the change control technology functionality. This should include testing the commands of the technology.
   - Validate the steps in the SCM change control process that utilize the change control technology functionality. Update the process as appropriate.

4. Import any existing baseline items into the change control technology. For example, if requirements need to be managed, then import any existing requirements into the change control technology.

5. Assign personnel who will become change control board (CCB) members. See Section 3.2.3 of Chapter 3 for more on this topic. The CCB member names are defined in the application SCM plan or SCM design specification.

6. Train the CCB members. CCB members must have the appropriate training and application knowledge to understand how to evaluate a change request and determine a course of action (see Section 8.4). Ensure the training includes a review and discussion of the CCB conduct guidelines (see Section 6.2.1).

Roles:

- SCM manager – task lead
- SCM engineer
- Application owner
- Project manager
- CCB

Considerations:

- This change control super-task combines all change control tasks and may be completed separately from other tasks in this book if the focus is change control.
- The change control technology and the problem management technology may be based on the same technology and have fields that differentiate them (e.g., a Change field versus a Problem field).
- For more on the topic of problem management, consider reading the 'Change Control' chapter in [Bays 1999].

Output:

- Established and operationally-ready change control infrastructure:
  - Installed change control technology
  - Tested change control commands, functionality, and applicable process steps
  - Personnel assigned and trained to play the roles of change control board (CCB) member and change control technology administrator

7.4. *Establish the SCM Release Engineering Infrastructure*

This 'super-task' provides the high-level steps to establish an effective release engineering infrastructure. Infrastructure includes processes, technology, and training. The importance of this task is to have a consistent and reliable infrastructure that will ensure the integrity of the release package as it approaches and enters the production baseline.

Key Steps:

1. Review the selected SCM release engineering technology (from Section 4.2). If a technology has been chosen, then complete this task.
2. Assign and train a release engineer on the technology and process steps associated with the release migration and installation. See Section 8.1 for more on providing the appropriate administrator training.
3. Set up the release engineering technology.
   - Install the technology as per the installation instructions from the vendor.
   - Configure the technology to meet the process needs as defined in Section 6.7. This may include (but is not limited to) defining the servers and/or SCM version control repository to acquire the deliverables from and the server(s), location, or media on which to place the release package.
   - Test the release engineering technology functionality. This should include testing the commands of the technology.
   - Validate the steps in the SCM release process that utilize the release engineering technology. Update the process as appropriate.

Roles:

- SCM engineer (release engineer, production/operations personnel) – task lead
- SCM manager
- Application owner

Considerations:

- Release engineering technology is synonymous with deployment, installation, and migration.
- This release engineering super-task combines all release engineering tasks and may be completed separately from other tasks in this book if the focus is release engineering.

Output:

- Established and operationally-ready release engineering infrastructure:
  - Installed release engineering technology
  - Tested release engineering commands, functionality, and applicable process steps
  - Personnel assigned and trained to play the release engineer role

7.5. *Establish the Global SCM/Development Infrastructure*

This "super-task" provides the high-level steps for establishing an effective global SCM/development infrastructure. If distributed development occurs on an application, it is important to establish an infrastructure that supports the process of developing application release deliverables across sites.

Key Steps:

1. Review the selected SCM version control/build management technology (from Section 4.2) and the distributed access technology identified in the global SCM/development strategy (from Section 5.3). If a technology or strategy has not been defined, then complete the appropriate task(s).
2. Implement the distributed access technology identified in Section 5.3:
   - If the technology approach selected is 'remote client snapshot', perform the following:
     - Assign and train a distributed access technology administrator. It is recommended that this role be played by the same person/group that supports the SCM version control technology.
     - Establish the SCM version control technology on the remote client.
       - Install it on the client as per the installation instructions from the vendor.
       - Checkout or retrieve the code baseline to the remote client.
       - Validate the code baseline on the remote client. This may involve a compare of the code sizes, test build, test of the functionality, etc. The process of validating the code baseline to a remote client should be consistently applied to all remote clients in this distributed access infrastructure.
     - Implement and validate the recommended branch/merge approach from Section 5.3.
     - Assign and train a code integrator as needed by the roles and responsibilities described in the distributed roles and responsibilities output from Section 5.3.
     - Establish communication channels amongst code integrators, distributed access administrators, and SCM version control administrators across all sites.
   - If the technology approach selected is 'remote server repository', perform the following:
     - Assign and train a distributed access technology administrator. It is recommended that this role be played by the same person/group that supports the SCM version control technology.
     - Establish the remote server repository technology.
       - Install the SCM version control technology on the remote server as per vendor instructions.
       - Install the remote server repository technology on the local and remote servers as per vendor instructions.
       - Define the replication frequency.
       - Replicate the code repository to the remote server
       - Validate the replication of the code repository.

- Populate the remote clients from the remote server where the replicated code repository exists. Validate the code baseline on the remote client. This may involve a test build, comparing the sizes of the code items, testing the functionality, checking in code back to the remote server, etc. The process identified to validate the code baseline to a remote client should be consistently applied to all remote clients in this distributed access infrastructure.
        - Establish periodic repository replications (include all items or only changes) from the remote server to the local server and from the local server to the remote server at a defined frequency.
    - Implement and validate the recommended branch/merge approach from Section 5.3.
    - Assign and train a code integrator as needed by the roles and responsibilities described in the distributed roles and responsibilities output from Section 5.3.
    - Establish communication channels amongst code integrators, distributed access administrators, and SCM version control administrators across all sites.
- If the approach selected is 'terminal services', perform the following:
    - Assign and train a distributed access technology administrator for the terminal services technology. It is recommended that this role be played by the same person/group that supports the SCM version control technology.
    - Establish the terminal services technology on the local terminal services server or client. Follow the installation instructions from the vendor.
    - Install the terminal services client on the remote client. Validate that the remote client personnel can access the local terminal services server or client and the corresponding local development technology.
    - Implement and validate the recommended branch/merge approach from Section 5.3.
    - Assign and train a code integrator as needed by the roles and responsibilities described in the distributed roles and responsibilities output from Section 5.3.
    - Establish communication channels amongst code integrators, distributed access administrators, and SCM version control administrators across all sites.
- If the approach selected is 'terminal emulator', perform the following:
    - Ensure the remote login capability exists on the appropriate remote servers and clients.
    - Validate that the remote client personnel can access the code and utilize the same tools for development as the local personnel.
    - Implement and validate the recommended branch/merge approach from Section 5.3.
    - Assign and train a code integrator at the local site as per the roles and responsibilities described in the distributed roles and responsibilities output from Section 5.3 with a focus on merging.

Roles:

- SCM manager – task lead
- SCM version control administrator (SCM engineer)

- Distributed access administrator (may be played by SCM engineer)
- Code integrator (best handled by personnel who are very familiar with the code)
- Application owner

Considerations:

- This global SCM/development super-task combines all distributed site tasks and may be completed separately from other tasks in this book if the focus is on distributed development. However, this task should be undertaken in conjunction with its predecessor task that defines the global SCM/development strategy (see Section 5.3).
- If the remote client snapshot approach is selected, the SCM version control technology being used must be able to support this approach. This should be a functional requirement when evaluating SCM version control technologies.
- If the remote server repository approach is selected, the SCM version control technology being used must be able to support an automated repository replication to all sites. This should be a functional requirement when evaluating SCM version control technologies since not all support this capability.
- While there are similarities between distributed development and parallel development, they are not the same. Parallel development occurs when two or more different releases are being worked on at the same time or two or more personnel are working on the same item at the same time. Distributed development is when personnel from two or more sites are working on the same release or different releases of the same application.
- Developing an application from distributed sites implies that there is project management personnel trained in managing distributed and parallel development efforts, who plan for the impact of branching and merging activities and, most importantly, understand the importance of communication and collaboration in a challenging global environment.
- Ensure the SCM merge process is customized to support the global SCM/development infrastructure (see Section 6.5).

Output:

- Established and operationally-ready global SCM/development infrastructure:
  - Installed distributed access technology
  - Tested distributed access technology functionality and appropriate branch/merge functionality in the version control technology
  - Personnel assigned as code integrators and assigned and trained as distributed access administrators

7.6. SCM Technology Implementation Phase Completion Checklist

The items in this checklist may be used to determine if SCM tasks have been completed in this phase:

- Has an SCM version control/build management infrastructure been established?

- If more than one application is to be placed under SCM version control, have the applications been reviewed for complexity and implementation readiness to determine the best candidate application with the most favorable chance of successfully transitioning into the SCM version control repository?
- Has any time been spent in restructuring and/or refining the application code structure?
- Has the SCM version control/build management technology been installed according to the installation processes?
- Has all of the code been imported into the SCM repository?
- Has a backup and recovery process been developed?
- Have user workspaces been established as per a standard process?
- Has an SCM problem management infrastructure been established (to include processes, roles and responsibilities, technology, and training)?
- Has an SCM change control infrastructure been established (to include processes, conduct guidelines, roles and responsibilities, technology, and training)?
- Has an SCM release engineering infrastructure been established (to include processes, roles and responsibilities, technology, and training)?
- Has a global SCM/development infrastructure been established (to include processes, roles and responsibilities, technology, and training)?

8. SCM Training Phase

The SCM training phase focuses on the SCM training needed for those administering or using the SCM technology or processes.

8.1. Provide SCM Technology Administrator Training

This task includes steps to ensure the specified personnel receive the appropriate SCM technology administrator training. SCM technology may refer to version control/build management, problem management, change control, release engineering, or global SCM/development technology. This task may be repeated for each SCM technology that requires administrator training.

Key Steps:

1. Identify SCM technology administrator training requirements (SCM technology being used, beginners/advanced level, specialization, cost, schedule needs, location, etc.)
2. Identify the SCM technology administrator training courses and their scheduled dates made available by technology vendors and training vendors.
3. Obtain approval for the identified training and associated costs.
4. Register for the training course that fulfills the most training requirements specified. Consider scheduling just-in-time training. If training is taken too early, the materials learned can be forgotten over time.
5. Attend SCM technology administrator training.

6. Document who took the training in the SCM Training section of the SCM Design Specification document or in a location where it is readily available for review. For more on this topic, see Section 5.1.7.

7. Optional – consider having the personnel who attended the training write a summary that includes an evaluation of the course (e.g., what was good/bad, what was missing, etc.) so that others may review it when deciding to take the course. Store the training summaries in an easily accessible location for others to find.

Roles:

- SCM engineer (SCM technology administrator) – task lead
- SCM manager
- Application owner

Considerations:

- Consider contacting SCM professionals to identify someone who has taken the course under consideration and solicit their opinions of the course.
- The SCM technology administrator should take the SCM technology administrator training prior to installing the SCM technology.
- This task may be omitted if the assigned SCM technology administrator already has that specified training.

Output:

- Personnel trained as an SCM technology administrator
- Updated 'Who has taken SCM Training' table within the SCM design specification document
- Optional – Training summary

8.2. Prepare SCM Technology User Training Materials

This task includes steps to evaluate the benefit of preparing training materials in-house and the steps for preparing in-house SCM technology user training materials for any application team personnel who are required to use an SCM technology.

Key Steps:

1. Evaluate the cost/benefit of whether SCM technology user training will be done by a vendor or handled by an in-house resource. Perform the following steps:
   - Determine if there is an SCM technology user training course offered by a technology vendor and/or a training vendor. If so, identify the cost per course. Then calculate the cost of sending all users to the vendor SCM technology user training course (cost of the course multiplied by the number of users that will be trained).

- If no vendor training is offered, then in-house training materials should be prepared for training the users (go to step 2).
- Determine if the application owner will fund the cost of vendor training for users. Use the calculated cost from the above step.
  - If so, schedule the vendor training for the users (see Section 8.3).
  - If not, go to step 2 below. However, ensure the opportunity is taken to explain to the application owner how much money will be saved by performing training in-house.

2. Identify the Instructor for the SCM technology user training course. In many cases, this will be the SCM engineer. The SCM engineer and the SCM manager should work together to prepare the in-house training if this is the approach that is determined.

3. Prepare in-house SCM technology user training materials. Perform the following steps:
   - Determine the logistics of the training course. This includes the:
     - Training format – Define the presentation format, online format, quick guide format, handouts, etc.
     - Length of course – Consider limiting it to less than four hours (1–2 hours is ideal).
     - Training facility – Define the needs of the training session. For example, this may include a screen for a slide presentation and computers for exercises. Consider the size of the training location.
   - Prepare the training materials (in the defined training format). Document the following:
     - The purpose of the SCM technology
     - The benefits of the SCM technology
     - The roles and responsibilities of the user
     - SCM technology basic concepts
     - SCM technology key user commands
     - Process by which the users will use the technology. Consider input from the SCM processes that may include the technology user commands (see Section 6, the SCM process phase) and the branch naming convention and branching and merging process flow (see Section 5.1.6).
     - SCM technology exercises including the key user commands that the users may walk-through in an 'exercise' section of the training.
   - Perform a practice SCM technology user training session using the training materials. Include a couple of project and SCM personnel for feedback. Update training materials as appropriate.
   - Place the training materials in the application team's document repository for future use.

Roles:

- SCM engineer – task lead
- SCM manager

- Application owner
- Key developer

Considerations:

- If you are sending the users to vendor SCM technology user training, the vendor will have the materials prepared. However, consider sending an SCM engineer to evaluate the SCM technology user training course prior to moving ahead with the vendor training option.
- There is a cost saving by preparing the SCM technology user training internally. However, ensure the training is well developed and adequate for the needs of the user. Also ensure the instructor has training experience to more effectively train the users.
- Consider preparing an SCM technology user commands 'quick guide'. This is typically a one page document which a user may place in their work area for quick reference.

Output:

- Decision to train in-house (with internal resources) or utilize a vendor
- If in-house, output includes:
  - SCM technology user training materials
  - Training course logistics (location, facilities, course length, etc.)
  - SCM processes that support the training materials
  - Training materials in the application team repository

8.3. Provide SCM Technology User Training

This task includes steps to ensure that each user has a basic understanding of the SCM technology.

Key Steps:

1. Confirm management support (specifically from the application owner) for user training. This provides leverage to insist that all users are trained.
2. Identify all potential users of the SCM technology. This may include (but is not limited to) development, QA/test, and management personnel.
3. Determine the best time to train users. Typically, the best time to train personnel (and to transition to a new SCM technology) is after the end of a project release or in the early phases of a project release. Consider just-in-time training since the users will have a better chance of retaining the knowledge from training.
   - If SCM technology user training is being given by the vendor, register all appropriate users for the vendor class that aligns with the best time to schedule training.

- If SCM technology user training is being prepared and given internally, schedule just-in-time training for all appropriate users. This may mean scheduling several classes.
4. Notify users of the scheduled SCM technology user training course including when and where it will occur. Indicate the management support for the training. Consider including an overview of what they can expect from the training.
5. Conduct the SCM technology user training course:
   - Appropriate personnel attend the course.
   - If in-house, the instructor trains the users utilizing the materials prepared in Section 8.2 and relevant SCM processes.
6. Document who took the training in the 'Who has taken SCM Training' table within the SCM Training section of the SCM design specification document or in a location where it is readily available for review. For more on this topic, see Section 5.1.7.
7. Optional – Provide management with a list of who has taken the training and who has not.

Roles:

- SCM engineer – task lead
- SCM manager
- Instructor (may be the SCM engineer)
- Users (appropriate personnel) who attend training

Considerations:

- It is preferable that the person performing the internal training has training experience to more effectively train the users.
- Whether training is done internally or by a vendor, it is unlikely that all users can be trained at the same time due to project commitments. Consider scheduling several training sessions.
- It may be advantageous to video tape a user training session. This can be used as a training resource when a new person joins the application team.

Output:

- SCM technology user training course(s) held and taken by appropriate personnel.
- Updated 'Who has taken SCM Training' table within the SCM Training section of the SCM design specification document.

8.4. Prepare and Provide Change Control Board (CCB) Training

This task provides steps to ensure that those involved with the Change Control Board (CCB) have a basic understanding of the change control process and supporting artifacts. Specifically it makes those on the CCB aware of the roles, process, and the conduct guidelines for controlling baselines.

Key Steps:

1. Identify the instructor for the CCB training course. In many cases, this will be the SCM manager. The SCM manager and possibly the application owner should work together to prepare the CCB training.
2. Prepare the Change Control Board Training materials. Perform the following steps:
   - Determine the logistics of the training course. This includes the:
     - Training format – Define the presentation format, online format, quick guide format, handouts, etc.
     - Length of course – Consider limiting it to two hours.
     - Training facility – Define the needs of the training session and consider the size of the training location.
   - Prepare the CCB training materials (in the training format). Document the following:
     - The purpose of a CCB
     - The benefits of a CCB
     - The roles and responsibilities of a CCB and who in the training course plays which role
     - The baselines to which the CCB will apply change control
     - A walk-through of the change control process. If it does not exist, see Section 6.2.
     - A demonstration of the change control technology. If it does not exist, see Section 7.3.
     - A walk-through of the change control board conduct guidelines. If they do not exist, see Section 6.2.1.
     - The change request form (CRF). If one does not exist, customize the example in Section 14.1 of the Appendix.
     - An exercise simulating a CCB meeting that reviews two (or more) change requests.
   - Review the training materials with the application owner and project manager(s). Update training materials as appropriate.
   - Place the training materials in the application team's document repository for current and future use.
3. Provide CCB Training:
   - Confirm management support (specifically from the application owner) for CCB training. This provides leverage to insist that all CCB personnel are trained.
   - Identify all CCB members. Consider reviewing the CCB Members section of the 'SCM Roles and Responsibilities' table within the SCM design specification or SCM plan (if one exists).
   - Determine the best time to conduct the CCB training. Typically, the best time to train CCB personnel is in the beginning phase of a project release.
   - Notify CCB personnel of the scheduled CCB training course including when and where it will occur. Indicate the management support for the training. Consider including an overview of what they can expect from the training.
   - Conduct the CCB Training course:
     - All CCB personnel attend the course.

- Instructor trains the CCB personnel utilizing the CCB training materials with relevant processes and artifacts.
- Document who took the training in the 'Who has taken SCM Training' table within the SCM Training section of the SCM design specification document or in a location where it is readily available for review. For more on this topic, see Section 5.1.7.

Roles:

- SCM manager – task lead
- Application owner
- Instructor (may be the SCM manager)
- Change control board (CCB) members who attend training

Considerations:

- It is best to have all CCB members on the training course so that they may play their roles while they are in the training and perform the exercise together, thereby getting experience in their role within the CCB context.
- A good way to test the change control processes, conduct guidelines, and supporting artifacts is by including an exercise simulating a CCB meeting that reviews two or more change requests within the training materials.

Output:

- CCB training materials (stored in the application team repository)
- CCB training course taken by CCB personnel
- Updated 'Who has taken SCM Training' table within the SCM Training section of the SCM design specification document.

8.5. SCM Training Phase Completion Checklist

The items in this checklist may be used to determine if SCM tasks have been completed in this phase:

- Has the SCM technology administrator attended SCM technology administrator training?
- Have SCM technology user training materials been developed (if training is handled in-house)?
  - Have the appropriate users attended SCM technology user training?
- Have CCB training materials been developed?
  - Have CCB members taken CCB training?
- Has the 'Who has taken SCM Training' table within the SCM Training section of the SCM design specification document been updated to indicate who has taken SCM training (technology administration training, user training, or CCB training)?

9. SCM System Testing Phase

The SCM system testing phase focuses on validating the functionality and usability of the SCM system via a functional test and a user acceptance test. The tasks in this phase are not just limited to testing the SCM vendor technology but include the testing of automation within the SCM system and of SCM processes that are used within the application context.

9.1. Perform Functional Test of SCM System

This task includes steps that ensure all appropriate SCM commands, functions, scripts, are operating as expected and results are communicated to the appropriate personnel. This includes testing commands within the SCM processes that use SCM technology. This functional test is separated in to two phases: testing SCM technology and testing SCM processes that utilize the SCM technology. The user acceptance test (see task in Section 9.2) should not be performed until the functional test meets the success criteria.

Key Steps:

1. SCM Technology – These steps will be utilized *iteratively* for each of the SCM technologies being tested.
   - Identify the SCM technologies being used as part of the overall SCM system.
     - Create a functional test plan per SCM technology that should include a test table and overall measurable test success criteria. The test table may include the following columns:
       - Commands/Scripts
       - Expected Output/Results
       - Actual Output/Results
       - Comments
   - Document the commands and scripts (one row each) in the Commands/Scripts Column that will be used regularly to ensure they work as stated. In the same row, document the expected output (e.g., from commands, response times, etc.) in the Expected Output/Results column.
   - Below the test table in the test plan, determine and document the overall measurable test success criteria. Consider what an overall 'passing' grade is for the test. Examples of passing grades include (but are not limited to):
     - 100% of all commands/scripts work successfully and 80% of commands respond at an expected performance level.
     - 100% of user commands and 80% of administration commands/scripts work successfully and 100% respond at an expected performance level.
   - Identify personnel that can perform the tests. Consider using testers or SCM engineers.
   - Perform tests as per the test plan.
   - Document results in the Actual Output/Results column along with any opportunities for improvement in the Comments column. This may include improving the system resources (e.g., more RAM, better CPU, etc.) or rewriting a script for faster response times.

2. SCM Processes – These steps will be utilized *iteratively* for each SCM process that utilizes SCM technology and, therefore, needs tested.
   - Identify the SCM processes that involve SCM technology steps (those that utilize commands from the technology as part of the Description column in the process steps table).
   - Create a functional test plan for each SCM process that utilizes commands from SCM technologies. Each test plan should include a test table and overall measurable test success criteria.
     - To create the test table, copy the Description column of the process steps table from the SCM process into the test plan document. The Description column should include the commands being tested. Also add three corresponding columns called:
       - Expected Output/Results
       - Actual Output/Results
       - Comments
       Note: The end result is a test table that has four columns.
     - Document the expected output from running the commands in the Expected Output/Results column.
     - Below the test table in the test plan, determine and document the overall measurable test success criteria. Consider what the overall 'passing' grade is for the test. A passing grade may mean (but is not limited to):
       - 100% of the descriptions in the process steps were actually needed and worked as expected.
       - 80% of the description in the process steps produced the expected output (from the Expected Output/Results column).
   - Identify personnel that can perform the tests. Consider using SCM coordinators or SCM engineers.
   - Perform the tests as per the test plan.
   - Document the results in the Actual Output/Results column along with opportunities for improvement in the Comments column. This may include rewriting the process, assigning different roles, or considering different output.
3. Present the test results to the SCM manager, application owner, and project manager(s). Discuss opportunities for improvements.
   - From the Comments column, determine which opportunities for improvement should be completed prior to transitioning to the new SCM system or process.
   - Determine the effort and schedule to perform these improvements.
   - For each SCM technology from step 1, determine if the test was successful enough to perform the user acceptance test (see next task).
4. Perform fixes and changes as recommended (from the opportunities for improvement ideas). Retest as appropriate.
5. If the functional test is successful, perform the user acceptance test (see Section 9.2).
6. Place the results in the application team's document repository for future reference.

Roles:

- SCM engineer – task lead
- SCM manager
- testers

Considerations:

- For objectivity purposes, it is better to have a tester who was not involved with setting up the SCM system. However, for expediency, it may be advantageous to have an SCM engineer or someone who is familiar with the SCM system to perform the tests. Determine which is more important for this situation.
- Consider collecting performance data on command and script response times in order to ensure performance improvements are actually being made.

Output:

- SCM technology functional test results
- SCM process functional test results
- Test results reviewed with appropriate management
- Opportunities for improvement identified and scheduled

9.2. Perform User Acceptance Test of SCM System

This task includes steps that provide a limited set of users with the opportunity of testing SCM technology commands for improvements. This task should not be performed until the SCM technology functional test is successful (see Section 9.1).

Key Steps:

1. The steps below will be utilized *iteratively* for each SCM technology being user acceptance tested.
2. Identify all SCM technologies being used as part of the overall SCM system.
3. Create a user acceptance test plan per SCM technology that should include a test table and overall measurable test success criteria. The test table may include the following columns:
   - Commands/Scripts
   - Results
   - Comments
4. In the Commands/Scripts column, document the main commands and automated scripts that will be performed by the users of the SCM technology. Consider documenting them in the order in which they use the SCM technology.
5. Identify personnel that can perform the test (consider those who will use the SCM system).

6. Perform the tests as per the user acceptance test plan. Document the results and add any opportunities for improvement in the Comments column (specifically areas that improve ease of use for user commands and scripts). The Results column is where the users will comment on the degree to which commands are easy to use, easy to understand, and work as expected.
7. Present results to the application owner and project manager.
8. Present user acceptance test results to the application owner and project manager(s). Discuss opportunities for improvements.
   - From the Comments column, determine which opportunities for improvement should be completed prior to transitioning to the new SCM system.
   - Determine effort and schedule to perform these improvements.
9. Perform any fixes and changes as recommended. Retest as appropriate.
10. Place the results into the application team's document repository for future reference.

Roles:

- SCM engineer – task lead
- SCM manager
- Users who perform the user acceptance tests

Consideration:

- Ensure you listen attentively to any improvement opportunities from the prospective users of the system. Small changes that improve ease of use may have a significant impact on the adoption of the SCM system.

Output:

- SCM technology user acceptance test results
- Test results reviewed with appropriate management
- Opportunities for improvement identified, scheduled, and started

9.3. Perform Final Import

This task includes steps to incorporate the latest configuration items (and identified versions) within the current development baseline into the new SCM technology that supports the baseline. Typically there is a divergence between when the items are first imported into the SCM version control repository (from the task in Section 7.14) and when the SCM system is cut-over for actual team use (in Section 10). Therefore, there is a need to update the new baseline with the latest items.

Key Steps:

1. Compare the latest items from the current development baseline with the items in the baseline within the new SCM version control technology. Identify any differences and select the items for addition to the new SCM technology.

2. Import and/or checkin any changed development baseline item(s) to the new SCM technology repository. Use either the:
   - import function of an SCM technology (see Section 7.1.4)
   - SCM version control process (see Section 6.4).
3. Label the latest development baseline. Upon the completion of importing or checking in the items, baseline the items by attaching a label to the specified versions (see Section 7.1.4).
4. Iterate through the above steps as necessary. Depending on the time it takes to transition to the new SCM technology, the above steps may have to be completed again (if any changes have occurred in the current development baseline).

Roles:

- SCM engineer – task lead
- SCM manager
- SCM coordinator

Considerations:

- The ultimate goal of this task is to ensure the latest items are in the new SCM technology repository prior to transitioning to the new SCM system.
- This task can be use to align any baseline of items from the current to the new system. This may include requirements baseline, problem management baseline, etc.

Output:

- Updated baseline in the new SCM technology

9.4. SCM System Testing Phase Completion Checklist

The items in this checklist may be used to determine if SCM tasks have been completed in this phase:

- Have all SCM technologies been functionally tested and have improvement opportunities been identified and scheduled?
- Have all appropriate SCM processes been functionally tested and have improvement opportunities been identified and scheduled?
  - Have the functional test results been reviewed with appropriate management?
- Have the SCM technologies been user acceptance tested and have improvement opportunities been identified and scheduled?
  - Have user acceptance test results been reviewed with appropriate management?
- Have the latest items from the current baseline been imported or checked into the baseline within the new SCM technology repository and has the updated new baseline been labeled?

10. SCM System Transition Phase

The SCM system transition phase focuses on performing a final review of the SCM system and the tasks involved with transitioning into the new SCM system.

10.1. Conduct an SCM System Readiness Meeting

This task includes the steps to determine if the SCM system is ready for active use. It allows all stakeholders who will benefit from the SCM system to perform a final review of all aspects of the system. It concludes with an agreement that the system is ready.

Key Steps:

1. Identify the stakeholder participants for the SCM system readiness meeting. This should include all SCM personnel, the application owner, applicable project manager(s), QA/test manager, and other impacted personnel.
2. Schedule the SCM system readiness meeting. Identify the best time for full attendance.
3. Review areas to ensure a successful transition to the new SCM environment. Determine if testing and operational readiness is acceptable. These areas include (but are not limited to):
   - Functional readiness – review any functional test results (see the output of task in Section 9.1).
   - User acceptance readiness – review available user acceptance results (see the output of task in Section 9.2).
   - Personnel trained in SCM technology – verify that the appropriate application team personnel have been trained or scheduled for just-in-time training in the SCM technology (see Section 8.3).
   - Updated Development baseline – verify that the latest items are in the SCM technology or will be just prior to cut-over (see Section 9.3).
4. Verify that SCM staff will be ready to provide the intensive support needed immediately after cut-over. Tasks may include resolving issues, setting up any additional workspaces, additional training, etc. (see Section 10.4 for more on this topic).
5. Identify if there are any issues or risks large enough to prevent the SCM system from being transitioned for use by the application team. If so, create improvement tasks to resolve or change part of the SCM system to make it acceptable. Complete the tasks. Communicate to the stakeholders that the tasks have been completed.
6. Get agreement from stakeholders that the SCM system is ready for use by personnel.
7. Identify a specific SCM system cut-over date and time. Ensure it does not conflict with a scheduled release (i.e., during the test and release phases of a project lifecycle).

Roles:

- SCM manager – task lead
- Application owner
- Stakeholders (SCM staff, project manager(s), test manager, etc.)

Considerations:

- An evening or weekend may be the best time to cut-over to a new SCM system.
- Consider postponing lesser priority SCM tasks for SCM personnel to focus on the cut-over.

- If SCM technology user training has not occurred, consider performing it immediately prior to the transition (i.e., just-in-time training). For more on this topic, see Section 8.3.

Output:

- Agreement that the SCM system is ready for use
- A specific date and time scheduled for the SCM system cut-over

10.2. Prepare Notification for SCM System Cut-Over

This task includes steps that provide awareness to those who will be using the new SCM system stating when the system will be operational and when they are expected to begin using the system.

Key Steps:

1. Define information needed for the SCM system cut-over notification. This may include:
   - Identifying applications being impacted
   - Indicating a high-level reason and benefit for the new SCM system
   - Indicating the specific SCM system cut-over date/time
   - Identifying SCM personnel to contact if problems occur
2. Prepare the SCM system cut-over notification (this may be in an email or standard notification format used to communicate this type of information). More than one communication channel may be used.
3. Identify the distribution list (users who are being impacted and stakeholders).
4. Send the SCM system cut-over notification to the distribution list.

Roles:

- SCM manager – task lead
- Application owner

Considerations:

- Consider sending the notification at three different times (e.g., 2 weeks before cut-over, 3 days before cut-over, and 4 hours before the cut-over).
- It may be best for the application owner (or sponsor of the new SCM system) to send out the first notification.

Output:

- SCM system cut-over notification prepared and sent to the distribution list

10.3. Cut-Over to New SCM System

This task includes steps that should occur for the cut-over to the new SCM system. This may be considered the final validation of the system. This task assumes at least one SCM system cut-over notification was sent (from task 10.2).

Effectively, the task of cut-over to the new SCM system is a milestone because the system should already be operational. This is validated and a notification effectively opens the SCM system to users.

Key Steps:

1. Ensure any recently modified items in the current development baseline are imported into the new SCM technology repository (see Section 9.3 for more details).
2. Lock the old SCM system (if appropriate and if possible). This is to ensure that the users now use the new SCM system.
3. Validate that all appropriate workspaces are created for users in the context of the latest project release (see Section 7.1.5).
4. Perform a final verification of the common SCM system user commands within a new workspace (see Section 9.2). This is an abbreviated version of the full user acceptance test.
5. Prepare and send a notification to all users and stakeholders that announces that the SCM system is 'open' and can be used by application personnel. Ensure the notification identifies the problem management process to use or SCM personnel to contact if problems occur. This final notification should be almost the same as the initial notification discussing the cut-over (see Section 10.2).

Roles:

- SCM manager – task lead
- SCM engineer

Consideration:

- The more effective the validation, the fewer the problems, the easier it is for personnel to adopt the SCM system, and the less intensive is the support that will be needed (see Section 10.4).

Output:

- Notification that the SCM system is operational and 'open' for use
- Cut-over to new SCM system has occurred (i.e., system is fully operational)

10.4. Provide Intensive Support of SCM System for Initial Weeks

This task includes steps to proactively ensure that there is intensive technical and procedural support available for the users immediately after the cut-over (see task "4.10.3 - Cut-Over to New SCM System") and within the initial two to four weeks of using the new SCM system.

Key Steps:

1. Immediately after the cut-over to the new SCM system, SCM personnel should be prepared to provide intensive support. SCM personnel respond to user requests and issues regarding the new SCM system. This may include requests for minor changes, resolving issues, setting up additional workspaces, providing additional training, consulting, and advice.
2. The SCM manager continuously monitors the SCM requests and issues and ensures the SCM personnel are responding to requests in a timely manner. When the number of SCM requests and issues has dropped to what may be considered the 'normal' level, this intensive support period can be considered ended.

Roles:

- SCM personnel (e.g., SCM engineer and SCM coordinator) – task lead
- SCM manager

Consideration:

- The period of intensive support will vary according to the success of the SCM training, experience level of the users, the testing of the SCM technology and SCM processes, and the preparation time and effort.

Output:

- Intensive support period ended
- SCM system is running relatively smoothly

10.5. SCM System Transition Phase Completion Checklist

The items in this checklist may be used to determine if SCM tasks have been completed in this phase:

- Has the SCM system readiness meeting been held and were appropriate personnel in attendance?
  - Has there been agreement from the stakeholders that the SCM system is ready?
  - Has a specific date and time been identified for the SCM system cut-over in relation to the current project lifecycle phase?
- Has the SCM system ready notification been sent out to the appropriate personnel?
- Have SCM requests and issues been monitored after the cut-over to ensure there is adequate support and to identify when the intensive support period is over?

5

Establish SCM Tasks on a Project

1. Focusing on the Project Level

This chapter of the book focuses on SCM tasks that may be included at the project level. As mentioned in Section 4 of Chapter 1, a project is a set of tasks whose aim is to deliver a changed (new/modified/deleted) set of functionality or deliverables (otherwise known as a release). In order for the project to create quality deliverables in a controlled manner, it is important to include SCM tasks in the project plan because they provide key functions for controlling changes. As stated in [IEEE 1987], the 'effectiveness of the SCM processes increases in proportion to the degree that its disciplines are an explicit part of the normal day-to-day activities of everyone involved in the development and maintenance efforts.' This, in part, implies that there is management commitment to include SCM at the project level, that personnel are trained, and that the team has adopted or are willing to adopt SCM processes and technology.

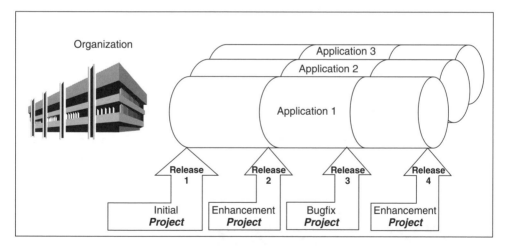

Figure 5.1   The Project Level

Software Configuration Management: Implementation Roadmap   M. E. Moreira
© 2004 Mario E. Moreira   ISBN: 0-470-86264-5 (HB)

1.1. Project Level Phases

This chapter is divided into chronological phases that parallel the phases of a typical project lifecycle (consider customizing them to fit the lifecycle and terminology used within the organization). The phases include:

- Project Planning and Requirements – the phase where a project plan is created and requirements gathering occurs for the project release.
- Design – the phase where the requirements are translated into designs.
- Development – the phase where coding occurs and project deliverables are created.
- Test – the phase where the project deliverables are tested.
- Release – the phase where the project deliverables are released into production.

The SCM tasks may be inserted into any project lifecycle method including (but not limited to) waterfall, incremental, and iterative. The diagram below appears linear but in many cases, there is movement back to previous phases based on the method used or needed.

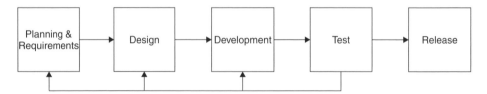

Figure 5.2   Project Level Process Flow

1.2. How to Use this Chapter

It is important to walk through each phase in this chapter and review each task in each phase. Consider customizing the task name to the one that best aligns with the terminology used within the workplace. When reviewing a task, consider customizing it in a manner that may improve the implementation or adoption.

Determine which SCM tasks will be undertaken for the particular effort according to the level of maturity of the organization or project team. For example, if the organization is not yet ready for SCM audits, do not consider performing the SCM audit tasks. After the tasks have been identified, work with the project manager to incorporate the SCM tasks into the project plan (see Section 2.1). Use the task name (or a similar name that is meaningful to project personnel) as the task description in the project plan.

2. Project Planning and Requirements Phase

In this early phase of the project, it is important to ensure that SCM tasks are incorporated into the project plan. It is also important that project requirements are managed by a change control process and approved by a group of stakeholders (the CCB). This section provides tasks that address these areas.

2.1. Add Appropriate SCM Tasks to the Project Plan

This task provides steps to ensure that appropriate SCM project level tasks are added to the project plan.

Key Steps:

1. Review all SCM tasks in this chapter.
2. Select which SCM tasks should be added to the project plan according to how much can be adopted by application/project personnel. See Section 23 of the Appendix for a list of all SCM tasks in this chapter.
3. Incorporate the selected SCM tasks into the appropriate sections of the project plan as per the project lifecycle method (waterfall, incremental, iterative, etc.). If a project planning process exists, use it as the basis for adding the SCM tasks.

Roles:

- Project manager – task lead
- SCM manger

Considerations:

- The project manager and SCM manager should work together to determine the appropriate SCM tasks to be added to the project plan.
- For SEI CMM compliance, it is important to have SCM tasks in project plans and include SCM review, SCM audit, and CCB tasks.
- If there is a standard project plan template within the organization, consider adding SCM tasks into the template. This increases the chances of integrating SCM into the project and improves the overall adoption and acceptance of SCM at the application and organization level.
- There may be other SCM tasks needed if the project must comply with certain contractual or certification level commitments.

Output:

- Project plan with SCM tasks included

2.2. Provide an SCM Overview to the Project Team

This task includes steps that provide the project team including managers with an overview of SCM, the SCM personnel and their roles, the SCM roles and responsibilities for the project personnel, and how SCM will be applied to the project. It will also discuss the SCM plan or SCM design specification, the SCM processes, and other SCM artifacts. Overall, it provides the project team with an introduction to SCM within the project context.

Key Steps:

1. Identify the instructor for the SCM Overview session. This may be the SCM manager.
2. Determine the logistics of the session. This includes the:
   - Training format – The delivery format may include (but is not limited to) the presentation format, online format, quick guide format, handouts, etc. (or a combination of those formats).
   - Length of session – Consider limiting it to 1 hour.
   - Training facility – The training facility may need technology (projector, laptop, etc.) and you should also define the size of training space.
3. Prepare an SCM Overview presentation (in the defined training format). Ensure the overview includes the following sections:
   - Introduction of SCM staff to project team
   - SCM overview
     - A brief description of SCM (see Section 1 of Chapter 2)
     - The fundamentals of SCM (see Section 2 of Chapter 2)
     - The benefits of SCM (see Section 3 of Chapter 2)
   - A review of the SCM policy, should it exist (see Section 3.1 of Chapter 3)
   - A review of the SCM design specification or SCM plan should they exist (see Section 5.1 of Chapter 4)
   - The roles and responsibilities of the project team as they relate to SCM (see Section 3.2.2 of Chapter 3)
   - Relevant SCM processes where the project team plays a role (see the processes in Section 6 of Chapter 4)
   - A review of the SCM technology – what it is and who is expected to use it (see Section 4.2 of Chapter 4)
4. Schedule the SCM Overview session with project personnel. Ensure the project manager and his manager are in attendance to show commitment to SCM.
5. Conduct the SCM Overview session. During the session, walk-through the SCM Overview presentation created above. Answer questions as appropriate.
6. Store the SCM Overview presentation in the application document repository, informing the project team of its location for future reference.

Roles:

- SCM manager (with SCM engineer and SCM coordinator input) – task lead
- Project manager and project team
- Application owner

Considerations:

- This should be one of the early tasks in the project lifecycle to ensure SCM expectations are set for the project team and that they have a solid understanding of SCM roles and tasks.
- Consider asking the application owner to send the message about the scheduled SCM Overview session to ensure attendance for the training.

Output:

- SCM overview presentation (presented to the project team)

2.3. Update the CCB Member List

This task includes steps to update the current list of CCB members and ensure they are trained in the change control processes and conduct guidelines. Some members of the CCB may change because of changes to the project (personnel changes, project scope, etc.), to the application (product scope or refocus, etc) or to the organization (organization restructuring, personnel changes, etc).

Note: This assumes that a CCB and Change Control Infrastructure have already been established at the application level. If not, go to Section 7.3 of Chapter 4.

Key Steps:

1. Review the current list of CCB members (if one exists). For more on this topic, see Section 3.2.3 of Chapter 3).
2. Validate and update the CCB member list for this project with respect to the roles. This may include adding, removing, or reassigning certain roles.
3. Provide CCB training to new members to ensure they are familiar with the SCM change control process and CCB conduct guidelines.
   - For steps to perform CCB training, see Section 8.4 of Chapter 4.
   - Document who took training in the 'Who has taken SCM Training' table within the SCM Training section of the application's SCM design specification or in a location where it is readily available. For more on this topic, see Section 5.1.7 of Chapter 4.
4. Store the updated CCB roles and responsibilities list (which may reside within the SCM design specification or SCM plan, etc.) in the application document repository.

Roles:

- SCM manager – task co-lead
- Project manager – task co-lead
- Application owner

Considerations:

- The project manager and SCM manager should work together to update the CCB member list and ensure the new CCB members are trained and ready to support their roles.
- The application owner should always be a member of the CCB for that application.

Output:

- Assigned and updated CCB roles and responsibilities list (in the SCM design specification, SCM plan, etc.) stored within the application document repository

---

2.4. Review and Authorize the Requirements Baseline for this Project Release

This task provides steps to ensure that a requirements baseline exists for this project release and that the baseline has been approved.

Key Steps:

1. Identify the requirements baseline for this project release.
2. Estimate the work effort for the requirements within the requirements baseline for this project release. Use an estimation process (if one exists).
3. Prioritize and rank the requirements within the requirements baseline for this project release. This ensures that the high priority requirements are identified and receive the primary focus and resources.
4. Validate that the requirements specified can be targeted for this project release. Review the estimates, priority, and rank together. Ensure that the requirements can be developed in the given timeframe desired. Update the requirements baseline as appropriate.
5. Approve the requirements and the requirements baseline for this project release using the SCM Change Control Process (from Chapter 4 Section 6.2) and Change Control Board Conduct Guidelines (from Chapter 4 Section 6.2.1).
6. Define the release criteria. This may be defined by the number of requirements that must be met within each priority level and the number of defects of each severity level that will be allowed. An example is 100% of priority 1 and 2 and 50% of priority 3 requirements completed and with no severity 1 defects and no more than ten severity 2 defects.
7. Communicate the requirements list and release criteria to the project team personnel so the team is aware of the functionality to be developed.
8. If the requirements list resides in an automated technology, ensure the requirements are updated as per the above steps. If the requirements list resides in a document, place the document in the document repository.

Roles:

- CCB (which should include the project manager and the SCM manager) – task lead

Considerations:

- Once requirements are approved for this project, the SCM change control processes are used to manage changes to the requirements baseline throughout the project lifecycle.
- If a requirements engineering/management process exists at the application level or for the project, consider using it if it helps to identify and validate the requirements for this project release, but ensure it includes the CCB (or similar) roles and responsibilities.
- The release criteria will be needed in Section 6.1 when you review and authorize the release for production.
- This task is important for SEI CMM compliance.
- For more on the importance of establishing a requirements baseline, consider reading the 'Requirements Jeopardy', chapter in [Brown *et al.* 1999].

Output:

- Estimated, prioritized, validated, and approved requirements baseline for this project release
- Release criteria
- Updated requirements baseline stored in requirements technology or document repository

2.5. *Update the Application Inventory*

This task provides steps to review and update changes to the application inventory to ensure the latest pieces of the application are identified to validate the integrity of the application and the project release.

Key Steps:

1. Review the current application inventory list. If no application inventory exists and this is the first time that this task is being performed, see Section 5.2 of Chapter 4.
2. Update the application inventory as appropriate with added (new), deleted, or modified items.
3. Place the updated application inventory list into the application document repository.

Roles:

- SCM engineer – task lead
- Project manager
- Technical lead

Considerations:

- Consider reviewing this application inventory with several project team and system administration personnel to validate the items.
- This task is important for SEI CMM compliance.

Output:

- Updated application inventory stored in the application document repository

2.6. *Perform a Project-Level SCM Risk Assessment*

This task provides steps for performing an SCM risk assessment in order to identify and mitigate risks that may impact the success of SCM and the project release.

Key Steps:

1. Identify an SCM risk list. Consider using the SCM risk list template found in Section 1 of the Appendix.
2. Perform the SCM risk assessment following the steps in Section 2.4 of Chapter 4. The high level steps include: scheduling a meeting, identifying and documenting the SCM risks, reviewing and prioritizing risks with the project manager, and adding mitigation actions of selected risks to the project plan or appropriate tracking list.

Roles:

- SCM manager – task lead
- Key project team members (including project manager)

Considerations:

- If this project is over six months (or so), consider performing periodic SCM risk assessments.
- For more on the topic of risk, review Section 2.4 of Chapter 4.

Output:

- SCM risk list template
- SCM risks identified and prioritized
- Mitigation action of selected risks in project plan (or similar tracking list)

2.7. Project Planning and Requirements Phase Completion Checklist

The items in this checklist may be used to determine if SCM tasks have been completed in this phase:

- Have appropriate SCM tasks been added to the project plan?
- Has an SCM overview been presented to the project team?
- Has the CCB roles and responsibilities list been reviewed, validated, and updated as appropriate?
- Has a requirements baseline been defined, reviewed, and authorized by the CCB?
- Has the application inventory been reviewed and updated?
- Has a project-level SCM risk assessment occurred?

3. Design Phase

In the design phase of the project lifecycle, it is important to verify that all SCM infrastructure is in place and a code baseline is established for development to occur. This section provides tasks that address these areas.

3.1. Perform SCM Capacity Planning for Project Needs

This task includes steps to ensure there are appropriate system resources allocated for the project release.

Key Steps:

1. Review disk space allocation for the:
   - SCM repository: Review the project requirements and determine if new application functionality will be created which may require adding capacity (to support new code, deliverables, documents, etc.) to the system in which the SCM version control repository resides.
   - User workspaces: Determine if the existing user workspace capacity is adequate or if more disk space is needed. This is important if the workspaces are in a centralized location.
   - Build/release workspaces and environments: Determine if the existing build/release workspaces and their supporting environments are adequate for the needs of the project release.
   - Staging areas: Determine if the existing staging areas are adequately sized for the expected size of the release deliverables.
2. If current capacity must be changed (added/removed) determine new capacity needs. If applicable, update the Application Environment Details section within the SCM design specification if one exists (see Section 5.1.3 of Chapter 4).
3. Identify if current RAM meets the needs of the project.
4. If additional diskspace or RAM is required, work with system administrators to expand, reconfigure, or acquire the item(s) needed.
5. Place updated documents (e.g., the SCM design specification) into the application document repository.

Roles:

- SCM engineer – task lead
- Technical lead
- System administrator

Consideration:

- In general, capacity should be reviewed on a periodic basis.

Output:

- Capacity is expanded, reconfigured, or acquired (as appropriate)
- Updated Application Environment Details section in the SCM design specification document

3.2. Establish the Development Baseline Project Branch

This task provides steps to define the specific versions within the development baseline where coding may begin for this project release. It is also used to validate the integrity of the baseline prior to the development phase beginning. This may include exercising existing SCM processes and ensuring the new development baseline can build, compile, or link without errors and is tested in a limited manner.

Key Steps:

1. With key project personnel, conduct a meeting and discuss the development baseline that will become the baseline for the new release.
   - Identify the previously released baseline of code. There may be a label in the SCM version control repository that identifies the source code and version of the items that derived the previous release.
   - Identify any changes to the development baseline since the previous release. Changes may be made due to defects in a release. Review any items in bugfix branches or any other branches where bugfixes or changes may have occurred.
   - Determine the overall composition of the new development baseline (which will become the new project branch). Determine which bugfixes and other changes should be included into the new development baseline.
2. Integrate all changes to create the new development baseline for the project release. The branching structure and steps suggested below may vary depending on the defined branch types, branch naming convention, and structure that are defined for this application.
   - Create a project release branch for this baseline of code and create an integration branch off the project release branch. For more on this topic, see Section 5.1.6 of Chapter 4.
   - Create a workspace (or a private branch) off the integration branch. For more on this topic, see Chapter 4 Section 7.1.5.
   - Merge any identified bugfixes (and any other changed items from other branches) into the private branch using the SCM merge process (if it exists). For more on this topic, see Chapter 4 Section 6.5.
   - Validate that all changes work together. At this point, the baseline from the previous release plus the changes from bugfixes and other changes should physically or virtually reside in the workspace (private branch). Validation may include:
     - Building the code (if code includes a compile/build aspect). Perform the following:
       - Review the SCM build process. Determine if it meets the need of this project release. If not, update the process as appropriate. For more on this topic, see Section 6.6 of Chapter 4.
       - Perform a build from the workspace. If build errors occur, modify the appropriate code items until it compiles without errors (if possible).
     - Testing the code. This may include performing a brief level of functional testing.

- Once the merged items are validated, checkin the changes to the private workspace branch. Then merge the items from the private branch to the integration branch and then to the project release branch.
- Tag the baseline of code with a recognizable development release baseline label. For more on this topic, see Section 5.1.5 of Chapter 4.

3. Notify all project personnel associated with the project release about the new development baseline and the name of the branch off which they will be working.

Roles:

- SCM engineer – task lead
- SCM manager
- Project manager
- Technical lead

Considerations:

- The step of reviewing the SCM build process may be done in parallel with the step of performing a build of the merged items. This is because changes to the SCM build process may be identified while building the new development baseline.
- This task is important for SEI CMM compliance.

Output:

- Identified development baseline (with development release baseline label)
- Created 'project release' branch and 'integration' branch
- Verified SCM build process (if applicable) and updated if changes were needed
- Project personnel have been notified of the new development baseline and the name of branch off which they will be working

3.3. Train Project Personnel in the SCM Technology

This task includes steps to ensure that project personnel who have not been trained (and are not experienced) in the SCM technology that is being used on the project have the opportunity to be trained.

Key Steps:

1. Identify which project personnel have not been trained in the SCM technology.
2. Identify the SCM training approach (will the training be done by a vendor or handled by an in-house resource). This is based on the evaluation step in Chapter 4 Section 8.2.
3. Schedule and register those personnel who have not yet taken the specified SCM technology training course(s). Consider just-in-time training since the users will have a better chance of retaining the knowledge from training.

4. Notify personnel of the scheduled SCM technology user training course.
5. Conduct the SCM technology user training course
   - Personnel attend the course. Validate attendance.
   - If in-house, the instructor trains personnel utilizing the SCM technology user training materials prepared in Section 8.2 of Chapter 4
6. Document who took training in the 'Who has taken SCM Training' table within the SCM Training section of the SCM design specification (see Chapter 4 Section 5.1.7).

Roles:

- Instructor (may be the SCM engineer) – task lead
- Users (appropriate project personnel)

Consideration:

- For more details on this task, consider reviewing the steps in Section 8.3 of Chapter 4.
- This task is important for SEI CMM compliance.

Output:

- SCM technology user training course(s) taken by appropriate project personnel.
- Updated 'Who has taken SCM' training table in the SCM Training section of the SCM design specification document.

3.4. Create User Workspaces for Project Release

This task includes steps to ensure that the appropriate project personnel have workspaces backed by the appropriate branch (i.e., the correct branch that represents the working development baseline).

Key Steps:

1. Determine which project personnel require workspaces.
2. Determine the process for creating workspaces (e.g., commands, naming conventions and locations). Consider using the steps in Section 7.1.5 of Chapter 4.
3. Create the workspaces from the appropriate branch of the development baseline (see Chapter 5 Section 3.2). This task may be done by the SCM engineer or Project personnel.
4. Test an actual workspace to ensure the SCM system functions as expected.

Roles:

- SCM engineer – task lead
- Project personnel (if they create their own workspaces)

Consideration:

- Creating the workspaces may be done by either the users or SCM personnel.
    - If users create their own workspaces, then the SCM engineer should document brief instructions that provide steps for creating workspaces.
    - If SCM personnel create workspaces, then they should notify users of new workspaces when they are created.

Output:

- Created workspaces for project personnel

3.5. Design Phase Completion Checklist

The items in this checklist may be used to determine if SCM tasks have been completed in this phase:

- Has SCM capacity planning occurred for this project?
- Has a project release branch that corresponds to the latest development baseline been established for the project?
- If applicable, has the SCM build process been verified (and updated as appropriate) for this project?
- Have project personnel been trained on the SCM technology?
- Have user workspaces been created for appropriate project personnel?

4. Development Phase

In the development phase of the project lifecycle, it is important to identify the build, merge, and release packaging tasks. This section provides tasks that address these areas. The build, merge, and packaging tasks may be done iteratively through this phase. While not explicitly a task, it is also expected that version control steps will occur during the task of developing items.

4.1. Perform Project Build/Compiles

This task includes steps to perform project builds/compiles. It is based on the SCM build process. It is applicable when the code being developed needs a build/compile step to produce release deliverables. It is also an iterative task in that it may occur regularly until the project release package is ready for production.

Key Steps:

1. Determine build schedule. This includes the time of day when builds will occur and the frequency of build.

2. Perform builds as per the schedule determined above and as per the SCM build process (if no process exists, see Section 6.6 of Chapter 4). SCM build process steps may include:
   - Establish a build workspace; acquire the CIs for the build; compile/build/link/translate.
   - Verify results – examine the build log for errors and omissions; contact appropriate project personnel about errors and omissions requesting resolution; rebuild as required.
   - If no build errors occur, capture built deliverables. This may include checking in and labeling the deliverables in the SCM version control system.
   - Create and send a build summary/log of build status (number of build errors, one line extract for each error, items that have changed, etc.).

Roles:

- SCM engineer – task lead
- Key developers

Considerations:

- This is an iterative task but should only be listed once in the project plan.
- It is recommended that you automate the build process.
- It is recommended that official project release builds occur in a clean room workspace.

Output:

- Compiled/built deliverables
- Build summary/log

4.2. Perform Merging Activities

This task includes steps to merge a version of a configuration item from one branch to another, provided they have the same ancestry. Merging implies that branches exist and are used for development. Merging is needed when parallel or concurrent development is occurring on the same set of code. It is also an iterative task in that it may occur several times until the project release is ready for production.

Key Steps:

1. If merging activities are formal, determine the merge schedule (e.g., time of day) and frequency (e.g., weekly, daily, etc.)
2. Perform merges as per the schedule determined above, or ad hoc if informal, as per the SCM merge process (if no process exists, see Section 6.5 of Chapter 4). SCM merge process steps may include:

- Identify the target branch you will move to (should be an ancestor of the current branch).
- Merge from the target branch to your branch. Note: merging it to your branch allows for more time within your branch to resolve conflicts (but it may be merged the other way).
- Resolve any logical lines of conflict (do this with the person that made the change to the configuration item prior to you).
- Compile/build (if appropriate), test, checkin, merge from your branch to target branch; rebuild and retest as appropriate; checkin to target branch (some SCM technologies consolidate the function of merge and checkin).

3. For awareness, communicate with project personnel after a significant merge task has been completed.

Roles:

- Project lead and technical staff (to perform merge steps) – task lead
- SCM engineer (provides merge process understanding and troubleshooting)

Consideration:

- It is appropriate to assign the task of merging to the personnel who are most familiar with the items being merged. This is particularly true when there are logical lines of conflict and a correct line item must be selected in order for the merged item to work properly.
- This is an iterative task but should only be listed once in the project plan.

Output:

- Merged and checked in code
- Communication of merge (as appropriate)

4.3. Create a Release Package

This task includes steps to create a release package for testing or for production. It is iterative in that it may occur several times for testing purposes until the project release package is ready for production.

Key Steps:

1. Identify the set of deliverables (code, documents, etc.) required for test or production. Effectively, these are release items that are added to an existing application running in production or if this is the first release, then it is all of the release items needed to create a fully functional and operational application.
2. Determine and create the release structure where the deliverables will live (typically this mirrors the structure as it will reside in production). The structure may live in a LAN directory or in an SCM version control repository.

3. Populate the release structure. Perform the following:
   - If it is on a LAN, copy the appropriate items into their respective directory locations.
   - If it is in a version control repository, checkin the deliverables to the appropriate location.
   - Note: according to the SCM build process, compile/build release deliverables are captured in the SCM version control repository.
4. Tag the deliverables (and corresponding source) with a label that identifies the application and release number.
   - If it is on a LAN, then rename the top level directory with the name of the application and release number, and increment the number to differentiate between the numerous release packages that may be prepared before one is ready for production.
   - If it is a version control repository, tag all items with a release label as per the label naming convention found in the SCM design specification document. For more, see Chapter 4 Section 5.1.5.
5. At this point, the release package has been created and can be copied, compressed, tarred, checked out (if in the version control repository), or whatever method is used to acquire the release deliverables and migrate them into a test or production area.

Roles:

- SCM engineer – task lead
- Technical lead
- Project manager

Considerations:

- This is an iterative task but should only be listed once in the project plan.
- It is recommended that you automate the release packaging task since it may occur numerous times. This may reduce the errors in deriving the release package.

Output:

- An identified and stored release package that is readily available for testing or production
  - If a release package is in a version control repository, the release deliverables are tagged with a release label
  - If a release package is in a LAN directory, the deliverables are in a defined directory structure

4.4. Create Draft Release Notes

This task includes steps to create draft release notes in preparation for the final release package. It may be an iterative task in that it may be updated several times during the test phase until the project release package is ready for production.

Key Steps:

1. Acquire a release notes template (if one exists) and complete the sections with information that is currently available. If no release notes template exists, see Chapter 4 Section 6.7.1 and create one for this project. Also consider reviewing the template in Section 19.1 of the Appendix.
2. Complete at least the following sections:
   - Name of the company
   - Product/application name
   - Release number
   - Release date
   - Known features of release
   - Installation instructions
   - Note: there may be many other items included in the release notes.
3. Review draft release notes with the Project Manager and QA/Test Manager. Update as appropriate

Roles:

- SCM engineer – task lead
- Project manager
- QA/test manager

Considerations:

- It is recommended that a release notes template is created at the application level because it can be reused for future project releases therefore reducing release notes creation time.
- A template also provides the customer with a consistent format for receiving the new release information which provides a sense of consistency and repeatability from the workplace.
- This is an iterative task but should only be listed once in the project plan.

Output:

- Draft release notes

4.5. Perform an SCM Audit

This task includes steps to assess if users of the SCM system are following the SCM processes and if the deliverables being developed can be identified in the SCM version control repository and traced to a change request (requirements) or problem request (defect) to ultimately verify the integrity of the CIs and commitment to using the processes.

Key Steps:

1. Acquire the SCM audit process document. If no SCM audit process exists, see Section 6.8 of Chapter 4 and create one for this project release (or for the application).
2. Perform the SCM audit as per the SCM audit process.
   - Determine what to audit and when
   - Select the audit team (this should include members of the project team)
   - Prepare for audit – collect audit artifacts such as the SCM process audit checklist (see Section 20.1 of the Appendix) and the SCM baseline audit checklist (see Section 20.2 of the Appendix)
3. Perform audit – complete the appropriate sections of the checklists.
   - Discuss the selected questions with project personnel; document results; indicate if the area passed or failed; and include a recommended action if improvement is needed.
   - Report results (consider using the SCM status report template in Section 21.1 of the Appendix).
4. Review findings with the project team (including project manager).
5. Identify tasks for improvement.
6. Store audit results in the application team repository.

Roles:

- SCM coordinator – task lead
- Audit team (personnel from the project)

Considerations:

- The SCM audit should be a collaborative effort with the project team.
- This task may be done more than once through a project lifecycle depending on the duration of the project. However, it should only be listed once in the project plan.
- This task is important for SEI CMM compliance.

Output:

- Completed audit with SCM audit results
- Review of SCM audit results with project team (including project manager).
- Improvement tasks identified

4.6. Perform an SCM Review

This task includes steps to summarize the SCM status of a project and a consistent method of reviewing SCM status with project management for awareness, problem resolution, and SCM improvements.

Key Steps:

1. Acquire the SCM oversight process. If no SCM oversight process exists, see Chapter 4 Section 6.9 and create one for this project release (or for the application).
2. Perform the SCM review per the SCM oversight process.
   - Schedule an SCM review session with the project manager.
   - Prepare the SCM status report (see Section 21.1 of the Appendix for an example of an SCM Status Report template). Document all SCM status since the last review. Consider including accomplishments, significant issues and risks, budgetary and staffing needs, completed training, audit results, etc.
   - Conduct the SCM review with project management and address issues, risks, budgetary and staffing items as appropriate.
   - Open problem requests to track outstanding issues to closure.
   - Store the SCM status report in the application team repository.

Roles:

- SCM manager – task lead
- Project manager
- Optional – Application owner

Considerations:

- This task may be done several times depending on the duration of the project. However, it should only be listed once in the project plan.
- Consider including date information in the name of the status report (e.g., SCM Status-050604)
- This task is important for SEI CMM compliance.

Output:

- SCM review has occurred with the project manager
- Outstanding issues are open as problem requests in the problem management system.

4.7. Development Phase Completion Checklist

The items in this checklist may be used to determine if SCM tasks have been completed in this phase:

- If applicable, are project compiles/builds occurring as expected and/or as per the SCM build process?
- If applicable, are merging activities occurring as expected and/or as per the SCM merge process?
- Are release packages being created in a consistent manner?

- Have draft release notes been created?
- If applicable, are SCM audits occurring as per the SCM audit process?
- Are reviews of SCM status occurring with the project manager as per the SCM oversight process?

5. Test Phase

In the test phase of the project lifecycle, SCM provides support for migrating the release package into a test region. It is also the phase where the release package and accompanying release notes are finalized in preparation for the release phase. This section provides tasks that address these areas.

5.1. Migrate the Release Package to the Test Regions

This task ensures the release package is migrated to the test region(s) in a consistent manner.

Key Steps:
1. Determine which release package (i.e., baseline of deliverables) in the SCM version control repository or LAN directory is needed for migration to the test region(s). The release package should be appropriately identified (see Section 4.3).
2. Identify the test region (e.g., system and location on the system) to which the release package will be migrating and the technology used for performing the migration.
3. Migrate the release package from the SCM version control repository or LAN directory to the identified test region.
4. Verify that all items in the release package were successfully migrated to the test region.
5. Notify the test personnel that the release package has been successfully migrated.

Roles:
- SCM engineer – task lead
- Test personnel
- Project manager

Considerations:
- Any proposed changes or fixes to the release package while in test should go through the change control or problem management process for consideration into this release and must make its way back into the SCM version control repository so the next release package includes these changes.
- This is an iterative task but should only be listed once in the project plan.
- It is recommended that you automate the release migration process with an SCM release engineering technology since it may occur numerous times. For more on this topic, consider reviewing Section 4.1.4 of Chapter 4.

Output:
- Test region populated with release package

5.2. *Prepare Final Release Package*

This task includes steps to create and finalize a release package for production. This task is effectively part of the SCM release process as prescribed in Section 6.7 of Chapter 4.

Key Steps:

1. Identify components of the final release package. This should include:
   - The current release package (see Section 4.3).
   - Changes made during test (see Section 5.1).
2. Incorporate (checkin) changes made to the release package during testing into the SCM version control repository so that the new 'latest' (or final) release package includes these changes.
3. Review the set of deliverables (code, documents, etc.) required for production to ensure it includes everything that is needed.
4. Tag the deliverables (and corresponding source) that are in the SCM version control repository with a label that identifies the application and release number.
   - If it is a LAN structure, then rename the top level directory with the name of the application and release number.
   - If it is a version control repository, tag all items with a release label as per the label naming convention found in the SCM design specification document. For more, see Section 5.1.5 of Chapter 4.
5. At this point, the 'final' release package has been created and is ready for migration into staging and production using the appropriate process and technology.

Roles:

- SCM engineer – task lead
- Technical lead
- Project manager

Considerations:

- This is the first step of the SCM release process as prescribed in Chapter 4 Section 6.7).
- Validate the final release package with the project manager, technical leads, and testers.
- The final release package should be created using the appropriate SCM processes.

Output:

- Final release package
   - If a release package is in a version control repository, the deliverables are labeled with a release label
   - If a release package is in a LAN directory, the deliverables are in a defined directory structure

5.3. Create Final Release Notes

This task includes steps to update and finalize the release notes for this release. This task is effectively part of the SCM release process as prescribed in Chapter 4 Section 6.7.

Key Steps:
1. Review draft release notes (see Section 4.4).
2. Identify areas of change based on the test phase and any impact to the requirements baseline or installation instructions.
3. Update the final release notes to address changes made (from the preceding step or other known changes).
4. Review final release notes with the application owner, project manager, and QA/test manager.

Roles:

- SCM engineer – task lead
- Project manager (and possibly the application owner)
- Test manager

Considerations:

- This is the second step of the SCM release process as prescribed in Chapter 4 Section 6.7.
- This becomes the version of the release notes that is presented to the Change Control Board (CCB) meeting that authorizes the release.
- There may be a marketing or documentation group that manages the final versions of any documents (e.g., the release notes, etc.) that are delivered to customers.

Output:

- Final release notes

5.4. Submit a Change Request for the Release

This task includes steps to create and submit a change request that documents the proposed change to the production baseline (i.e. the release). It also ensures that documents that support the release are ready for review should the CCB want to review them with the change request. This task is effectively part of the SCM release process as prescribed in Chapter 4 Section 6.7.

Key Steps:
1. Create a change request using the appropriate form and/or change control technology. The change request should include the application name, project release number, planned installation/release date, and a description of the change (this may be in the form of the release notes).

2. Submit the change request.
3. Collect supporting documents that indicate the readiness of the release. This may include:
   - A release package inventory to identify deliverables in the package.
   - Test report(s) to ensure that the appropriate level of testing occurred, the test success criteria were met, and pass/fail results are identified.
   - An installation plan for clear installation steps to establish a production baseline.
   - A backout and restore plan to ensure there are clear steps to recover the previous production baseline (in case the new release is problematic).

Roles:

- Project manager – task lead

Consideration:

- This is the third step of the SCM release process as prescribed in Chapter 4 Section 6.7.

Output:

- Change request (for release package)
- Documents supporting the change request, to include release package inventory, test report(s), installation plan, backout and restore plan

5.5. Test Phase Completion Checklist

The items in this checklist may be used to determine if SCM tasks have been completed in this phase:

- Have release package migrations to the test region(s) occurred as expected and as per a standard process?
- Has a final release package been created?
- Have final release notes been created?
- Has a change request for the release been created and submitted?
  - Have documents that support the change request been collected?

6. Release Phase

In the release phase of the project lifecycle, it is critical to review and authorize the release for production and to use a consistent process for installing and verifying the release. It is also the phase where the bugfix branch is created and cleanup occurs. This section addresses these areas.

6.1. Review and Authorize the Release for Production

This task includes steps for the CCB to review the change request for the proposed release, compare the release package to the requirements baseline, and authorize (approve or reject) the release package. This task is effectively part of the SCM release process as prescribed in Chapter 4 Section 6.7.

Key Steps:

1. Review the change request for this release and supporting release documents. This may include a release package inventory, test report(s), an installation plan, and a backout and restore plan.
2. Review the established release criteria. Validate that the functionality in the release package aligns with the requirements and release criteria. See Section 2.4 where the release criteria are defined.
   - Identify if all appropriate requirements have been met as per the release criteria or that there is a good reason that a requirement has not been met.
   - Identify if all appropriate defects have been fixed as per the release criteria or that there is a reason that remaining defects have not been fixed.
3. The CCB decides (approves or rejects) if the release package is ready for production.
   - If approved:
     - Update the change request with the approval.
     - Notify those personnel involved with migrating the release package into production of the impending installation.
     - Communicate the CCB approval decision to appropriate personnel.
   - If not approved:
     - Identify areas that need to be changed to get approval.
     - Communicate the reason for rejection to the project manager and appropriate staff requesting a timeframe to make adjustments for an acceptable release package. Note: This typically initiates a shortened revisit of the development, test, and release phases again to make the appropriate changes.
4. Modify the release notes as appropriate (see Section 5.3).

Roles:

- Change Control Board – task lead

Considerations:

- This is the fourth step of the SCM release process as prescribed in Chapter 4 Section 6.7.
- This part of the SCM release process points to the SCM change control process. If no SCM change control process exists, consider creating one (see Chapter 4 Section 6.2).
- There may be instances when part of the release package is not approved due to insufficient testing or not passing certain tests that support key requirements. If this occurs, the release package must be re-packaged and labeled to include only the deliverables that will be placed into production. This may also cause a rebuild and re-test to occur if pieces of the release package cannot be removed without impacting other parts of the release.

- If a backout and restore plan does not exist, consider creating one due to the advantages it gives of recovering from a problematic release installation.
- This task is important for SEI CMM compliance.

Output:

- CCB decision (approval or rejection) for the release package

6.2. Install Release Package Into Production

This task includes steps for installing the release package into production creating a new/updated production baseline per the installation plan. This task is effectively part of the SCM release process as prescribed in Chapter 4 Section 6.7. It assumes an SCM release engineering technology is in place. If not, see Chapter 4 Section 7.4.

Key Steps:

1. Place the approved release package into a staging area using the SCM release engineering technology or similar mechanism.
2. Install the release package into production (creating a new/updated application production baseline) using the SCM release engineering technology or similar mechanism. Depending on the target of the release package, the installation plan may include one of the following approaches:
   - If the release target is media (such as a CD), then place all release deliverables onto target media.
   - If the release target is a production server, then:
     - Prior to installing the release deliverables, copy the previous production baseline to a backout and restore area so that it may be quickly placed back into production (for recovery purposes).
     - Place release deliverables into the appropriate location within the production server and production baseline.
3. Notify appropriate personnel that the release package is in production.

Roles:

- SCM engineer (production/operations personnel or similar group) – task lead

Considerations:

- This comprises steps 5 and 6 of the SCM release process as prescribed in Chapter 4 Section 6.7.
- It is recommended that you automate the installation process with a release engineering technology for installation and deployment of the release package.

- The term 'in production' has various meanings depending on the context of production. It may mean 'in an execution location on a production server' or 'packaged on production media such as a CD' or in a number of other production locations.

Output:
- Release package in the production baseline (media, server, etc.)

6.3. Verify Migration of Release Package Into Production

This task includes steps for verifying and validating that the release package that has been installed into production operates as expected. This task may be a combination of functional testing and user acceptance testing. This task is effectively part of the SCM release process as prescribed in Chapter 4 Section 6.7.

Key Steps:
1. Verify the release placed into production (from Section 6.2). Depending on the target of the release package, the verification steps may include (but are not limited to) one of the following approaches:
   - If the release target is media (such as a CD), then:
     - Validate that all release deliverables are on the media.
     - Perform installation steps from the installation plan (if it exists) to ensure the new release of the application installs properly on the target system.
     - Perform test(s) to ensure that the new release deliverables are operating properly.
   - If the release target is a production server, then:
     - Validate that all release deliverables are in production.
     - Perform tests to ensure that the new release deliverables are operating properly.
   - Whether the release target is media or a production server, if minor changes are made to the release deliverables, ensure the CCB is notified and, if approved, label the new CIs in the SCM version control repository. If severe problems occur, notify stakeholders to discuss potential resolutions or begin planning for a backout and restore of the previous release of the application.
2. Notify stakeholders and the project team that the release package has been successfully tested (assuming a successful validation of the release).

Roles:
- QA/test personnel – task co-lead (for validating the release package)
- Project manager – task co-lead (for notifying stakeholders and project team of success)

Considerations:
- This comprises steps 7 and 8 of the SCM release process as prescribed in Chapter 4 Section 6.7.

- Depending on the criticality and complexity of the application, this verification step may take several hours to exercise the important functionality.
- If the target is a production server, ensure that the backout and restore plan is readily available in case the new release does not operate as expected and the previous release (or production baseline) must be restored.

Output:
- Verified production baseline (new release package in production)
- If any changes were made to the release deliverables, adjust the release label to the appropriate version of items
- Notification to stakeholders and project team

6.4. Establish a Bugfix Branch and Create Workspaces

This task provides steps to establish a bugfix branch and corresponding workspaces to allow for corrective action of the new release to begin. Once a release is in production, it is not uncommon for defects to be reported within a short period of time. With this in mind, bugfix branches and corresponding workspaces should be created immediately to handle issues with the new release of the application.

Key Steps:
1. Based on the release label and any adjustments made to it, hold a meeting and discuss what will become the baseline for the Bugfix branch.
   - Identify the release label (see Section 5.2) and the development baseline it represents.
   - Identify any changes made during the validation of the release in production (see Section 6.3).
   - Identify changes to the release since it was installed into the production baseline.
2. Merge any changes into the production baseline. Label as appropriate (see Chapter 4 Section 5.1.5).
3. Create the new Bugfix branch from this new production baseline. Create a Bugfix branch for this baseline of code off the branch where the release resides. For more on branch types, see Chapter 4 Section 5.1.6.
4. If a defect is found and recorded, create the appropriate Private bugfix workspace branch off the new Bugfix branch.
   - Determine which team members require Private bugfix workspaces.
   - Determine the process for creating workspaces (see Chapter 4 Section 7.1.5).
   - Create the workspaces needed as determined above. This task may be done by the SCM engineer or development staff.
     - If users creates workspaces, the SCM engineer should document brief instructions for the users that provide steps for creating workspaces.
     - If the SCM engineer creates the workspaces, notify users.
5. Test an actual workspace to ensure that it includes the items from the new release.

6. Notify all appropriate personnel associated with bugfix tasks of the new Bugfix branch and workspaces they may be working from.

Roles:

- SCM engineer – task lead
- Technical lead

Considerations:

- In some cases, multiple private bugfix workspace branches may be created for each individual working on corrective actions.
- The SCM problem management and/or change control process should be used to support any bugfix activities for the application.

Output:

- Bugfix branch off the branch where the release resides
- Private bugfix workspace branches for the appropriate personnel
- Notification of the bugfix branch and private workspace branches

6.5. Clean Up Unnecessary User Workspaces

This task provides steps that focus on the cleanup of unneeded workspaces after the new release is in production.

Key Steps:

1. Review the list of current private workspace branches.
2. Determine which workspaces may no longer be needed. This step may be done with key project personnel.
3. Notify all project personnel of the identified and potentially unneeded workspaces requesting if they can indicate if any are still needed or if any items in those workspaces are needed.
4. Cleanup workspaces:
   - Remove needed items from workspaces to a safe area. Notify appropriate personnel of this location for retrieval.
   - Remove all other items from unneeded workspaces.
   - Remove workspaces.

Roles:

- SCM engineer – task lead
- Project personnel

Considerations:

- Prior to removing workspaces, consider disabling them for up to four weeks to check that they really are not needed.
- If this task does not occur at this time, it will have to occur in the future to reduce the amount of unneeded items and clutter in the workspace area.
- This task increases disk space and reduces the number of workspaces to manage.

Output:

- Deleted workspaces

6.6. Perform a Postmortem

This task provides steps that focus on learning from the SCM problems on the just-completed project release. The benefit is to identify any areas that can be improved for more effective SCM on the next project release.

Key Steps:

1. Identify a lessons learned template. If one does not exist, consider using the template found in Section 2 of the Appendix. Make a copy of the lessons learned template for this postmortem task calling it the '<Project Release Name> SCM Lessons Learned List'.
2. Perform the SCM lessons learned postmortem.
   - Schedule a meeting with key project personnel involved with SCM tasks.
   - In the meeting, document the SCM problems that occurred during the project into the '<Project Release Name> SCM Lessons Learned List'. For each problem:
     - Identify the impact of the problem (e.g., who or what was impacted) and the level of impact to the project (low, medium, or high, where high indicates an impact to the delivery schedule of the project).
     - Identify an improvement that can be made that may reduce the chances of the problem occurring on the next project and state the benefit of that improvement.
3. Determine which improvement tasks from the '<Project Release Name> SCM Lessons Learned List' should be worked on, given SCM resource availability.
4. Assign and schedule the selected improvement tasks. Consider adding these improvement tasks (or the problems they stem from) into the problem management system should one exist.
5. Track until closed.

Roles:

- SCM manager – task lead
- SCM and key project personnel (i.e., those who performed some level of SCM task)

Considerations:

- Consider identifying the effort savings that each improvement task may have, as input to determining which improvement task should be worked on.
- For more on the topic of lessons learned/postmortem, consider reading:
  - 'Postmortem Planning' in [Brown *et al.* 1999]
  - [Kerth 2001]

Output:

- Identified, assigned, and scheduled improvement tasks to reduce or eliminate SCM problems

6.7. Release Phase Completion Checklist

The items in this checklist may be used to determine if SCM tasks have been completed in this phase:

- Has the release package been reviewed and authorized by the CCB for the production baseline?
- Has the release package been installed into production as per the SCM release process?
- Has a verification of the new release package in production occurred?
- Were a Bugfix branch and workspaces established after the release was placed into production?
- Was a cleanup activity performed to remove unneeded workspaces?
- Was an SCM lessons learned session conducted where areas of improvement were identified?

Bibliography

Adler, Paul and Shenhar, Aaron (Fall 1990) 'Adapting your Technological Base: The organizational challenge'. *Sloan Management Review*, pp. 25–37.

Bays, Michael E. (1999) *Software Release Methodology*. Prentice Hall PTR.

Berczuk, Stephen P. with Appleton, Brad (2002) *Software Configuration Management Patterns: Effective teamwork, practical integration*. Addison Wesley Professional.

Bounds, Nadine M. and Dart, Susan (2001) *Configuration Management Plans: The beginning to your CM solution*. Software Engineering Institute, Carnegie Mellon University. Online at www.sei.cmu.edu/legacy/scm/papers/CM_Plans/CMPlans.MasterToC.html.

Brown, William J., McCormick, Hays W., and Thomas, Scott W. (1999) *AntiPatterns and Patterns in Software Configuration Management*. John Wiley & Sons Ltd.

Dart, Susan (2000) *Configuration Management: The missing link in web engineering*. Artech House.

Institute of Electrical and Electronics Engineers (1998) *IEEE Std 828–1998 Software Configuration Management Plans*.

Institute of Electrical and Electronics Engineers (1987) *IEEE Std 1042–1987 Guide to Software Configuration Management*. Withdrawn.

Kerth, Norman L. (2001) *Project Retrospectives: A handbook for team reviews*. Dorset House.

Leon, Alexis (2000) *A Guide to Software Configuration Management*. Artech House.

Mikkelson, Tim and Pherigo, Suzanne (1997) *Practical Software Configuration Management: The latenight developer's handbook*. Prentice Hall PTR.

Myers, Jr, Charles R., Maher, Jr, John H., and Deimel, Betty L. (1995) *Managing Technology Change*. Presentation. Software Engineering Institute, Carnegie Mellon University.

Paulk, Mark C., Curtis, Bill, Chrissis, Mary Beth, and Weber, Charles V. (1993) *Capability Maturity Model for Software*, Version 1.1. CMU/SEI -93-TR-24. Software Engineering Institute, Carnegie Mellon University.

Appendix

This appendix includes numerous SCM templates, processes, and examples which are referenced in prior sections of this book. These items may provide a solid starting point in creating customized items for the needs of the organization, application, and project. Each item in this chapter has a corresponding file on the CD which accompanies this book.

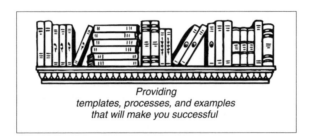

Providing
templates, processes, and examples
that will make you successful

Figure A.1 Templates

1. SCM Risk List Template

Organization:				Application:					
Date:				**Project:**					
Risk #	Risk Category	Description	Root Cause	Impact	Severity	Probability	Mitigation Action	Status	Status Date

Software Configuration Management: Implementation Roadmap   M. E. Moreira
© 2004 Mario E. Moreira   ISBN: 0-470-86264-5 (HB)

Definitions that Support the Risk List Template

- Risk# – Unique identifier of the risk (increase as you find risks)
- Risk Category – Category of the risk (see examples of risk categories below which may be adapted)
- Description – Condition of the risk in relation to its category (e.g., no sponsorship, schedule too aggressive, etc.)
- Root Cause – Known or suspected root cause of the risk
- Impact – What may be impacted should the risk materialize into a problem
- Severity – How broad an impact the risk may have should it materialize into an issue (Small, Medium or Large)
- Probability – The chance that a risk will turn into a problem (Low, Medium or High)
- Mitigation Action – A task that can be initiated to lower the probability of the risk occurring or reduce the severity of the impact
- Status – The current status of managing the risk (include all status statements in chronological order)
- Status Date – When the risk was last discussed

Examples of Risk Categories

Risk Category	Examples of Risk Conditions
Personnel/Resources	Number (not enough/too many), experience (not enough)
Estimates	Inadequate, no information
Scope	Creep, no control
Technological Issues	High integration, many platforms, poor network, new/unproven technology, multi-site
Management Dependencies	No input, not available
Sponsors	Not available, too much control
Policies	Not available, ambiguous
Schedule	Too aggressive, too loose
Location	One, many

Note: this Risk List template can be used for other disciplines in addition to SCM.

2. Lessons Learned Template

Project Name:			Release #:	
Date:			Date of Release:	
Problem	Impact	Impact Level	Improvement	Benefit of Improvement

Definitions that support the Lessons Learned Template

- Problem – Issue, defect, or non-compliance that had a negative impact on the project
- Impact – Describe the negative impact of the problem (schedule slipped by X days, cost overrun by $X, etc.)
- Impact Level – determine the level of the impact (High, Medium or Low) of the problem on the project
- Improvement – recommended improvement idea to eliminate or reduce the problem
- Benefit of Improvement – quantify or qualify the benefit of the improvement

Note: this Lessons Learned template can be used for other disciplines in addition to SCM.

3. SCM Glossary

Term	Definition
Audit Process	A repeatable process for assessing compliance to SCM processes and technology and determining the integrity of application baselines.
Baseline	A collection of similar configuration items at a specific time. Examples may include (but are not limited to) requirements, functional, development, environment, and production baselines.
Build Process	A repeatable process of generating deliverables from code.
Change	An action that causes an addition, modification, or deletion of a configuration item.

Term	Definition
Change Control Board (CCB)	Members, who represent the interests of all groups who may be affected by changes to the baselines, review and authorize changes to the baselines and authorize the creation of products. Typical CCBs authorize changes to the requirements baseline and the production baseline, although the CCB can be used to control changes to any baseline a project deems necessary.
Change Control Process	A repeatable process for controlling changes to important baselines of an application from submission to closure.
Change Request Form (CRF)	Form used to request a change to an important baseline (typically the requirements and production baselines). The CRF is a supporting work product used by the Change Control Process.
Configuration Item (CI)	An entity that contributes to, or is the result of, a deliverable. A CI is subject to one or more levels of SCM rigor (identification, version control, and change control).
Defect	A deviation in code such that it does not meet requirements or function as expected.
Draft	Draft refers to items in a state of development. They are not ready for public use, not having the release-ready functionality.
Identification Process	A repeatable process of identifying CIs to establish baselines which enable management of the CIs.
Label	An attribute used to define a baseline of items. Within an SCM version control tool, this attribute is used to define a development baseline of code.
Library	See *Repository*
Merge Process	A repeatable process of merging a version of a configuration item from one branch to another, provided that they have the same ancestry
Problem Management Process	A repeatable process for documenting, tracking and resolving problems.
Problem Request Form (PRF)	A form used to report a problem, defect, or non-conformance. The PRF is a supporting work product used by the Problem Management Process.
Release Package	A specific set of items (a collection of versioned configuration items) derived from requirements changes (and/or bugfixes) that represents release deliverables entering a production baseline.

Term	**Definition**
Release Process	A repeatable process for managing changes into the production baseline.
Report Process	A repeatable process for showing SCM data relating to an organization, application, or project that can be acted upon to promote continuous improvement.
Repository	A secure place to store configuration items.
Review Process	A repeatable process for documenting and reviewing SCM activity.
Revision	See *Version*
Software Configuration Management (SCM)	Practice which maintains the integrity and traceability of configuration items (CIs) throughout the software lifecycle. SCM is comprised of *identifying* CIs, systematically *controlling* (version control, configuration control, build management, and release engineering) changes to the CIs, periodically *auditing* baselines of CIs for integrity and accuracy, and *reporting* on the status of the CIs.
SCM Design Specification	A document that defines the SCM technical and process design and infrastructure for establishing an SCM application environment. It defines the policy, roles, processes, and activities that support SCM.
SCM Plan	A document that defines how SCM will be implemented including policy, roles, processes, and activities that support SCM.
SCM Technology	An SCM product that provides SCM technical functionality and supports SCM processes. There is no single SCM technology. Common SCM technologies include version control/build management, problem management, change control, release engineering, and multiple site development technologies.
Traceability	The degree to which a relationship can be established between two or more items within a lifecycle that have a predecessor–successor relationship with one another.
Version	An identified and uniquely numbered configuration item.
Version Control Process	A repeatable process for version controlled changes to any baseline.

4. SCM Policy Template

Objective

This policy defines the doctrine for Software Configuration Management (SCM). The purpose of SCM is to establish and maintain the integrity of deliverables throughout a lifecycle using the four fundamental components of SCM (i.e., Identification, Control, Audit, and Report). Applying SCM allows the organization to effectively control all aspects of change, controlling such items as code, tools, documents, requirements, configurations, change requests, and deliverables. It also allows for repeatability of processes and the ability to track requirements through design, code, test, and final deliverables.

Scope

This policy applies to all applications and their respective projects within the organization.

Authority and Compliance

This policy is authorized by senior management. Compliance with this policy will be evaluated through an independent audit process. Results will be provided to the appropriate personnel and non-compliance and other issues will be submitted to the problem management system.

Policy Declaration

SCM Roles and Responsibilities

Responsibility for SCM shall be divided among SCM personnel, the application owner, project managers, and the users of SCM. SCM personnel and the application owner shall provide the direction, policies, and strategies in order to provide effective SCM. SCM personnel shall be responsible for implementing the SCM directives. Project managers must ensure the team is adhering to the appropriate use of the SCM processes and technology. Application and project personnel must comply with SCM policy and processes and use the prescribed SCM technologies.

SCM Processes

SCM processes shall be implemented and utilized throughout an application lifecycle for repeatability and consistency. The common SCM processes include identification, problem management, change control, version control, build, audit, and review.

SCM Technology

The SCM group shall establish and maintain a version control repository for securing configuration items for the application. The standard SCM version control technology is <SCM technology name>.

5. SCM Plan Template

Objective

The objective of the SCM Plan is to provide details for establishing and managing SCM for the <organization name or <application/product name> team>.

To implement an SCM system successfully, the SCM Plan must include: SCM terminology; reference documents; SCM roles and responsibilities and an organizational structure (relative to SCM); SCM tasks (a list of activities to be undertaken); and SCM policy and processes. In a nutshell, the SCM Plan is the focal point for all other SCM documents, activities, and efforts.

Scope

This SCM Plan applies to all applications and their respective projects.

SCM Terminology

The following are the common and consistent SCM terminology and acronyms to be used within the scope of the SCM policy. <Either place the SCM terminology and acronyms here or point to a location where SCM terminology and acronyms reside. For more on this topic, see Chapter 3 Section 4.2>

SCM and Related Documents

The following documents are used in relation to SCM within the organization or for this application.

Reference Documents

The following are non-SCM documents that may impact SCM <examples are included>.

Name of Document	Location
<IEEE/EIA 12207.2>	<path on server or website>
<MIL-STD-973>	<path on server or website>
Organization Project Planning Standards	<path on server or website>
Organization Coding Standards	<path on server or website>
Organization Test Plan Template	<path on server or website>

SCM Policy and Standards

The following documents provide guidance and direction for SCM:

Name of Document	Location
SCM Policy	<path on server, website address>
SCM Technology Standard	<path on server, website address>

SCM Processes and Templates

The following documents provide step-by-step guidance for enacting SCM processes:

Name of Process/Template	Location
<List SCM processes>	<path on server, website address>
<List SCM templates>	<path on server, website address>

SCM Organizational Structure

The SCM organization will report directly to the application owner.

SCM Roles and Responsibilities

Below are the roles and responsibilities for performing SCM activities. <Assign a name to each role in the table below. This provides accountability for the SCM roles and responsibilities. Included are roles that should have some level of SCM responsibility. For more on this topic, see Chapter 3 Sections 3.2.2 and 3.2.3 Note: one person may play multiple roles. The name assigned to a role may change. If so, document the change in this section.>

Role	Name	Responsibilities
Senior Management	<Name(s)>	<include specific responsibilities>
Application Owner	<Name(s)>	<include specific responsibilities>
Project Manager	<Name>	<include specific responsibilities>
SCM Manager	<Name>	<include specific responsibilities>
SCM Coordinator	<Name(s)>	<include specific responsibilities>
SCM Engineer	<Name(s)>	<include specific responsibilities>
System Administrator	<Name(s)>	<include specific responsibilities>

Role	Name	Responsibilities
CCB Member Key roles include: • Chairperson • Coordinator • Application Owner • Project Manager • Requestor • QA/Test Representative • Release Engineer • Technical Representative • Document Representative • Production Representative	\<Name(s)\>	\<Describe overall responsibility of the CCB and specific responsibilities of each CCB role, Indicate if the role is mandatory or optional\>

SCM Activities

This section details the activities necessary to implement SCM successfully. SCM activities (or tasks) may be: placed in a software project plan (at the project level), an SCM implementation plan (at the application level) when a new SCM system is being implemented or an existing SCM system is being improved; added to an SCM problem list that is regularly reviewed and; worked on, or included in an SCM risk list to manage and mitigate risks to prevent them from turning into problems.

Identification Activities

The appropriate personnel must establish baselines, utilize appropriate label naming conventions, and store applicable items into a repository.

Control Activities

The appropriate personnel must apply the appropriate problem management, version control, change control, build, and release processes to the project and they must utilize the appropriate SCM version control, problem management, change control, and release engineering technologies.

Audit Activities

The appropriate personnel must apply the SCM audit process to the project on a periodic basis.

Review Activities

The appropriate personnel must apply the SCM report and oversight process for reporting and reviewing the status of SCM activities.

6. SCM Analysis Investigator Template

General Information	
Application Name(s):	Current Release(s) of Application(s):
Group/Organization:	Date:
SCM Lead (include phone):	Signing Authority for funding SCM effort (include phone):
Process Overview	
Does an SCM Design Specification or SCM Plan exist?	
Are SCM Roles and Responsibilities defined and the names of people assigned to each role indicated?	
How are SCM issues managed? Is there an SCM problem management process or technology used?	
Does an SCM Change Control process exist?	
Is there an active Change Control Board in place to manage and control important application baselines?	
Do any other SCM processes exist (Version Control, Build, Release, etc)? If so, where are they?	

Is a release migration path defined (how is the release package created in development and migrated through production – include process and technology used – also include if parallel or linear development, branching/merging process, build process, migration process, production installation process):
Does SCM training exist (for users)?
Technology Overview
Development Platform(s):
Production Platform(s):
Coding Language(s):
Development Tool(s):
Number of people (dev/qa/sup) working in the SCM system (within the next year):
Approximate size of each application (LOC or number of modules or small/medium/large):
Build and Run-time Application Dependencies:
What SCM Version Control Technology is in use?
If none, has one been selected?
Where does the SCM Version Control code repository reside (if in use – specify server)?
If none, where does the current code reside?
If SCM technology is in use, how was it selected (evaluated, inherited, or ad hoc)?
Is an SCM Release Engineering technology used to migrate the release package into production?
What SCM technologies are used for other applications within the organization?

7. SCM Analysis Summary Template

General Information	
Application Name(s):	Current Release(s) of Application(s):
Group/Organization:	Date:
Strengths	
<include at least 5>	
Opportunities for Improvement	
<include no more than 3 biggest areas of improvement>	
Comments:	

8. SCM Implementation Project Plan Template

Phase	Task	Task Owner	Dependency	Start Date	End Date	Estimated Effort
Analysis	Assess the Implementation Readiness					
	Prepare High-Level Estimates for the SCM Project					
	Perform an SCM Analysis					
	Perform an Application-Level SCM Risk Assessment					
Planning	Develop an SCM Implementation Project Plan					

Phase	Task	Task Owner	Dependency	Start Date	End Date	Estimated Effort
	Establish a Document Infrastructure					
	Establish Application Level SCM Metrics					
	Project Contingency					
Technology Selection	Evaluate and Select an SCM Technology					
	Determine Number of SCM Technology Licenses Needed					
	Prepare Purchase Justification for SCM Technology					
	Acquire Selected SCM Technology					
	Project Contingency					
Design	Create an SCM Design Specification					
	Establish a Master Application Inventory					
	Define a Global SCM/Development Strategy (if applicable)					
	Project Contingency					
Process	Develop an SCM Problem Management Process					
	Develop an SCM Change Control Process					
	Prepare Change Control Conduct Guidelines					
	Develop an SCM Identification Process					

Phase	Task	Task Owner	Dependency	Start Date	End Date	Estimated Effort
	Develop an SCM Version Control Process					
	Develop an SCM Merge Process					
	Develop an SCM Build Process					
	Develop an SCM Release Process					
	Prepare a Release Notes Template					
	Develop an SCM Audit Process					
	Develop an SCM Oversight Process					
	Develop an SCM Report Process					
	Project Contingency					
Technology Implementation	Establish the SCM Version Control/Build Management Infrastructure					
	Determine Transition Order of Applications into the SCM Technology					
	Define/Redefine the Application Code Structure					
	Install the SCM Technology					
	Import and Baseline the Application into the SCM Technology					
	Establish User Workspaces					
	Establish the SCM Problem Management Infrastructure					
	Establish the SCM Change Control Infrastructure					

Phase	Task	Task Owner	Dependency	Start Date	End Date	Estimated Effort
	Establish the SCM Release Engineering Infrastructure					
	Establish the Global SCM/Development Infrastructure (if applicable)					
	Project Contingency					
Training	Provide SCM Technology Administrator Training					
	Prepare SCM Technology User Training Materials					
	Provide SCM Technology User Training					
	Prepare and Provide Change Control Board (CCB) Training					
Test	Perform Functional Test of SCM System					
	Perform User Acceptance Test of SCM System					
	Perform Final Import					
	Project Contingency					
Transition	Conduct an SCM System Readiness Meeting					
	Prepare Notification for SCM System Cut-Over					
	Cut-over to New SCM System					
	Provide Intensive Support of SCM System for 2–4 Weeks					
	Project Contingency					

9. SCM Technology Evaluation Requirements List Template

Note: add SCM Technology columns as needed (for the number of SCM technologies being evaluated)

Organization:			For What Application(s):	
Date:			Evaluation Participants:	

Functional Requirements	Weight	SCM Technology A Raw Score	SCM Technology A Weighted Score	SCM Technology B Raw Score	SCM Technology B Weighted Score
<requirement>	0	0	0	0	0
<requirement>	0	0	0	0	0
<requirement>	0	0	0	0	0
<requirement>	0	0	0	0	0
Subtotal			0		0
Implementation and Integration Requirements	Weight	SCM Technology A Raw Score	SCM Technology A Weighted Score	SCM Technology B Raw Score	SCM Technology B Weighted Score
Expertise required	0	0	0	0	0
Ease of Implementation	0	0	0	0	0
Family of Integrated Tools	0	0	0	0	0
Ease of Integration	0	0	0	0	0
Subtotal			0		0
Customer Support Requirements	Weight	SCM Technology A Raw Score	SCM Technology A Weighted Score	SCM Technology B Raw Score	SCM Technology B Weighted Score
Response Time	0	0	0	0	0
Willingness to Help	0	0	0	0	0

		SCM Technology A Raw Score	SCM Technology A Weighted Score	SCM Technology B Raw Score	SCM Technology B Weighted Score
Location	0	0	0	0	0
Subtotal			0		0
Cost Requirements	**Weight**	**SCM Technology A Raw Score**	**SCM Technology A Weighted Score**	**SCM Technology B Raw Score**	**SCM Technology B Weighted Score**
Overall Price	0	0	0	0	0
Consulting Costs	0	0	0	0	0
Subtotal			0		0
Overall Total			0		0

9.1. SCM Technology Evaluation Summary Template

Organization:	**Platform:**
SCM Technologies evaluated:	**Date**:

Benefits/Risks Section:
Benefits:
1st Choice–<list benefits>
2nd Choice–<list benefits>
Risks:
1st Choice–<list risks>
2nd Choice–<list risks>

Requirements Summary Section:

FUNCTIONAL REQUIREMENTS

	<1st Choice SCM Tool Name>	<2nd Choice SCM Tool Name>
Subtotal		

<Provide the main reason(s) why the 1st choice was selected over the 2nd choice>

IMPLEMENTATION/INTEGRATION REQUIREMENTS

	<1st Choice SCM Tool Name>	<2nd Choice SCM Tool Name>
Subtotal		

<Provide the main reason(s) why the 1st choice was selected over the 2nd choice>

CUSTOMER SUPPORT REQUIREMENTS

	<1st Choice SCM Tool Name>	<2nd Choice SCM Tool Name>
Subtotal		

<Provide the main reason(s) why the 1st choice was selected over the 2nd choice>

COST REQUIREMENTS

	<1st Choice SCM Tool Name>	<2nd Choice SCM Tool Name>
Subtotal		

<Provide the main reason(s) why the 1st choice was selected over the 2nd choice>

SCM Technology Selection Section:

OVERALL

	<1st Choice SCM Tool Name>	<2nd Choice SCM Tool Name>
Total		

The SCM Technology Selected is: <Name the SCM Technology selected>

10. SCM Design Specification Template

Objective

The objective of the SCM Design Specification is to provide details for establishing and managing SCM for the <organization name or <application/product name> team>. It also provides direction for preparing, designing, implementing, and maintaining an SCM environment.

To implement an SCM system successfully, the SCM Design Specification includes: SCM Roles and Responsibilities, SCM Terminology, Application Environment Details, Application Environment Change Policy, SCM System Details, Label and Branch Naming Conventions, SCM Activity Management Documents (SCM Implementation Plan, Problem List, and Risk List), SCM Training, and SCM Processes. In a nutshell, the SCM Design Specification is the focal point document for implementing and maintaining SCM on an application/product.

Scope

This SCM Design Specification applies to all projects of a respective application.

SCM Roles and Responsibilities

Below are the roles and responsibilities for performing SCM activities. <Assign a name to each role in the table below. This provides accountability for the SCM roles and responsibilities. Included are roles that should have some level of SCM responsibility. For more on this topic, see Chapter 3 Sections 3.2.2 and 3.2.3 for information on responsibilities. Note: one person may play multiple roles. The name assigned to a role may change. If so, document the change in this section.>

Role	Name	Responsibilities
Senior Management	<Name(s)>	<include specific responsibilities>
Application Owner	<Name(s)>	<include specific responsibilities>
Project Manager	<Name>	<include specific responsibilities>
SCM Manager	<Name>	<include specific responsibilities>
SCM Coordinator	<Name(s)>	<include specific responsibilities>
SCM Engineer	<Name(s)>	<include specific responsibilities>

Role	Name	Responsibilities
System Administrator	<Name(s)>	<include specific responsibilities>
CCB Member Key roles included: • Chairperson • Coordinator • Application Owner • Project Manager • Requestor • QA/Test Representative • Release Engineer • Technical Representative • Document Representative • Production Representative	<Name(s)>	<Describe overall responsibility of the CCB and specific responsibilities of each CCB role, Indicate if the role is mandatory or optional.>

SCM Terminology

The following are the common and consistent SCM terminology and acronyms to be used on this application. <Either place the SCM terminology and acronyms here or point to a location where SCM terminology and acronyms reside. For more on this topic, see Chapter 3 Section 4.2>

SCM and Related Documents

The following documents are used in relation to SCM for this application. <This section may already exist in an SCM Plan for the application. If so, reference that SCM Plan here. Otherwise, complete this section.>

Reference Documents

The following non-SCM documents may impact SCM.

Name of Document	Location
<IEEE/EIA 12207.2>	<path on server or website>
<MIL-STD-973>	<path on server or website>
Organization Project Planning Standards	<path on server or website>
Organization Coding Standards	<path on server or website>
Organization Test Plan Template	<path on server or website>
Application Requirements List	<path on server or website>

SCM Policy and Standards

The following documents provide guidance and direction for SCM.

Name of Document	Location
SCM Policy	<path on server, website address>
SCM Technology Standard	<path on server, website address>

SCM Processes and Templates

The following documents provide step-by-step guidance for enacting SCM processes.

Name of Process/Template	Location
SCM Technology User Guide (includes Version Control and User Build Process)	<path on server, website address>
SCM Technology Administration Guide (includes Build and Release Process)	<path on server, website address>
Change Control Process	<path on server, website address>
Problem Management Process	<path on server, website address>
Audit Process	<path on server, website address>

Name of Process/Template	Location
Review Process	\<path on server, website address\>
Backup and Recovery Process	\<path on server, website address\>
SCM Design Specification	\<path on server, website address\>
Master Application Inventory	\<path on server, website address\>

SCM Activity Management Documents

This section provides SCM activity and task based improvement documents for SCM such as implementation plans, problem lists, and risk lists that are used to manage SCM on a task-oriented basis for an application.

SCM Activity Management Documents	Location
\<Application/Product\> SCM Implementation Plan	\<path on server, website address\>
\<Application\> SCM Problem List, Problem Management Tool, or Problem Management Website	\<path on server, website address\>
\<Application\> SCM Risk List	\<path on server, website address\>
Other	\<path on server, website address\>

Application Environment Change Policy

This section provides the basis for environment change control guidelines for authorizing changes to any part of the application environment baseline (including the SCM system) that may impact the integrity of the application deliverables.

Policy Statement	Before any change to any item that is part of the application environment (including the SCM system) can happen, change control with the appropriate authorization must occur. This is to ensure that there is no loss of productivity in case the environment change impacts other items within the application environment.
Process	\<Indicate the Application Environment Change Control Process . Consider customizing the SCM Change Control Process Template in Section 14 of the Appendix. For more details, see Chapter 4 Section 6.2.\>

Items to Manage	\<Consider the following\> • Server operating system changes • Server hardware changes • Technology used for application development and testing • SCM related technology • Network changes that impact the servers in which the application items reside
Who Authorizes Changes	\<Identify who authorizes the changes. This is typically the Application Owner (or representative) and SCM Manager but may include others like the System Administration personnel.\>

Application Environment Details

This section provides information on the application logistics and the SCM servers used for application development. This information helps determine if the environment is adequate to establish a robust SCM infrastructure and provides input to designing the SCM system.

Application Information

\<Make a copy of the following table for each application that will reside in the shared SCM system\>

Application Name:	**Organization:**
Estimated Size (MB/GB) of code base:	Estimated Size (MB/GB) of application install base:
Build-time dependencies with other applications:	
Run-time dependencies with other applications:	

Server Information

\<Identify any servers and information that will be used as part of the SCM system. This provides an overview of where the SCM technology may be installed, where the repositories will live, where the application gets built, etc. Make a copy of the following table for each SCM server that is used within the application environment and part of the SCM system.\>

Server Name:	• Server Function: <SCM technology installation, repository, build, licenses, etc.>
<server name>	• Machine Type: <manufacturer and model>
	• OS Version: <operating system and release number>
	• Location: <location of server–city/site, area of the building, floor, etc.>
	• IP Address: <network address for system>
	• RAM: <RAM on server>
	• Domain: <name of domain which the system is in>

Data on Disk	Size of Disk	Mapping or Mount point
User workspace areas	<list sizes>	<path/map to user workspaces>
SCM technology executable area	<list sizes>	<path/map to executable area>
SCM technology repository area	<list sizes>	<path to SCM technology repository>

SCM System Details

This section provides information on the installation aspects of an SCM technology. <Complete one table per SCM technology, but particularly for the version control/build management technology>

SCM Environment Details	<SCM technology name>
SCM Technology and Release Number	<SCM technology and release number>
SCM Technology Installation Location	<server and installation directory path>
SCM Technology Repository Location	<server and top level repository directory path. Note: may refer back to the "Server Information" section earlier in the SCM Design Specification.>
SCM Technology Run-time Location	<server and run-time directory path>
Build Server(s) and Build Location(s) (if applicable)	<server and build/packaging directory path(s)>

SCM Environment Details	**<SCM technology name>**
SCM Technology License Location and Amount	<server, location of licenses, and number of licenses>
SCM Technology Administrator Account	<admin account name and group name>
SCM Technology Build Engineer Account (if applicable)	<admin account name and group name>
User Workspace Location(s)	<server(s) and path to workspaces – consider standardizing this location across workstations and/or on a central server>
Workspace Naming Convention	<userid-application-release-type – consider standardizing the naming convention to the user id, the application name, the release they are working on, and the type of work (latest, bugfix, etc.)>

Label Naming Convention

This section provides the standard label naming convention used for placing tag attributes on baselines of code within the SCM version control repository.

Label Type	**Naming Convention**
Development Release Baseline Label	<application name-DR#>
Nightly Build Label	<application name-NB>
Engineering Build Label	<application name-EB#>
Internal Pre-release Packaging Label	<application name-PR#>
External Release or Production Packaging Label	<application name-R#>
Bugfix Label	<application name-R#-Bug#>
Other	

Branch Types and Branch Naming Convention

The following table of information provides the standard branch types and naming convention.

Branch Type	Naming Convention
Private Branch	\<This branch naming convention may include the release number of what is being worked on and whether it is off an integration branch and/or a shared branch. It will also include the user's id to distinguish it from other user's private branches. Example: /main/rel#/int/user_private or /main/rel#/int/shared/user_private\>
Shared Branch	\<This branch naming convention may include the release number of what is being worked on, the integration branch identifier, and the shared branch identifier. Example: /main/rel#/int/shared\>
Integration Branch	\<This branch naming convention may include the release number and an integration branch identifier. Example: /main/rel#/int\>
Project Release Branch	\<This branch naming convention may simply be the project release number of what is being worked on. Example: /main/rel#\>
Main Branch	\<This branch naming convention may simply be the main branch. Example: /main\>
Bugfix Branch	\<This branch naming convention may include the main branch with the appropriate release and bugfix identifier either for a set of bugfixes or for a specific bugfix. Example: /main/rel#-bugfix or /main/rel#-bugfix#\>
Site Branch	\<This branch naming convention may include the release number and the site identifier. Example: /main/rel#/int/site1\>
Other	

Branch and Merge Process Flow Diagram

The following is a branch and merge process flow diagram that will be used for this application and the projects that create the release deliverables.

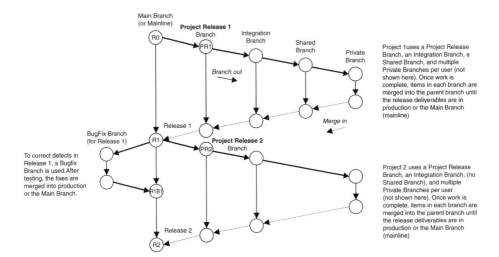

Figure A.2   Branch/Merge Process Flow

SCM Training

List of SCM courses available

The following is a list of SCM courses offered <either in-house or by a vendor> that can be delivered to the application team members. <Three examples are provided.>

SCM Course	Length	Description	Who should Attend	Where to Register
<Change Control Board Training>	2 hours	Provides an overview of the application's Change Control Process, Conduct Guidelines, and case study used in a role playing exercise.	CCB members	SCM Manager
<SCM Technology User Training>	1 hour	Provides an overview of the SCM technology and the user commands	SCM Engineers, Application Team	SCM Manager
<SCM Administra- tion Training>	2 days	Provides SCM technology administrator training.	SCM Engineers	<www.vendor.com>

Who has taken SCM Training

The following are the application team members who have taken SCM courses.

SCM Course	Date	Name
<name of SCM course>	<date>	<names or attendees>

11. Master Application Inventory Template

Application Information

Application Name:	Application Owner:
Organization:	SCM Manager:
Version #:	Last Date Updated:

Application Baseline Definition

Baseline Category	SCM Rigor	Items found within Baseline
Functional	Identify, Version Control, Change Control	Documents–*Plan, Process, Standard, Specification, Template, Guideline*
Requirements	Identify, Version Control, Change Control	Requirements
Development	Identify, Version Control	Code
Test	Identify, Version Control	Test cases
Environment	Identify, Change Control	Infrastructure

Application Inventory List

Baseline	Name	Version/Release Number	Description	Location

12. Global SCM/Development Strategy Template

Objective

The primary purpose of the global SCM/development strategy is to identify and evaluate the best approach to performing development across distributed locations.

Distributed Analysis

This section identifies the characteristics of each application being developed across distributed sites. <Identify the application(s) that will be developed concurrently across different sites and define the application characteristics in the appropriate columns. Analyze and document the following (included are two examples)>

Application Name	# at Site 1[1]	# at Site 2	# at Site 3	Lifecycle[2] Phases	Complexity[3]
<Application 1>	20	8	n/a	Dev thru Test	High
<Application 2>	5	5	2	Design thru Dev	Low

[1]Number of personnel at each site
[2]Lifecycle phases include: Planning, Requirements, Design, Development, Test, and Release
[3]Complexity of the development technology used (complexity level examples below)
- Low complexity technologies have low RAM requirements, low network dependency or few network transactions, and ASCII text based development. Examples include C, C++, Perl, and Cobol.
- High complexity technologies have high RAM requirements, high network dependency or constant network transactions, and object-based development. Examples include development technologies driven by IDEs.

Distributed Direction

This section uses the application characteristics defined in the analysis section above to determine the distributed access technology, code availability, and branch/merge approach for each application. <Consider and document the following (included are two examples)>

Application Name	Distributed Access Technology	Code Availability	Branch/Merge
<Application 1>	Distributed Site/Remote Client Snapshot	Section of code per site	Private Branch backed by Site Branch
<Application 2>	Single Site/Terminal Services	All code	Private Branch backed by Integration Branch

Distributed Roles and Responsibilities

Below are the roles and responsibilities for performing multiple site development activities. <Assign a name of a person to each role in the table below. This provides accountability for the distributed development tasks.>

Role	Responsibilities	Name
Code Integrator	• Establish the site branches (as needed) as per the branch naming convention. • Merges the code from site branch to either a local site branch or local integration branch. • Note: A member of the application team who is very familiar with the code may play this role.	<Name(s)>
Project Manager	• Identify how many developers will work on the application at each site • Determine when, in a project lifecycle, the additional sites begin and end their work • Identify the complexity of the development technology used for application development (in conjunction with the SCM Manager)	<Name>

Role	Responsibilities	Name
	• Identify the code availability approach • Ensure there is a well-defined communication and collaboration process across sites (in conjunction with the application owner)	
Application Owner	• Determine the most appropriate distributed access technology (in conjunction with the SCM Manager) • Ensure there is a well-defined communication and collaboration process across sites (in conjunction with the project manager(s))	\<Name\>
SCM Manager	• Identify the complexity of the development technology used for application development (in conjunction with the project manager) • Determine the most appropriate distributed access technology (in conjunction with the application owner) • Determine the branch types and branch naming convention	\<Name\>

13. SCM Problem Management Process

Objective

To provide a repeatable process for documenting, tracking and resolving problems.

Scope

This process applies to all projects related to this application.

Problem Type

This process applies to the following problem types: defects, issues, and non-compliances.

Severity Levels

The severity levels used in this process are:

• Severity 1 = Critical with no workaround
• Severity 2 = Critical with workaround

- Severity 3 = Major with workaround
- Severity 4 = Minor with workaround

State Transition

The state transitions used in this process are:

- New – a problem has been identified and a problem request has been opened (this state may be called 'Opened').
- Assigned – the problem has been reviewed by the appropriate management and assigned to an appropriate change agent.
- Fixed – the development staff member has completed the activities involved with resolving the problem.
- Tested – a test staff member has verified that the problem is resolved.
- Closed – management has reviewed the problem status and closed the problem.

Steps

Step	Role	Description	Output
1	Requester	Submit a problem request on a Problem Request Form (PRF)	Submitted Problem Request
2	Project Manager	Review New Problem Requests • Review/update the severity of the problem and the estimated effort of correcting the problem. • Update the Problem Request (if appropriate) Note: reviews of new PRFs may be done in a batch or on a periodic basis instead of on an individual basis	Review of Problem Request
3	Project Manager	Determine if Action is Required • If yes, assign PRF to appropriate change agent • If no (the originating problem may be found to be working as designed or the	A decision, Change Agent assigned

Step	Role	Description	Output
		PRF is a duplicate of an existing and active PRF), update log to that effect and go to step 6	
4	Change Agent	Resolve the Problem	Problem has been resolved
5	Test Personnel	Validate the Resolution was Successful • If yes, update and the PRF • If no, return PRF to change agent with a reason indicating why it did not meet expected results. Repeat Step 4	Validation Updated PRF
6	SCM Coordinator	Close the Problem Request	Closed PRF

13.1. Problem Request Form Template

<This problem request form is an example of a document used to capture problems. It can be customized and renamed to fit its function (Problem Ticket, Problem Submission Form, etc.). It may be duplicated in an automated tool.>

Section 1: To be completed by the Requestor

Requestor Name:		Requestor Phone Number:	
Problem Type:		Date Opened:	
Brief Problem Summary:			
Where problem was found:			
Is this an Emergency (Yes/No)	Severity (select one): Low	Medium	High
Detailed Problem Info:			

Section 2: To be completed by the Manager and Change Agent

Manager who owns problem space:	
Problem Assigned to:	
Estimated Effort/Cost Impact:	
Severity Update: (select one): Low	Medium High
Status:	
Date Fixed:	Date Tested: Date Closed:

14. SCM Change Control Process

Objective

To provide a repeatable process for controlling changes to items in important baselines of an application from submission to closure.

Scope

This process applies to all projects related to this application.

Baselines

This process applies to the requirements, environment, and production baselines.

Priority Levels

The priority levels used in this process are:

- Priority 1 = must do, critical
- Priority 2 = great benefit
- Priority 3 = some benefit
- Priority 4 = minor benefit

State Transition

The state transitions used in this process are:

- New – a change has been identified and a change request has been opened (this state is often called 'Opened').
- Analyzed – the change has been analyzed for clarification of change request and estimated effort.
- Reviewed – the change has been reviewed by the Change Control Board (CCB) and a decision has been made
  - If accepted, the state remains at 'Reviewed' in preparation for assigning the change to the appropriate personnel.
  - If rejected, the state changes to 'Closed'.
  - If more information is needed, the state changes to 'New' so that it can be further analyzed.
- Assigned – the change has been assigned to the appropriate personnel (change agent).
- Completed – the change agent has completed the activities involved.
- Tested – a test staff member has verified that the change is completed as requested.
- Closed – the CCB has reviewed the change status and closed the change.

Steps

Step	Role	Description	Output
1	Requester, SCM Coordinator	Submit Change Request • Requester fills out a CRF to request a change and submits it. • Change Coordinator logs the request.	Submitted Change Request
2	Analyst	Perform Analysis of Change Request • Determine if the change request is an emergency. If so, review any existing protocols, perform minute analysis, implement change, verify change, close change request, and go to Step 3. • Identify impacts of making the change (to items in the baseline). • Estimate effort and cost of making the change. • Determine priority of the change. • Update CRF with this information.	Completed Analysis with impacts, effort and cost Updated CRF

Step	Role	Description	Output
3	SCM Coordinator	Distribute CCB Agenda and new CRFs for Review • Prepare CCB agenda. • Send the CCB agenda and new CRFs to the CCB members in advance of the next CCB meeting.	CCB Agenda, CRF(s) with analysis results
4	CCB Members	Determine Status of Change Request(s) • The CCB discusses each Change Request and determines the decision. • Approve–go to Step 5. • Reject–go to Step 9. • Pending Information–more information is needed before a decision can be made–go to Step 2. • Escalate–cannot decide as a group–escalate to escalation point/senior management.	Decision for each CRF
5	SCM Coordinator	Update CRF(s) and Distribute CCB Minutes • Update the Change Requests with decision, create CCB minutes and distribute the minutes. • Forward all approved Change Requests to Project Manager	CCB Minutes, Change Requests with decision
6	Project Manager	Assign Change Request and Re-Estimate Effort • Assigns a change agent to the CRF for implementing the change. • Reviews estimated effort from Step 2 and re-estimates as appropriate. Update project plan if effort is significant.	Updated effort estimate, Change Agent assigned
7	Change Agent	Implement Change to the appropriate item(s) • Note: utilize appropriate SCM processes to implement the change (e.g., version control, etc.).	Change is made

Step	Role	Description	Output
8	QA/Test Personnel	Verify Change is implemented as requested • If successful, update CRF. • If unsuccessful, the CRF is returned to the change agent with a reason indicating why it did not meet expected results. Return to Step 7.	Verification Results and Updated CRF Summary Log.
9	SCM Coordinator	Close Change Request • Include the closed CRF in next CCB agenda for awareness. • Note: if you are releasing the CIs into the production baseline, use the release processes for proper implementation.	Closed Change Request

14.1. Change Request Form Template

<This change request form is an example of a format used to capture change request information. It can be called any name that is representative of its function (Change Ticket, Change Submission Form, Change Entry, etc.). The form shown below is an example of a manual change request form and may be duplicated in an automated tool.>

Section 1: To be completed by the Requestor

Requestor Name:		Requestor Phone #:	
Application Name:		Date Requested:	

Brief Change Summary:	

Release of Application being run:		Change type Add		Change		Delete	
Is this an Emergency (Yes/No)		Priority Low		Medium		High	

Detailed Change Info:	

Section 2: To be completed by the Analyst

Analyst Name:	
Estimated Effort/Cost Impact:	
Personnel Impact:	
Dependencies:	

Priority Update: Low ☐   Medium ☐   High ☐

Additional Analysis:	

Section 3: To be completed by the Manager and Change Agent

Manager who owns problem space:	
Problem Assigned to: (indicate name):	
Updated Estimated Effort Impact:	

Section 4: This section to be completed by CCB Coordinator or Chairperson

Date of CCB Meeting: ☐   Approve ☐   Reject ☐   Pending ☐   Escalate ☐

If Rejected, provide reason:	

Priority Update: Low ☐   Medium ☐   High ☐

Target Release Number:	
Additional Information:	

14.2. Change Control Board (CCB) Conduct Guidelines Template

CCB Overview

CCB Span of Control	<e.g., Application name(s)>
Baselines under CCB Control	<e.g., Requirements, Production, Environment, etc.>

CCB Meeting Logistics

Frequency of Meetings	
Meeting Time/Day	
Length of CCB meeting	
Length of Time needed to discuss each CRF	
Time period prior to CCB meeting that CRFs must be submitted to CCB Coordinator	
Time period prior to CCB meeting that CRFs and CCB agenda must be sent	
Method for prioritizing CRFs	

CCB Meeting Process

The following is a sample meeting agenda/process. Adapt it to fit your particular CCB meeting.

Step	Activity
1	Review minutes from last CCB meeting
2	Review Emergency CRFs (if any)
3	Discuss new and pending CRFs and determine a decision (e.g., voting)
4	Assign newly approved CRFs to change agents
5	Review newly closed CRFs since the last meeting
6	Review the change metrics from the last meeting
7	Review all documented action items resulting from the last CCB meeting

Voting Privileges (e.g., some CCB members have more weight than others)

Voting Approval Method (e.g., consensus, number of votes, quorum, other)

Waiving Policy

Waiving Allowances	

CCB Technology

CCB Technology/Repository Location	

Escalation

Who participates in a Change Request disagreement?	
Who ensures a resolution is reached regarding Change Request disagreements?	

CCB Meeting Closure

Time period between approval of CRF and the notification to the Change Agent	
Time period between end of CCB meeting and distributing the meeting minutes	

15. SCM Identification Process

Objective

To provide a repeatable process for identifying CIs to establish baselines which enable management of the CIs.

Scope

This process applies to all projects related to this application.

Steps

Step	Role	Description	Output
1	Project Manager, SCM Engineer	Identify CIs for the Application • Identify and document application CIs in an application inventory list. • Assign a level of SCM rigor to each CI in the list (e.g., identification, version control, change control).	Application Inventory List
2	SCM Engineer	Align CI Name with Naming Conventions (Optional) • If naming conventions exist for specific types of items, modify the name to align with naming convention.	Renamed CIs
3	SCM Engineer, Application/Project Team	Place CI into the Baseline • Using the appropriate process, place the CI into the appropriate baseline. This may require: • a version control process for adding to the development (code) baseline • a release process and change control process for installation into a production baseline • a requirements management process or change control process for creating and managing a requirements baseline	CI in the baseline

16. SCM Version Control Process

Objective

To provide a repeatable process for version controlled changes to any baseline.

Scope

This process applies to all projects related to this application.

Steps

<Note: the Description may include the checkout and checkin commands of an SCM technology.>

Step	Role	Description	Output
1	Project personnel	Checkout Item • Transfer a copy of an existing configuration item (CI) from an appropriate repository to the work area.	Checked out configuration item (CI)
2	Project personnel	Change Item • Change applicable CI(s) per change request or problem request. • Perform the appropriate testing to meet the checkin criteria. This may include a build (if applicable), unit test, code review, etc.	Changed and validated CI
3	Project personnel	Checkin Item • Place a modified copy of the CI into the appropriate baseline. • A unique copy (i.e., version) must be developed	A CI checked into the repository
4	Project personnel	Increment the version number for this item • Automated – The versioning is handled automatically if an SCM version control technology is used. • Manual – for a manual system, consider a convention which includes major version, minor version, and draft version identifiers.	CI with unique version identifier

17. SCM Merge Process

Objective

To provide a repeatable process for merging a version of a configuration item from one branch to another, provided that they have the same ancestry.

Scope

This process applies to all projects related to this application.

Steps

<Note: Consider including the specific merge commands and examples.>

Step	Role	Description	Output
1	Project personnel	Identify the target branch to move to • Note: This should be an ancestor of your current branch.	Identified branch
2	Project personnel	Merge from the target branch to your branch • If there is nothing to merge (the version is the same as the version in the other branch), go to Step 5. • If it is a trivial merge (no logical lines of conflict and no compiling is required), then go to Step 4. • If it is a trivial merge (no logical lines of conflict and compiling is a standard step), go to Step 3. • If there is a merge conflict (logical lines of conflict), go to Step 2a. • Note: merging to your branch allows for more time within your branch to resolve conflicts (if any).	Merged CI
2a	Project personnel	Resolve any logical lines of conflict • Identify the logical lines of conflict and determine which line should go into the new version of the CI. Consider doing this with the person that made the change to the version of the CI in the target branch. • If compiling is a standard step of the development process, go to Step 3. • If compiling is not a standard step of the development process, complete the merging step and go to Step 4.	Conflict resolved, Merged CI
3	Project personnel	Compile/Build (if appropriate) • <Indicate the specific command and provide an example.> • If code is normally built, then rebuild to ensure it compiles properly. Rebuild and fix until a clean compile occurs (no build errors).	Clean recompile
4	Project personnel	Test the changes as appropriate.	Tested CI

Step	Role	Description	Output
5	Project personnel	Checkin CI to create a new version	CI in the baseline
6	Project personnel	Merge from your branch to the target branch • \<Indicate the specific command and provide an example. Assumes no merge conflict if Steps 2–4 occur\>	Merged CI in the target branch
7	Project personnel	Checkin to target branch • \<Indicate the specific command and provide an example. Note: some SCM technologies consolidate the function of merge and checkin.\>	CI in the target branch

18. SCM Build Process

Objective

To provide a repeatable process of generating deliverables from code.

Scope

This process applies to all projects related to this application.

Steps

Note: assumes an SCM version control repository has already been established.

Step	Role	Description	Output
1	SCM Engineer	Identify specific workspace • Verify that it is a clean room workspace (i.e., that there are no items in the workspace other than what belongs).	Clean room workspace
2	SCM Engineer	Acquire the code for the Build • This may involve a checkout of the versioned code or establishing a virtual workspace that displays the code.	code in workspace

Step	Role	Description	Output
3	SCM Engineer	Build code • Perform compile/build process using the specified compilers and tools.	Programs, Binaries, Executables, etc.
4	SCM Engineer	Validate Deliverables and Results • Identify that the build was successful. • Determine if expected deliverables were built (compare with expected deliverables). • Correct as needed.	Validation of deliverables
5	SCM Engineer	Capture Deliverables • This may include checking in and labeling the deliverables into the SCM version control system	Deliverables packaged
6	SCM Engineer	Summarize and Send a Build Summary • Create a summary of the results of the build. • Send build summary to the appropriate personnel	Build summary

19. SCM Release Process

Objective

To provide a repeatable process for managing changes to the production baseline.

Scope

This process applies to all projects related to this application.

Steps

Step	Role	Description	Output
1	SCM Engineer	Identify Deliverables that make up the Release Package • This would include names and locations of code, documents, installation scripts, etc. This may be based on a label found within the SCM version control repository.	Release Package Inventory or similar list

Step	Role	Description	Output
2	SCM Engineer	Prepare Release Notes	Draft Release Notes
3	Project Manager	Submit a Change Request • The Change Request documents the proposed change (or release package) to the production baseline. • Also, collect documents that support the Change Request and the readiness of the release such as: Release Package Inventory; Test Report(s); Installation Plan; Backout and Restore Plan	Change Request for Release, Supporting Release documents
4	CCB	Determine Status of Change Request • Review the change request and ensure the release criteria have been met. Effectively, determine if the release package includes: • the specified requirements (e.g., 100% of priority 1 and 2 and 50% of priority 3 requirements from the requirements baseline of this release) • only the defects allowed by the release criteria (e.g., no severity 1 defects and no more than 10 severity 2 defects). • Determine the decision. • Approve (i.e., authorize the Release Package for the production baseline). • Reject–discuss what needs to be corrected in order for approval to occur. • Review and update Release Notes as appropriate.	Decision on Change Request
5	SCM Engineer	Migrate the approved Release Package into a Staging Area	Staged Release
6	SCM Engineer	Install Release Package into the Production Baseline	Release in production baseline

Step	Role	Description	Output
		• Depending on the target of the release package, installation steps will include one of the following approaches: • If release target is media (such as a CD), then place all release package onto the target media • If the release target is a production system, then: • Copy the current production baseline to a backout and restore area so that it can quickly be placed back into production (for recovery purposes) • Place release package into the appropriate location within the production baseline. • Notify appropriate personnel that the release package is in the production baseline.	
7	QA/Test Personnel	Validate the Release Package in Production • Depending on the target of the release package, the verification steps will include one of the following approaches: • If the release target is media (such as a CD), then: • Validate that release deliverables are on the media • Perform an installation test (from the installation plan, if it exists) to ensure that the new release of the application installs properly on its target system. • Perform test(s) to ensure that the new release deliverables operate as expected. • If the release target is a production server, then: • Validate that all release deliverables are in production. • Perform test(s) to ensure that the new release deliverables operate as expected.	Validated release in production

Step	Role	Description	Output
		• If minor changes are made to release deliverables, ensure the CCB is notified. If severe problems occur, notify stakeholders to discuss resolutions or begin following the Backout and Restore plan and restore to the previous release.	
8	Project Manager	Notify Stakeholders and Project Team that the Release Package has been Successfully Installed and Tested • Assumes a successful verification of the release package • Place Release notes into application document repository	Notification of successful release

19.1. Release Notes Template

Company:	Product/Application:
Release Number:	GA Release Date:

New Features of this Release: <list features>

Defects Corrected in this Release: <list defects corrected>

Installation Plan (instructions):

20. SCM Audit Process

Objective

To provide a repeatable process for assessing compliance with SCM processes and technology and determines the integrity of the application baselines.

Scope

This process applies to all projects related to this application.

Steps

Step	Role	Description	Output
1	Project Manager, SCM Manager	Determine What To Audit and When • Consider questions for the audit (it may be all items on a checklist or selected checklist items). If checklists exist, utilize for consistency. • Determine specific date for the audit.	Audit questions, audit scheduled
2	Project Manager, SCM Manager	Select Audit Team • Select personnel for audit team from the project personnel. The audit team must include an SCM engineer, two key development staff members, and someone to act as recorder (collects information). • Assign roles to audit team members (who will audit what)	Audit team, roles assigned
3	Audit Team	Prepare For Audit • Schedule meeting times with project team members as appropriate. • Notify project manager and application owner that the audit has been scheduled.	Meetings scheduled, Notification sent
4	Audit Team	Perform Audit • Discuss selected audit questions with project personnel. • Document results. • Indicate if the area passed or failed, and include a recommended action if improvement is needed.	Audit completed

Step	Role	Description	Output
5	Recorder	Report Results • Document results in the SCM Status Report template or similar. The results should include what was being done well, identify areas of improvement, and indicate recommended actions. • Report results to the SCM manager, project manager and application owner (as per the SCM oversight process if applicable) • Open problem requests for any audit improvement items and track to closure. • Place a copy of the audit results into the application team document repository.	SCM Audit Report with Opportunities for Improvement

20.1. SCM Process Audit Checklist Template

Application:	Project Release Name:
Date:	Project Phase:
Audit Team:	

Audit Question	Results	Pass Yes/No	Recommended Action
Does an SCM plan or design specification exist for the application?			
Are SCM tasks found in the project plan?			
Is the SCM plan or design specification in the document repository?			
Are SCM roles and responsibilities clearly defined and a name assigned for each role?			
Is the version control process being used as defined?			
Are version number naming conventions being used on documents as defined?			

Audit Question	Results	Pass Yes/No	Recommended Action
Is the problem management process being used as designed?			
Is the change control process being used to manage baselines?			
Is the build process being used as defined?			
Is the release process being used as designed?			
Is training for SCM processes and technologies being offered?			
Are project personnel taking the appropriate SCM training?			

20.2. SCM Baseline Audit Checklist Template

Application:	Project Release Name:
Date:	Project Phase:
Audit Team:	

Audit Question	Results	Pass Yes/No	Recommended Action
Does a document repository exist?			
Does a version control repository exist?			
Are version control processes being used to modify items in the repository?			
Is information that is stored and accessed in the repositories properly protected, backed up, and recoverable?			
Is the appropriate level of SCM rigor being applied to the respective baselines?			

Audit Question	Results	Pass Yes/No	Recommended Action
Are labels applied in a structured manner to identify baselines of code at varying milestones?			
Can you obtain a list of the latest requirements baseline?			
Can you obtain a list of latest items in the production baseline?			
Randomly select five recently changed versions in the development baseline for the current project release. Can you trace the changes to the requirement(s) and/or defect(s) that they fulfill?			
For each deliverable planned for the production baseline, verify that all configuration items are contained in the development code baseline.			

21. SCM Oversight Process

Objectives

To provide a repeatable process for summarizing and discussing SCM activity with management.

Scope

This process applies to all projects related to this application.

Steps

Step	Role	Description	Output
1	SCM Manager	Schedule an SCM Oversight Session with Management	Meeting scheduled
2	SCM Manager	Prepare the SCM Status Report • Document SCM status since the last review. Consider including: accomplishments, significant issues	SCM Status Report

Step	Role	Description	Output
		and risks, budgetary and staffing needs, training completed, audit results, etc. If status report template exists, utilize for consistency. • Provide supporting SCM reports	
3	SCM Manager	Conduct SCM Oversight Session • Meet with Project Manager and optionally with the Application Owner. • Review current status of SCM activities, plans, milestones, and resources (budgetary and staffing). • Address issues, risks, improvements as appropriate.	Management Review
4	SCM Manager	Open Actions to track to Closure • Actions may be issues, risks, or improvement tasks. • If issue, add to problem list using the SCM problem management process. • If risk, add mitigation action to plan or action list. • If improvement, add to plan or action list.	Opened Action(s)
5	SCM Manager	Store SCM Status Report in Document Repository • Utilize a naming convention that distinguishes it from other status reports – consider a date convention.	SCM Status Report in repository

21.1. SCM Status Report Template

General Information

Application:	Reporting Period:	Project Stage:
Project Release:	Project Manager:	

SCM Training

Course	Date	List of Attendees	

SCM Activities

Number of Builds:		Number of Applications Supported:	
Number of Releases:		Number of Project Staff Supported:	
Current SCM Tasks/Projects:			
Changes to SCM Processes, Policy, etc			

SCM Resources (staff and budget)

SCM Staff: _____   SCM Workload: _____

Budget for SCM Technology: _____   In current budget?   YES ☐   NO ☐

SCM Achievements

SCM Audit

Was an Audit Performed?   Yes ☐   No ☐

If Yes, which type of Audit   Process ☐   Baseline ☐   Both ☐

Results:

Outstanding SCM Issues <or attach SCM problem report from Problem Management technology>

Problem #	Problem	Date Open	Action Required

22. SCM Report Process

Objective

To provide a repeatable process of exhibiting SCM data relating to an organization, application, or project that can be acted upon to promote continuous improvement.

Scope

This process applies to all projects related to this application.

Steps

Step	Role	Description	Output
1	SCM Manager	Identify SCM Data for generating Reports • This may include data from processes, audits, measures, training, etc.	Identified SCM Data
2	SCM Coordinator	Generate SCM Reports • For each data type, identify and prepare a standard report template. • Collect the data via the repeatable process. • Place the collected data into the specific SCM report template.	SCM Reports
3	SCM Coordinator	Distribute SCM Reports • Determine the appropriate personnel for each report distribution (or as per the SCM process need) • Determine frequency of distributing the reports (or as per the SCM process need) • Distribute reports to the appropriate personnel at the appropriate frequency	SCM Reports Distributed
4	SCM Coordinator	Store SCM Reports • Store the SCM reports in the application team repository (document repository or SCM repository) or as per the specific SCM process	SCM Reports in repository

23. SCM Tasks at the Project Level

Phase	Task
Planning and Requirements	Add Appropriate SCM Tasks to the Project Plan
	Provide an SCM Overview to the Project Team
	Update the CCB Member List
	Review and Authorize the Requirements Baseline for this Project Release
	Update the Application Inventory
	Perform a Project-Level SCM Risk Assessment
Design	Perform SCM Capacity Planning for Project Needs
	Establish the Development Baseline Project Branch
	Train Project Personnel in the SCM Technology
	Create User Workspaces for Project Release
Development	Perform Project Compiles/Builds (if applicable)
	Perform Merging Activities (if applicable)
	Create a Release Package
	Create Draft Release Notes
	Perform an SCM Audit
	Perform an SCM Review
Test	Migrate the Release Package to the Test Region(s)
	Prepare Final Release Package
	Create Final Release Notes
	Submit a Change Request for the Release
Release	Review and Authorize the Release for Production
	Install Release Package Into Production
	Verify Migration of Release Package into Production
	Establish a Bugfix Branch and Create Workspaces
	Clean Up Unnecessary User Workspaces
	Perform a Postmortem

About the Author

Mario E. Moreira has worked in the SCM field since 1986. He has experience with numerous SCM technologies and processes on a range of platforms in a variety of industries including commercial, government, and financial sectors. He has implemented various SCM technologies on over 75 applications/products which includes establishing global SCM infrastructures. He has experience in several process and quality related areas including SEI CMM. Mario has written many SCM-related articles and has spoken at several international SCM conferences. He has an MA in Mass Communication with an emphasis on communication technologies. Mario also brings years of project management, software quality assurance, requirements management, facilitation, and team building skills and experience.

Software Configuration Management: Implementation Roadmap   M. E. Moreira
© 2004 Mario E. Moreira   ISBN: 0-470-86264-5 (HB)

Index

Software Configuration Management: Implementation Roadmap M. E. Moreira
© 2004 Mario E. Moreira ISBN: 0-470-86264-5 (HB)